The Limits to Citizen Power

Anthropology, Culture and Society

Series Editors:
Professor Vered Amit, Concordia University
Doctor Jamie Cross, University of Edinburgh
and
Professor Christina Garsten, Stockholm University

Recent titles:

*Becoming Arab in London:
Performativity and the
Undoing of Identity*
RAMY M. K. ALY

*Community, Cosmopolitanism
and the Problem of Human
Commonality*
VERED AMIT AND NIGEL RAPPORT

*In Foreign Fields:
The Politics and Experiences of
Transnational Sport Migration*
THOMAS F. CARTER

*Dream Zones:
Anticipating Capitalism and
Development in India*
JAMIE CROSS

*A History of Anthropology
Second Edition*
THOMAS HYLLAND ERIKSEN AND
FINN SIVERT NIELSEN

*Ethnicity and Nationalism:
Anthropological Perspectives
Third Edition*
THOMAS HYLLAND ERIKSEN

*Fredrik Barth:
An Intellectual Biography*
THOMAS HYLLAND ERIKSEN

*Small Places, Large Issues:
An Introduction to Social and
Cultural Anthropology
Fourth Edition*
Thomas Hylland Eriksen

*At the Heart of the State:
The Moral World of Institutions*
DIDIER FASSIN ET AL.

*Discordant Development:
Global Capitalism and the
Struggle for Connection in
Bangladesh*
KATY GARDNER

*Anthropology and Development:
Challenges for the Twenty-first
Century*
KATY GARDNER AND DAVID LEWIS

*Organisational Anthropology:
Doing Ethnography in and
Among Complex Organisations*
EDITED BY CHRISTINA GARSTEN
AND ANETTE NYQVIST

*Border Watch:
Cultures of Immigration,
Detention and Control*
ALEXANDRA HALL

*Anthropology's World:
Life in a Twenty-First
Century Discipline*
ULF HANNERZ

*Humans and Other Animals:
Cross-cultural Perspectives on
Human–Animal Interactions*
SAMANTHA HURN

*Flip-Flop:
A Journey Through
Globalisation's Backroads*
CAROLINE KNOWLES

*The Anthropology of Security:
Perspectives from the Frontline
of Policing, Counter-Terrorism
and Border Control*
EDITED BY MARK MAGUIRE,
CATARINA FROIS
AND NILS ZURAWSKI

*The Gloss of Harmony:
The Politics of Policy Making
in Multilateral Organisations*
EDITED BY BIRGIT MÜLLER

*Contesting Publics:
Feminism, Activism,
Ethnography*
LYNNE PHILLIPS
AND SALLY COLE

*Food For Change:
The Politics and Values
of Social Movements*
JEFF PRATT AND
PETER LUETCHFORD

*Base Encounters:
The US Armed Forces
in South Korea*
ELISABETH SCHOBER

*Checkpoint, Temple, Church
and Mosque:
A Collaborative Ethnography
of War and Peace*
JONATHAN SPENCER,
JONATHAN GOODHAND,
SHAHUL HASBULLAH,
BART KLEM, BENEDIKT KORF
AND KALINGA TUDOR SILVA

*Race and Ethnicity in
Latin America
Second Edition*
PETER WADE

*The Capability of Places:
Methods for Modelling
Community Response to
Intrusion and Change*
SANDRA WALLMAN

*The Making of an African
Working Class:
Politics, Law and Cultural
Protest in the Manual Workers'
Union of Botswana*
PNINA WERBNER

The Limits to Citizen Power

Participatory Democracy and
the Entanglements of the State

Victor Albert

PlutoPress
www.plutobooks.com

First published 2016 by Pluto Press
345 Archway Road, London N6 5AA

www.plutobooks.com

Copyright © Victor Albert 2016

The right of Victor Albert to be identified as the author of this work has been asserted by him in accordance with the Copyright, Designs and Patents Act 1988.

British Library Cataloguing in Publication Data
A catalogue record for this book is available from the British Library

ISBN 978 0 7453 3612 1   Hardback
ISBN 978 0 7453 3617 6   Paperback
ISBN 978 1 7837 1797 2   PDF eBook
ISBN 978 1 7837 1799 6   Kindle eBook
ISBN 978 1 7837 1798 9   EPUB eBook

This book is printed on paper suitable for recycling and made from fully managed and sustained forest sources. Logging, pulping and manufacturing processes are expected to conform to the environmental standards of the country of origin.

Typeset by Stanford DTP Services, Northampton, England

Simultaneously printed in the European Union and United States of America

Contents

List of Figures and Tables	vi
List of Abbreviations	vii
Series Preface	viii
Acknowledgements	ix
Introduction	1
1 Democratisation, Reform and Participation in Brazil	22
2 Rituals and Ritualisation	41
3 Participatory Budgeting: Ritualisations of Petitioning and Power	66
4 Embedded Participatory Institutions: The Urban Development Council and the Housing Council	85
5 Shared Practices, Contrasting Ideologies	114
6 Backstage	143
Conclusion: Reimagining Participatory Democracy	167
Notes	188
References	192
Index	205

List of Figures and Tables

Figures

3.1	Participants making demands during the Parque Andreense assembly	72
3.2	Demands displayed on a projector screen	74
3.3	Attendees vote for investment priorities and regional representatives using electronic ballot machines	76
4.1	Spatial organisation in the UDC	90
4.2	Spatial organisation in the HC	104

Tables

3.1	Biennial cycle of the participatory budget	68
4.1	General agenda items for the UDC	95
4.2	General agenda items for the HC	106

List of Abbreviations

AEIS	Áreas de Especial Interesse Social (Areas of Special Social Interest)
ABC	the municipalities of Santo André, São Bernardo do Campo and São Caetano, a region of São Paulo
CESA	Centro Educacional de Santo André
FNRU	Fórum Nacional de Reforma Urbana (National Forum for Urban Reform)
HC	Conselho Municipal de Habitação (Housing Council)
MBC	Conselho Municipal de Orçamento (Municipal Budget Council)
MDF	Movimento de Defesa do Favelado (Movement for the Defence of Shanty-Town Inhabitants)
MDDF	Movimento de Defesa dos Direitos de Moradores em Favela (Movement for the Defence of Favela Inhabitants' Rights)
MNRU	Movimento Nacional de Reforma Urbana (Movement for Urban Reform)
PB	participatory budget
PDS	Partido Democrático Social (Democratic Social Party)
PFL	Partido da Frente Liberal (Liberal Front Party)
SEMASA	Serviço Municipal de Saneamento Ambiental de Santo André (Municipal Urban Sanitation Service of Santo André)
SERVCOOP	Cooperativa Habitacional dos Servidores Públicos de Santo André (Santo André Municipal Public Servants' Housing Cooperative)
UDC	Conselho Municipal de Política Urbana (Urban Development Council)
WMC	Conselho Municipal de Assistência Social (Welfare Management Council)
ZEIS	Zonas Especiais de Interesse Social (Special Social Interest Zones)

Series Preface

Anthropology is a discipline based upon in-depth ethnographic works that deal with wider theoretical issues in the context of particular, local conditions – to paraphrase an important volume from the series: *large issues* explored in *small places*. This series has a particular mission: to publish work that moves away from an old-style descriptive ethnography that is strongly area-studies oriented, and offer genuine theoretical arguments that are of interest to a much wider readership, but which are nevertheless located and grounded in solid ethnographic research. If anthropology is to argue itself a place in the contemporary intellectual world, then it must surely be through such research.

We start from the question: 'What can this ethnographic material tell us about the bigger theoretical issues that concern the social sciences?' rather than 'What can these theoretical ideas tell us about the ethnographic context?' Put this way round, such work becomes *about* large issues, *set in* a (relatively) small place, rather than detailed description of a small place for its own sake. As Clifford Geertz once said, 'Anthropologists don't study villages; they study *in* villages.'

By place, we mean not only geographical locale, but also other types of 'place' – within political, economic, religious or other social systems. We therefore publish work based on ethnography within political and religious movements, occupational or class groups, among youth, development agencies, and nationalist movements; but also work that is more thematically based – on kinship, landscape, the state, violence, corruption, the self. The series publishes four kinds of volume: ethnographic monographs; comparative texts; edited collections; and shorter, polemical essays.

We publish work from all traditions of anthropology, and all parts of the world, which combines theoretical debate with empirical evidence to demonstrate anthropology's unique position in contemporary scholarship and the contemporary world.

Professor Vered Amit
Dr Jamie Cross
Professor Christina Garsten

Acknowledgements

I am very grateful to a large number of people that made this book possible. In Australia, I must first of all recognise the efforts of my dear friend, Rowan Ireland. Rowan's selfless encouragement, support, and critical feedback belong to a kind of scholarly collegiality that seems to be disappearing from the modern academy. I hope that some of it has rubbed off on me. At La Trobe University, I would like to thank Anthony Moran for his constructive criticism, practical advice, generous spirit and friendship. Also at La Trobe were that coterie of Latin Americanists, including Barry Carr, Ralph Newmark, and the late Steve Niblo, who helped to shape this work through years of feedback, debate and discussions. Many thanks go to them and also to Chris Eipper and Karl Smith for their own important contributions to this project. Zuleika Arashiro has been a great friend and an important source of support and advice over the years as we each have criss-crossed each other's countries.

If I am indebted to a large number of people in Australia, the number is even higher in Brazil. The administration in Santo André gave me access I would never have been afforded in Australia. They were willing and accessible, forthright and accommodating. Without their co-operation I never would have been able to write this monograph. I was welcomed by the administration in Santo André based on the understanding, I believe, that it is important to have critical perspectives on local politics. My hope is that this book is received in the spirit in which I was received. I must particularly single out Robson at SEMASA for his friendship and help over the years. I am also, of course, forever in the debt of those *andreense* participants and social activists who gave of their time to a stranger, who took me in, dried me when I arrived soaking from a flash storm, fed me and trusted me like family. Perhaps the only way I can repay some of their hospitality and good will is to give a faithful rendering of what I experienced and the story the data tell. I would also like to acknowledge Thaisa de Andrade, Jefferson Mainardes and Robison Chagas in Ponta Grossa-PR, for their help and support.

This manuscript grew and took shape over a period when I was a Post Doctoral Fellow at the Digital Ethnography Research Centre, at RMIT University. I would in particular like to thank Tania Lewis for helping me to think in more sophisticated ways about politics and power (and for the posh lunches). I must also thank the Institute of Latin American Studies at La Trobe University for the honorary fellowship that provided me with the conditions that enabled this manuscript to take its final shape.

At Pluto Press, I would like to thank the editorial team, reviewers, and copy-editing staff for their professionalism, cordiality, and also for the improvements they made possible to the text.

My friends and family deserve more than the mention they can be given here. I am grateful to my partner, Masha, for those things in life that make my academic labours by comparison seem trivial. I would also like to thank Julita, Jorge, Max, Sebastian, and Sash for their love and support. Finally, however, I would like to dedicate this book to my parents, Eva and Geza, for being constants in life, and for allowing my own personal kinds of tacit understandings that I, at times, am able to recognise.

Victor Albert

Introduction

Participatory democracy has a venerable place in political history, and yet it has enjoyed a resurgence of popularity in recent years among social movements, activists and reformist politicians who seek to address an array of governance ills. The rise of transnational political actors, such as the EU, IMF and World Bank, have created a 'democratic deficit' by putting important decision-making processes beyond the reach of the voting public. The transformation of the political class into a moneyed and professionalised elite, especially in the Global North, has widened the gap between elected officials and rank-and-file party members, leading to diminishing membership rates and grassroots support for traditional political parties, challenging the representativeness and vibrancy of electoral democracy. In addition, the prevalence of patronage politics and clientelism, often identified with the countries of the Global South, continues to thwart the programmes of elected governments, and is particularly injurious for communities of little strategic electoral value. All of these problems and more are held to be remediable by instituting participatory democracy, by re-energising and recalibrating existing democratic institutions with the participation of the lay public.

The new-found enthusiasm for participatory democracy has been nourished by a florescence of participatory reforms in Latin America. New constitutions that encourage and mandate citizen participation have been promulgated; electoral parties supportive of participatory democracy have been elected, some with explicitly democratic socialist aims; and scores of localised participatory experiments have spread across the continent, garnering the attention of the international development community and global justice movement. The rhetoric of participatory democracy and the ambitious aims of some activists and progressive politicians have helped to cast some of these reforms in a redemptive light, as challenges to the very nature of politics and the distribution of political power. The success or failure of participatory reform is, however, often determined in mundane situations that seem to have little in common with the emancipatory language of participatory democracy.

This is a book about participatory democracy in the everyday, about how the promise of participation is realised or thwarted in the course of quotidian interactions between social activists, public servants and political appointees in Santo André, a medium-sized city that is part of Greater São Paulo, Brazil. Santo André and the industrial region of which it is a part was the birthplace of the Partido dos Trabalhadores (Workers' Party), a political party that championed participatory reforms in office, which would earn a kind of celebrity status that was remarkable even in a continent with so many other noteworthy innovations. I come to the history of the Workers' Party in a moment. But first it is fitting, in a study of participatory democracy in the everyday, for you to begin where I began, in the most familiar setting of my daily life in Santo André.

Santo André

In Santo André I stayed in an apartment on Avenida Portugal, in Jardim Bela Vista. It had two bedrooms and polished floorboards. The kitchen was covered in tiles, in the Portuguese style, and my small back porch gave out onto the car park of an adjacent shopping centre. From there I could see beyond the car park to Avenida Pereira Barreto, an avenue that leads from the city centre of Santo André to the neighbouring city of São Bernardo do Campo. Following Pereira Barreto towards São Bernardo do Campo, one is led to the large factories of São Bernardo, where at the end of the 1970s a number of famous strikes signalled the diminishing authority of Brazil's authoritarian regime that had been in power since 1964. They were strikes that form an important part of the historical narrative that activists in Santo André tell and retell about local opposition to the military regime and the eventual return to democracy in 1985.

Traversing Avenida Pereira Barreto and heading further towards the horizon from my apartment window leads to Parque Central. Redeveloped in 2005, it would be the envy of any Western city. It had lush, rolling slopes and a sandy jogging track that wound around its edges. A series of ponds and small lakes played home to different types of fish and scores of water birds, seemingly attracted by the former. When there was wind, and particularly on weekends, groups of children would congregate on one of the park's hills, where updrafts would take their brightly coloured kites far into the bright blue sky. At the base of the kite-runners' favoured slope, a well-trodden dirt ramp led over a concrete boundary fence and into Favela Gamboa II, a strip of informal housing that had been constructed under high-tensile power lines. It was much like innumerable other shanty settlements peppered about São Paulo: most of its residences had orange breeze-blocks for walls with concrete floors and corrugated fibreglass or aluminium roofs. Some of the houses functioned as shop fronts, and the owners could often be seen, leaning out of the shop window, laconically engaging in the community life of the *favela*, talking to the neighbours or reprimanding annoying kids. Sometimes passers-by would stop to buy some tapioca pancakes or sugar-cane juice. And there always seemed to be, emanating from one house or another, some kind of bass-driven tune whose rhythms gave the *favela* a pulsating life that contrasted with the manicured solemnity of the park. The juxtaposition of the patchwork architecture of the *favela* and the precise landscaping of the park was indicative of the strange intermingling of social classes in São Paulo's urban form.

Beyond the park, walking past its lakes and then up steep, labyrinthine side streets, I arrived at Cap. Mário Toledo de Camargo Road. A major arterial of the city, Mário Toledo always seemed a torrent of traffic, of heavy trucks that wheezed black smoke, and whose tyres left deep furrows in the tarmac. Arriving at Mário Toledo, I encountered a quite different built environment. It was unlike the park and the *favela*, and even some of Santo André's older suburbs, characterised by their two-storey gated homes. Here concrete was almost ubiquitous. It made up adjacent dividing walls, buildings, shops and, before it was demolished, the prominent rectangular frontage of the Bruno Daniel Stadium – home of the city's football team, the Ramalhão.[1] Along this stretch of the city, space was less intensively developed, and hence perhaps the prevalence of *pichação*, that angular graffiti script so common in Brazilian cities. Following Mário Toledo south, to its conclusion, I finally arrived at the so-called periphery – an expanse of working-class and informal housing that extends into the hills of the *serra*. This was one of my most common journeys during fieldwork. I came to the periphery to interview fieldwork colleagues, to visit neighbourhood associations and also to socialise. Yet this is not a work about life in São Paulo's outskirts, in the vein of other urban ethnographies (see Donna Goldstein 2003; Perlman 2010). It is about how the periphery is influenced from afar, by administrative decisions and deliberations, by attendant laws and policies, and most importantly, by the power relationships that decide whether its residents, and other members of the popular classes, partake in the governance decisions that come to influence their communities.

My most common fieldwork journey was thus not out along Pereira Barreto, nor past Gamboa II, along Mário Toledo and out into the periphery.

Rather, I would exit my two-tone mustard and bone-white building and follow Avenida Portugal north towards the centre of town. It was a downhill walk. I followed the path of the rains, past the 24 hour cafe, then the 24 hour bakery and finally the medical centre, where small bronze birds had their own seed-filled pagoda. It was only a ten-minute walk from my apartment to the Paço Municipal (City Square), a paved square with an expansive pond and fountain. The three largest buildings constructed thereon were themselves symbols of the trinity of political power. They looked austerely hard edged and functionalist. The judiciary, several floors high, was located to my immediate left, while the legislature, a more diminutive building, was to my right. Located on the far side of the square from my entry point was the fifteen-storey *prefeitura* (town hall), which housed the municipality's executive and dwarfed other buildings around it, reflecting, perhaps, its pre-eminence among the branches of government. In this book I will argue that, though more diffuse, fluid and multiform than the buildings on the Paço Municipal, there are other manifestations and enactments of state power that have become highly problematic for the democratising project undertaken by Workers' Party administrations in the city.

Participation in the Workers' City

Santo André is part of the ABC region of São Paulo. The acronym derives from the names of neighbouring municipalities: Santo (A)ndré, São (B)ernardo and São (C)aetano. In recent times the expression Greater ABC region has been used to also include the municipalities of Diadema, Riberão Pires, Mauá and Rio Grande da Serra, which are also identified with the common history of this area, the most heavily industrialised region in Brazil. The ABC region was the birthplace of the new, autonomous union movement, which was active in the creation of the Workers' Party (Sader 1988). The city is also recognised for historically having active civic associations and social movements, and it was in Santo André that one of São Paulo's most important urban popular movements of the 1980s emerged, the Movimento de Defesa do Favelado (MDF, Movement for the Defence of Shanty-Town Inhabitants) (Almeida 1992: 69, 82; Jacobi & Nunes 1983). The Workers' Party became the major electoral force in local politics in Santo André following democratisation, and by 2016 had failed to win the mayoral elections on only two occasions since 1988. Celso Daniel was the first Workers' Party mayor and the city's foremost political figure in the post-authoritarian period. A charismatic leader and a gifted intellectual, Daniel, on assuming office, immediately began experimenting with initiatives that elicited the participation of the wider public in matters of governance. It began in a tentative fashion during his first administration, and developed and became more complex over time. By the time I began my first stint of fieldwork in 2007, over two dozen participatory institutions were active in the city. There were 24 management policy councils, a participatory budget, a participatory planning programme called Cidade Futuro (Future City) and dozens of other attendant ad hoc assemblies and conferences. On average there was at least one participatory assembly per weekday, and at times many more. Despite the large numbers of participatory institutions in Santo André, it was the city's participatory budget that caught the attention of academics and activists alike.

Participatory Budgeting

Participatory budgets were first developed in Porto Alegre, in Brazil's southernmost state of Rio Grande do Sul, by the Frente Popular (Popular Front), a leftist coalition, after winning the 1988 elections. Headed by a Workers' Party mayor, Olivio Dutra, the Frente Popular developed a participatory budget (PB) in response to a history of demands, from various social actors and a confederation of local civic associations (União das Associaçõoes de Moradores de Porto Alegre), for the community to have a direct influence on the way the municipal budget is spent (Baiocchi 2005: 31; Goldfrank 2003: 33). The PB invited the lay public to determine investment priorities in a series of regional and thematic assemblies held around the city, which were then implemented by the government over the following year. The result transformed sections of the impoverished urban periphery (Abers 2000; Goldfrank 2003), led to increasing civic activism (Goldfrank 2007: 163) and drew international fame for the city which hosted five World Social Forums.

This case of participatory democracy, and several others inspired by it, caught the imagination of progressive scholars and activists around the world. Boaventura de Sousa Santos (1998) saw the PB as an example of redistributive democracy, and also argued that it was one of the most 'credible guiding ideas mobilising countless social movements and progressive NGOs around the world in their struggles against exclusion, dispossession and discrimination produced or intensified by neoliberal globalisation' (Santos 2005: 336). Rebecca Abers (2000) and William Nylen (2002) saw in the PB the potential for citizen 'empowerment'. Gianpaolo Baiocchi (2003, 2005) and Lígia Lüchmann (2002) interpreted the proliferation of participatory forums as burgeoning, deliberative 'public spheres' that had ignited a civil society which had been repressed by years of military rule. Leonardo Avritzer, similarly inspired by Habermas's work on the public sphere, and drawing on his close study of civic associations (Avritzer 1997; see also Avritzer 2003), developed the concept of 'participatory publics' (Avritzer 2002a; see also Avritzer & Wampler 2004). These were part of what might be called a hopeful wave of interest in participatory democracy, in which well-worn ideas about Brazilian politics, at least for some analysts and commentators, seemed to melt in the face of innovation. But less well developed, in some of the more celebratory evaluations of participatory reform, was an account of the key role of state actors and how continuities of state power persisted in the new spaces opened up for civil society.

Santo André's PB also attracted significant attention in the early years. Pedro Pontual (2000) posited that participants became educated citizens through taking an active role in the government of the city. Bruno Daniel, brother of the erstwhile mayor, Celso Daniel, similarly found the PB to be a 'space of learning' (Daniel 2003: 230) that improved 'accountability', but whose primary limitations were the scarcity of funds and the 'efficiency and efficacy' related to public spending (ibid.: 231). Claudio Acioly et al. argued that the PB 'provided an avenue for participation and communication to population groups that were traditionally excluded from public policy' (Acioly et al. 2003: 41), but held that there existed challenges to institutionalising the relationship between the PB and the city planning programme, Cidade Futuro while maintaining flexibility (ibid.: 84). These kinds of findings gave the impression of an administration at the forefront of innovation in democratic governance (Wampler 2007: 179), an impression strengthened by, as the mayor was wont to say, 'a cabinet full of trophies', awarded by a slew of government and non-government bodies.

The initiatives in cities like Porto Alegre and Santo André helped to breathe new life into participatory and deliberative democracy, and generated considerable enthusiasm for their transformative potential in Brazil and abroad. An initial wave of enthusiasm was part of what Leonardo Avritzer has called the 'laudatory phase' (Avritzer 2009: 174) of participation, a period that gave way to more sobering evaluations of the changes that had been wrought through participatory reform and that were yet possible (see Lavalle 2011). In part, the early ebullience was due to a selective focus on a series of exemplary cases (Wampler 2008: 61), but it was also due to an emphasis on civil society activity and a reluctance to account, at least in a sustained and theoretically informed way, for the role of the state in both enabling and conditioning projects of participatory reform. That is, of course, not to imply that the state and its constituent actors have a singular influence on the prospects of participatory democracy, either as the enablers of reform or as agents that constrain the influence of the public. However, it often left an array of powerful actors and the influence of political and administrative authority out of the analytical mix. Before outlining how such factors figure in the approach taken here, I locate the participatory reform effort in Santo André within a broader historical compass that also incorporates the experiences of other Latin American countries.

Participatory Democracy in Brazil

Institutions of participatory democracy emerged as part of a florescence of political experiments that followed Brazil's transition from military rule. In the early days of the authoritarian regime that began in 1964, there was little active support for the participation of ordinary citizens in institutions of governance. At a time when the country was experiencing record-breaking growth (during Brazil's 'economic miracle', from 1968 to 1972), the regime discriminated against the popular classes and brutally repressed opposition, helping to create the image of a polarised society (Assies 1994: 84; Gohn 1997: 282), one in which collaboration with the governing elite was considered both unproductive and disloyal to a popular movement fired by the autonomous and anti-capitalist ideology of Comunidades Eclesiais de Base (Catholic Base Communities) (Banck 1990; Singer 1983). Many popular actors, in practice, adopted more pragmatic postures in their private dealings with local state institutions, which provided vital resources (Cardoso 1983; Mainwaring 1987: 151).

The political polarisation that was exacerbated by repression began to diminish by the second half of the 1970s. A democratic transition that had been repeatedly postponed by successive military leaders finally became increasingly likely under the generals Ernesto Geisel, who became president of the republic, and the *éminence grise* of the 'decompression', Golbery do Couto e Silva. Some of the more draconian measures put in place by hard-line predecessors were repealed, such as the arbitrary detention of adversaries of the regime and prohibitions on the press and free assembly. The regime's liberalising rhetoric and a thawing of relations with the workers – symbolic opponents of the regime – helped restore the prospect of a return to electoral democracy (Stepan 1988: 33). The possibility of effective representation, buoyed by a resurgent, broad-based movement for democratic reform, helped allay the categorical disdain for formal politics publicly held by a number of important popular actors. Exclusion from institutional politics had, in any case, been a chastening experience for many urban social movements, for although the discourse of autonomy may have been born of an incisive appreciation of patterns in elite politics, it had failed to provide much needed goods and services for poor communities.

A new autonomous union movement that developed in contradistinction to the corporatist labour system also gained in strength during the latter half of the 1970s. The largest strikes in the country's history were held in 1978 and 1979 in the south-east industrial region of São Paulo, some of them just within walking distance from my apartment in Santo André. But even if the strikes failed to secure many of the workers' substantive demands, or provide the kind of impetus for political change attributed to them by some analysts (see Sader 1988), they did provide a heavily publicised, and therefore symbolic, challenge to the authority of the regime in what became a national wave of militancy that numbered supporters in the millions (French & Fontes 2005: 19). In 1979 and 1980, a series of meetings was held in São Paulo, led by some of the new unionists and leftist intellectuals, that culminated in the creation of a new political grouping, the Workers' Party, which was conceived as a manifestation of the social movements whose activities had gathered pace at the end of the 1970s (Brandão 2003: 38). It was socialist, but ideologically heterogeneous, maintaining independence from the USSR and uniting in its ranks Trotskyists, socialist democrats and others of a more conservative disposition under different 'factions'. By now, demands for citizen participation had widespread social support, and the Workers' Party became its foremost political advocate in elected office.

In 1985, the presidency was finally transferred to a civilian. The first presidential elections of the democratic era were held in 1988, the same year in which a new federal constitution was enacted. These are the customary registers of the democratic transition. Yet even in such formal markers of political renewal there were telling signs of continuity. After the untimely death of civilian president-to-be Tancredo Neves, the presidency somewhat symbolically passed to José Sarney, a man who only months earlier represented the Partido Democrático Social (PDS, Democratic Social Party), the party of the authoritarian government in Congress. Indeed, Frances Hagopian (1996: 213) argued that it was the traditional elite that maintained power during the political transition and that retained control over the design of the new democracy's political institutions. Many scholars and critical commentators thus interpreted the democratic transition as yet another episode of cosmetic regime change, of the kind analysed in the works of Florestan Fernandes (2005) and Caio Prado Junior (1965). Luiz Werneck Vianna used the Gramscian term 'passive revolution' to capture the way official regime change had an insignificant practical influence on Brazil's political economy (Vianna 1997: 53; see also Nogueira 1998: 270–90). According to such analyses, the need for substantive democratisation remained undiminished following the formal transition.

With the return to electoral democracy, the Workers' Party won a number of local elections, some of them in large cities. These became the source of enormous academic local and international attention for the implementation of policies and programmes that sought to confront many of the so-called 'traditional' characteristics of the new democracy. The Workers' Party administrations won accolades by combating inequality, breaking clientelist relationships that were pernicious for politically unimportant social groups, and developing channels for the participation of the lay public in government decision-making. The success of some of these administrations set against the backdrop of a conservative democratic transition only emphasised their accomplishments.

The Participatory Turn in Latin America

Participatory reform in Brazil was part of a wave of interest in participatory democracy that swept across Latin America at the end of the twentieth century. Just as in Brazil, this predilection to directly engage with state agencies in deliberative forums contrasts strongly with the strategies of earlier social and popular movements that called for autonomy from the state (Cameron et al. 2012a: 5). The willingness to participate in formal state institutions was in part a reaction to the changes to the political establishment that civil societies of the region had helped to effect. In the 1980s, military regimes were removed from office in Peru, Bolivia, Argentina, Uruguay, Chile and Brazil; the only South American country that did not liberate itself from military rule during this time was Paraguay, and even there the end of the Stroessner dictatorship led to political liberalisation (Remmer 1992: 4). However, the new democracies were the subject of often vociferous criticism, as formal political transition revealed a governance landscape ill-equipped for the manifold demands and heightened expectations of democratic government. Discontent with democracy was especially pronounced in the Andean region, where between 1992 and 2005 Colombia was the only country that did not have a presidential term cut short by popular and elite dissatisfaction (Mainwaring 2006: 13). Indeed, scholars of comparative politics have tended to explain the emergent interest in participatory democracy in terms of a failure of representative institutions to effectively incorporate excluded social sectors and their interests into the political system (Barczak 2001; Cameron et al. 2012a). The 'crisis of representation', weak political parties and the enduring influence of political patronage and clientelism, according to this reasoning, led to the search for alternative means of influencing state action. In a region with such diversity, it is unsurprising that there was significant variance among the participatory reforms pursued and realised in the new Latin American democracies.

Latin American polities are often informally rated according to the opportunities for citizen participation they allow. Whenever such comparisons are made, Chile and Mexico are generally held to be home to the least serious reform efforts (Cameron et al. 2012b: 241; Lupien 2015). Chile's democracy is generally praised by liberal scholars for its consolidated electoral system and representative institutions, but it was not until Michele Bachelet's presidency in 2006 that a discourse of popular participation was promoted at the national level, and among Latin American countries it still has, according to Pascal Lupien, 'one of the least participatory systems' (Lupien 2015: 3). Mexico's recent history of participatory governance goes back quite a bit further. Developed in 1983, the Sistema Nacional de Planeación Democrática (National System of Democratic Planning) provided a legal framework for the participatory institutions that were later developed. In order to comply with the national democratic planning framework, municipalities were obliged to develop two kinds of participatory institutions. First was the Comité de Planeación para el Desarrollo Municipal (Municipal Development Planning Committee), a committee formed by citizens to aid state officials to determine investment priorities, particularly in those cases where federal infrastructure funds were involved. Second was an array of different kinds of neighbourhood councils, which went by various names, and generally provided community-based guidance for the work of the planning and development committees (Montambeault 2011: 99–100). These were the forerunners of various types of consultative councils, which brought together expert and lay participants to deliberate on sectoral policies and were introduced at all levels of government. However, even the most successful of these councils, the Consultative Councils for Sustainable Development, had negligible policy impact, leading Felipe de la Jara and Ernesto Vera (2012: 91) to cast doubt on the influence and effectiveness of scores of other, less notable examples.

If Mexico and Chile provide examples of tentative participatory reforms, several of the Andean nations have drawn worldwide attention for their attempts to not only improve public policy and investment decision-making through increasing citizen participation, but to fundamentally reconfigure socio-political relations. Some of those nations which experienced a 'crisis of representation' (Mainwaring 2006) promulgated new constitutions around the turn of the century that encouraged and indeed mandated citizen participation. Between 1999 and 2009, new constitutions were passed in Bolivia, Ecuador and Venezuela that provided a number of new powers to lay citizens. Referendums assumed a more central role in each of these countries, as new constitutional provisions allowed for the approval and revocation of laws, international treaties and conventions and constitutional changes. The citizenry was granted new powers of oversight and accountability over state agencies, and also opportunities to propose new legislation and constitutional amendments (see Bruce 2008; Postero 2010). Further, new provisions were made to allow citizens to directly engage in policy-making and planning processes (Flores et al. 2011: 3–4). Among these cases, Venezuela's participatory reform efforts have drawn special attention for their ambitious scope and the broader revolutionary project of which they form a part.

Hugo Chavez assumed presidential office in 1999 and launched a broad based reform programme that sought to fundamentally reshape Venezuelan politics. Though his presidency marked a significant departure from the political status quo, it also built upon existing calls for substantive democracy that had been circulating since the 1980s. However, democratic reform of this kind did not have a serious political advocate until the Bolivarians assumed power (Maya & Lander 2011: 58). The Bolivarian project extended beyond the country's formal political institutions, seeking also to democratise society, with the aim of empowering citizens to become the active members of the 'protagonistic democracy' envisioned by revolutionary reformers. A key element of the reform programme was the Constitution, which, redrafted in 1999, foregrounded a much more active role for civil society in the national revolutionary project (Maya 2010: 100). A couple of the key participatory institutions that would be further developed when Chavez assumed power in 1999 had, however, already been in operation for some time.

The poor public services and environmental vulnerability of informal *barrios* in Venezuela had prompted various cooperative endeavours among residents that would become more enduring features of organisational life under the Bolivarians. The Mesas Tecnicas de Agua (Technical Water Roundtables) and Organizaciones Comunitarias Autogestionarias (Self-Managing Community Organisations), for example, grew out of collective organisations in the informal *barrios* in response to sanitation, infrastructure and water security issues. A so-called 'social consortium' emerged to address sanitation issues in Catuche, a *barrio* in Libertador, Caracas, in the 1990s, a project which caught the eye and attracted the support of the local mayor. The project also had input from academic staff at the Central University of Venezuela. On assuming office, Chavez appointed the Central University architect Josefina Baldó as president of El Consejo Nacional de la Viviendato (National Housing Council), a position from which she launched social consortia across the country (Maya 2010: 109–10). Under the minister of housing and habitat, Julio Montes, the social consortia were transformed in 2004 and 2005 into Self-Managing Community Organisations. These organisations had a similar remit to the social consortia – to combine technical expertise and community participation in order to address the infrastructural and sanitation problems of the *barrios* – but they were given more power. As a result of this change, the other actors involved in development projects had to work for, rather than with, the community (ibid.: 110).

The Consejos Comunales (Community Councils) are perhaps the best known participatory institution in Venezuela, and the most thoroughgoing attempt to realise the Bolivarian project at the community level. They are also relatively new, having been introduced following the passage of the Communal Councils Law in 2006, which was accompanied by a $1 billion investment that was to be managed by 'people's banks', also newly created (Maya & Lander 2011: 74). Under the vision for *poder popular* ('people's power') set out by Chavez, the Community Councils became the local nodes that would coordinate the existing participatory bodies as the 'fifth motor' of the Bolivarian revolution (McCarthy 2012: 131). Though they were described by Chavez as engines of socialist transformation, Community Councils are heavily regulated, and according to Margarita Maya (2010: 122) can be considered part of the Venezuelan state, given the encompassing stipulations of the Community Councils Law, which specifies and sanctions everything from their creation to their decision-making processes and organisational particulars. In order to access public funds, they must also be registered with a Local Presidential Commission for Popular Power, whose officers are personally appointed by the president, in effect giving the presidential office considerable influence over the network of state–society relations.

Latin America is home to a slew of highly differentiated participatory initiatives that have been implemented over the past 20 years. Yet even in this brief survey of participatory reforms, state power has figured as a problem, whether in the form of the constrained authority and reach of Mexico's Consultative Councils or as an extension of presidential power in Venezuela's Community Councils. Such cases highlight the importance of understanding how existing patterns of political and administrative authority shape the potential for participatory democracy. In the following section I elaborate the problematic of state power and outline how it will be addressed.

Participatory Democracy and the State

This book addresses a problem that is central to attempts to realise participatory democracy in spaces organised by the state. It is a problem that derives from the authority that states have acquired through evolutionary processes – and indeed political conflicts – that have cultivated legitimate spheres of action for their constituent bodies, in part through the development of elaborate jural codes and the organisation of political power around a central authority (Roscoe 1993). Rubbish collection, road and drainage works, the installation of crèches and sports centres, the construction and upkeep of public housing are, when not devolved to third parties, the mundane, unremarkable work of public bodies in mature democracies. The logic of surfacing one road rather than another, or of building a crèche rather than a sports centre, may be hotly debated, but the capacity of the government to make that decision rests on the often solid foundations of political authority that has accrued over time. Participatory democracy is problematic because, at least in theory if not always in practice, it challenges the singular authority of state and administrative officers to make decisions concerning the activities of the public administration. It is for this reason that Valdemir Pires observes a 'potential contradiction in advocating social control over the public administration' (V. Pires 2007: 17),[2] namely, that citizen participation proposes to intervene in the work of authoritative organisations with established structures of power. This potential contradiction may seem to be borne out, particularly in those institutions of participatory democracy where state officials tend to dominate their counterparts from the lay public.

But the role of state agencies and officials in participatory institutions is much more interdependent and mutually constitutive than this potential contradiction suggests. States provide the resources, technical expertise and organisational wherewithal that enable citizen demands to be fulfilled; and states also possess the attendant decision-making authority that citizens in participatory institutions seek to use for their own ends. Public officials sponsor and often organise participatory institutions, and may also be reflective interlocutors who engage in open-ended deliberation and advocate for the interests of social actors (Baiocchi 2005: 75). The relationship between emergent participatory reforms and state power is thus one of constriction and enablement, of continuity entangled with change (Cornwall & Shankland 2013).

States are not the 'almighty apparatuses, with almost total top-down control' they are sometimes made out to be (Nuijten 2003: 15). While a rhetoric of supreme authority might be formally employed by state actors, anthropological enquiry has revealed the diversity of state forms that operate on the ground, and their complex imbrications with social and community actors and their collective endeavours (Das & Poole 2004; Ferguson & Gupta 2002; Hansen & Stepputat 2001; Sharma & Gupta 2006; for Brazil, see Bevilaqua 2003; Bevilaqua & Leirner 2000; Castilho et al. 2014). In place of universalist structures, anthropological studies have focused rather on the cultural practices and symbolic devices through which state power becomes operational and normalised (Ferguson & Gupta 2002: 983). In part because 'the material substance of the state is diffuse and ambiguously defined at its edges' (Mitchell 2006: 169), anthropological writing has tended to represent the state as an only loosely mediated assemblage of practices. The characterisations of state agencies in this book, however, appear somewhat more coordinated because I examine a local, tightly knit organisational ensemble rather than 'the state' as a whole – organisations that have common command structures, shared professional norms, durable and predictable patterns of cooperation and, at least during formal occasions, give coherent public performances. The reality behind the scenes is another matter, and though this is also examined, I give considerable attention to the formal instances of participation, provided their defining role in what Dagnino, Olvera and Panfichi have called the 'participatory project' (Dagnino et al. 2006).

This book examines and explores how institutions of participatory democracy are layered into, shape and are shaped by existing patterns and structures of institutionalised power. To this end I borrow rather eclectically from a body of literature called the practice approach (or practice theory). The practice approach was developed to overcome analytical dualisms in social theory, and is thus well placed to help analyse the relations between 'state' and 'civil society' that are mobilised in participatory institutions (see Mitchell 2006: 180). Pierre Bourdieu and Anthony Giddens have made major contributions to this field of research (Postill 2010: 4). Both Bourdieu and Giddens sought an alternative to analytical dichotomies, such as agent and structure (for Giddens) and objectivism and subjectivism (for Bourdieu), that explained social action in terms of dualistic schemes that then required some, often mechanistic, form of mediation between them. Rather than conceiving of the acting subject as one who navigates a reified, pre-existing system, these practice theorists argued that the interwoven actions, praxis or practices of individual or collective actors at one and the same time helped to produce 'structures' or 'systems' (Ortner 1984: 148–9). The dualistic schemes that helped to set the parameters of Bourdieu's and Giddens's enquiries were collapsed into an interactive theorisation of social action in which the actor was 'always already' embedded in socially meaningful arrays of activities. Systems and structures are made and remade, according to this approach, through the interwoven actions or practices of individual and collective actors. The very meaning of the terms 'structures' and 'systems' for practice theorists is considerably different from those of their structuralist and functionalist forebears. For Giddens, for instance, systems 'amount to nothing more than a manifold of interconnected practices and their enduring cycles of reproduction' (Nicolini 2012: 48). Extending this insight to institutions of participatory democracy, we can argue that participatory reforms are implicated in the reproduction of the state, insofar as they create new bases of legitimacy, and inevitably recognise and legitimate certain features of state authority, just as they may allow social groups to destabilise, interrogate and intervene in others.

Theodore Schatzki, a social philosopher and a major figure in the further development of practice theory, identifies two key dimensions of the practice approach as conceived by Bourdieu and Giddens that are important for my approach to citizen participation. The first is an interpretation of practices as spatially and temporally extended manifolds of actions (Schatzki 1997: 285–6). Practices are interwoven activities that are sustained and mutually adjusted through their interrelations with a larger tapestry of social (and in this case political) practices. This refers in other words to the spatial and temporal organisation of practices, which are shaped by a larger field of practices, more or less geographically localised, and more or less repetitive or arrhythmic. The second is a focus on 'doing – the activity or energisation – through which action takes place' (ibid.: 286). It is in the doing or performance of interwoven activities that practices are actualised, sustained and modified. These two dimensions of practices are largely homologous, for it is only in and through embodied performances that larger, organised patterns of practices are realised and reproduced over time. As formal institutions that are organised by local state agencies, Santo André's participatory institutions are constituted through practices that serve to order and structure so-called participatory activities, though of course without over-determining them, since practices are never simply the sites of 'macro determinations ... that are impervious to the intervention of individuals' (Schatzki 2001: 14). Indeed, they are influenced by a number of factors, which are examined and explored in the analysis. Nonetheless, the patterns of interactive behaviour in Santo André's institutions warrant a focus on the organisation or configuration of practices (Nuijten 2003: 10–11; Ortner 2006: 5), understood here as emergent phenomena that unfold over time and which are inexorably shaped by state power.

Public meetings and assemblies are a crucial part of the empirical phenomena to be examined here, and a cornerstone of the construction of participatory democracy. I outline below their place in this study, and how they figure as sites in which broader challenges to participation can be made out.

The Form of Public Meetings and Assemblies

Public meetings and assemblies are important testing grounds for the promise of participatory democracy. Whatever determinations made therein can plainly be influenced by other, not immediately apparent, social and political interests, and by the effectiveness and efficiency of the administration. Ideally democratic public assemblies can have their determinations thwarted by an inefficient bureaucracy, by interfering elites, judicial prohibitions and complexities and so on. Yet if the meetings and assemblies are not democratic, if citizens are not actively influencing the decisions and conduct of the public administration rather than merely being offered a formal opportunity to do so, then an ideally liberal bureaucracy and an ideally efficient administration cannot salvage their democratic promise. An analysis of public meetings, as the principal, formal instantiations of participatory democracy contributes to an understanding of the effectiveness of participation. But they are more than just practical spaces where brokering, negotiation and deliberation take place between the stakeholders of participatory ventures. They also follow common patterns of organisation and have properties that allow some of the broader challenges of participation as well as the entanglements of the state to be examined.

In public meetings and assemblies, some participants play a more active and decisive role than others. They may speak for longer, hold sway over the meeting content, have comparatively greater influence over decision-making processes and moderate the contributions of others. These are disparities of power – disparities which pose an evident challenge to the promise of participation. Some coordination of deliberation and social intercourse is both inevitable and desirable in participatory assemblies if they are not to be chaotic. Yet most projects of citizen participation, and certainly those in Santo André, are not designed according to some democratic ideal plucked out of the ether. Rather, they draw from and are built upon existing practices that emerged coterminously with the development of the modern state (Van Vree 1999). Through examining how public meetings and assemblies are configured – their social form (see Abers et al. 2014) – we can see how existing sedimentations of power are woven into the grounded phenomena of participation. This social form

> contributes to the formation of public events, setting broad parameters of likelihood – the likelihood of certain operations being accomplished through certain forms of public events ... These structures have high degrees of replicability. That is, whenever a particular occasion is enacted, it is put together from more-or-less similar elements, it is performed by more or less the same cast of characters; and it passes

through more-or-less the same sequences of action. (Handelman 1990: 7, 12)

Public assemblies are, like other public events, made up of comparable social elements and characters, which contribute to their recursive and routinised character (Giddens 1979: 75, 77). This performative ritualisation is part of the reason why the form of citizen participation can become doxic (Bourdieu 1977) and taken-for-granted, and therefore escape the critical attention of lay participants who may be more preoccupied with the content of deliberations. Although the social form of the assembly furnishes an array of 'more-or-less similar elements' based on historically established practices, the way in which these elements are employed is not predetermined. Enactment represents the ability of organisers and participants to exercise agency and creativity in the organisation of the meeting – which will vary according to its size, its content matter and mode of presentation – and in deploying its formal elements.

The possible varieties of public assemblies and meetings, and their common elements and cast of characters, make them susceptible to comparative analysis. There have been numerous other comparative studies of citizen participation in Brazil (see Baiocchi et al. 2011; Ottman 2006; Ribeiro & Grazia 2003; Schönleitner 2006; Wampler 2007, 2008), but they have generally assessed the same type of participatory institution between different cities (one exception is Avritzer 2009). In this book I compare and contrast three participatory institutions managed by the same administration. Through comparing organising practices in public meetings and assemblies in different participatory institutions, and attendant ethnographic data, we can make out the broader dimensions of a governance logic that deploys and crystallises state power in some spaces and not others. The analysis is, through contrasting and comparing participatory institutions, able to move beyond an examination of situated practices to demonstrate the 'strategic selectivities' of state power in institutions of participatory democracy (Jessop 2008: 125–6). This enables, in other words, an examination of how political interests play out across a number of participatory institutions in the city.

Another relevant feature highlighted by Handelman (1990) concerns temporality. Participatory assemblies are sequenced, or rather, are routine enactments based on more-or-less established practices. In Santo André, members of participatory institutions have a biennial membership, which marks out a beginning and an end for a given cohort of councillors. They are, in a sense, teleological. In some participatory institutions, the teleological division of participation into successive stages enables the generation of 'emotional energy' (Collins 2004), as lay participants and their government counterparts fight to have their own personal and collective goals implemented, at times at the expense of others. Other participatory institutions may be better characterised by numbingly, bureaucratic routine, or indeed something more flexible and fluid altogether. Whichever the case, the initial phase is particularly important, as it helps shape the expectations of the future participants at a critical juncture. As I show in Chapter 2, the induction ritual, in which lay participants become official members of the participatory institution, dramatises the power of high status officials, formally locates elected citizens in a symbolic order, and introduces social constructs and spatial configurations that will become routine features of participatory assemblies. It helps establish and ritualise power relations and the configuration of practices that extend beyond the ritual itself (Bell 1992, 2009).[3] Apart from the long-term sequencing of assemblies over a biennial term, meetings also have an infra-meeting sequence. They have an internal logic that parses out and coordinates participation. A regulatory instrument as banal as a meeting agenda is one example of how an assembly may be organised and controlled, at the infra meeting level, without the explicit issuing of orders. In Chapters 3 and 4 I examine how different institutions organise their meetings and the instruments and techniques with which they are regulated.

Spatial organisation is a basic dimension of the organisation of practices in participatory institutions, for the manner in which individuals are positioned in relation to one another encourages certain patterns of interaction and engagement, while also discouraging others (see Hall 1963, 1966; Giddens 1984: 66–68; Lincoln 1994). The patterns of bodily positioning in participatory assemblies are consonant with established patterns of conduct that prevail in classrooms, press conferences, business meetings and academic symposia, to name just a few. But despite their ubiquity in modern, organisational life, and consequently their taken-for-granted nature, this spatial organisation has significance insofar as it helps to reproduce particular patterns of deliberation and social intercourse that are shaped by power (Lincoln 1994: 62). In Chapters 3 and 4 I identify two particularly common spatial forms of organisation in public assemblies and meetings, and use analytical distinctions developed by Edward Hall (1963, 1966) to demonstrate how spatial organisation contributes to generating different patterns of deliberation and interaction. These chapters draw largely on participant-observation carried out in public assemblies, fieldwork journal entries and documentary evidence collected over a period of 16 months from 2007 to 2008. Chapters 5 and 6 draw more extensively on in-depth interviews with social activists, participants from civil society and with public servants and political appointees.

In Chapter 5, the interviews reveal that despite behavioural regularities in the assemblies, there were quite dissonant interpretations of their desirability or indeed necessity. I relate these interpretations to different, and often contradictory, ideological orientations. At the risk of reifying the state/society distinction, it is important to note that public servants and political appointees, unlike their civil society counterparts, are exposed, and indeed socialised into, an organisational culture bound together by a coherent belief system that may be called 'administrative ideology' (Abravanel 1983: 274; Starbuck 1982: 3). Organisations are not just rational enterprises; like any other formal institution, they are made coherent by more-or-less consistent and cogent beliefs and values that give co-workers a shared sense of purpose and that justify their place in the social order. This ideology can, perhaps unsurprisingly, often put government representatives at cross-purposes with civil society participants, who may hold to divergent ideals, such as those of participatory democracy, which valorise the knowledge of the lay public and hold that state decision-making should be devolved to, or co-determined with, members of civil society. Among the interviewees, however, there is no simplistic adherence to one or the other ideological orientation. As their narratives make clear, some public servants, although perhaps complicit in their everyday work with the functioning and propagation of the administration, hold to ideals of participatory democracy and identify with civil society. Conversely, some civil society participants criticise what are seen as instances of manipulation in participatory assemblies, while also justifying certain aspects of the administrative ideology, such as the pre-eminence of specialist knowledge. In the analysis of these interviews, I identify clusters of ideological convictions, points of overlap and agreement but also of dissonance, among different civil society and government participants as they reflect on past activity in the three participatory institutions. This analysis allows me to reflect on how power imbalances are perceived, rationalised and inform different strategies and patterns of conduct that were examined in previous chapters.

The attention given to public assemblies in the book is warranted, since they are the primary forums in which citizens voice their concerns and articulate their interests. They are the principal grounded phenomena of projects of participatory democracy. Yet precisely because they are formal public events, participatory assemblies are often subject to formal and official codes of conduct. The performative imperatives of participatory assemblies can alter and shape the behaviour of participants and proscribe the airing of discomforting truths. They can be sanitised of much of the messy realpolitik that goes on behind the scenes. In Chapter 6 I use analytical distinctions popularised by Erving Goffman (1957) to explore the interaction between a formal, participatory front stage and an informal backstage. I do so through a series of case studies that examine the manner in which political clientelism, fear and financial rewards come to influence participants as they pursue both individual and collective interests.

In the Conclusion I consider some of the broader implications of the foregoing analysis, and consider how participatory reform might proceed given the interdependencies of participatory reform and state power. Using some of the insights from this practice approach to participatory democracy, I put forward some practical suggestions for participatory reform that may be useful for activists in Brazil, Latin America and even further afield. Drawing on another stint of ethnographic fieldwork in 2015, I finally examine the advances and effects of participatory reform in Santo André and the trajectory and changing political aims of the Workers' Party.

1
Democratisation, Reform and Participation in Brazil

In this chapter I develop further the history of Santo André's participatory institutions begun in the Introduction. The institutions examined here were developed by a single administration over a relatively short stretch of time. Although somewhat intertwined, they each have individual histories, which have conditioned and shaped the grounded manifestations of citizen participation in Santo André. Like those promulgated in the Andean countries of South America, Brazil's Constitution and associated legislation had a large impact on the form of participation in the new democracy that emerged from the end of authoritarian rule in 1985, at times specifying important organisational features and elaborating legal-bureaucratic discourses that would be employed throughout the federation and many of the attendant participatory institutions.

In the section below I give a brief history of the participatory reform programme at the national level that led to the proliferation of Conselhos Gestores de Políticas Públicas (management policy councils), the 'institutional type' of the Conselho Municipal de Habitação (Housing Council, HC) and the Conselho de Política Urbana (Urban Development Council, UDC). Given its direct relevance to the HC and the UDC, particular attention is paid to the urban reform movement and its efforts to influence the founding features of the new democracy. Against this broader historical backdrop, I elaborate the history of the Workers' Party in Santo André and its efforts to transform local governance in a way that was at least initially inspired by democratic socialism. The emergence of the UDC and the HC is also located within the context of the practical housing and urban development challenges that the city faced as a result of deindustrialisation. A history of the participatory budget (PB), the institution that would become the flagship of participatory reform in Santo André, is finally provided, which notes some of the significant changes that it experienced under a series of Workers' Party administrations.

Participatory Democratisation in Brazil

Brazil's democratic transition was a period marked by extensive negotiation over the juridical and political form of the new republic. One of the foremost concerns in the immediate, post-transition environment was the drafting of a new Constitution, a document that was to have an enormous impact on the proliferation of participatory institutions throughout the country. On 1 February 1987, 559 members of Congress, who had been elected the previous November, formed the National Constituent Assembly and began a long and highly contentious process of drafting a new constitution. The conservative bloc fractured when a politically significant group of the Partido Democrático Social (PDS, Democratic Social Party) left to form the Partido da Frente Liberal (PFL, Liberal Front Party), meaning that the drafting process was not dominated by one particular group (Reich 1998). Numerous conservative and progressive lobby groups strove, and succeeded, in having their interests formally secured in the new Constitution, resulting in a lengthy document, contradictory and unworkable in parts, that took a full 20 months to draw up (Reich 2007: 178).

The nation's capital, Brasilia, became the site of intense lobbying efforts by progressive forces determined that the conservative tenor of the political transition not extend to the formal features of the new republic. Coalitions between different social groups, such as labour unions, the left wing of the Catholic Church and social movement organisations, established lobbies in the city in 1986 and 1987. A number of popular 'caravans' were also organised that transported activists to Brasilia during the convention of the National Constituent Assembly to have their demands written into the new Constitution (Alvarez 1993: 200). Lobbying by a number of progressive actors succeeded in opening up the negotiations to popular initiatives. Consequently, individuals and social organisations were able to directly offer suggestions to the initial constitutional draft. Individual citizens were also able to give testimony to the 24 sub-commissions charged with drafting particular sections of the Constitution. In addition, popular amendments could be submitted to Congress provided they were undersigned by 30,000 registered voters and three social organisations (ibid.: 201).

When it was finally completed, sections of the so-called 'Citizens' Constitution' reflected the widespread antipathy held towards the authoritarian regime and its command-and-control method of rule. One of the largest political and administrative changes mandated by the new Constitution was a decentralisation of federal authority and control over resources to states and municipalities. Many believed a devolution of federal responsibilities and resources to sub-national political units would improve service delivery and transparency, and provide the conditions for deepening citizen participation. The political Left was also strongly supportive of decentralisation since it was seen as a necessary ingredient in maximising its influence on local state agencies (Melo & Rezende 2004: 49). As the specifics of decentralisation were nested in a more extensive opposition to centralised government, broad-based support ensured a vigorous reform agenda, formally initiated by the ratification of the new Constitution.

Following the promulgation of the Constitution in 1988, decentralisation proceeded apace. Increasing autonomy for sub-national governmental bodies was coupled with hikes in their share of federal funding. The proportion of federal funds distributed to municipalities leapt from 9.5 per cent in 1980 to 16.9 per cent in 1992. State governments received similar increases, with their share of federal funds reaching 31 per cent in 1992, up from 24.3 per cent in 1980 (Rolnik & Somekh 2000: 83). Control of important social services shifted markedly towards states and municipalities. By the mid 1990s, 58 per cent of municipalities had discretionary power over federal monies transferred for health. Meanwhile, 33 per cent were similarly able to use federal transfers for welfare as the municipality considered appropriate (Melo & Rezende 2004: 44). Although decentralisation did not affect every sub-national political unit uniformly, and although some resources and responsibilities have been recentralised (see Arretche 1999, 2010), this transfer of authority nonetheless represented a significant devolution of service provision responsibilities.

Decentralisation was coupled, in the Constitution, with the legislative mandating and general encouragement of citizen participation in different areas of governance. From its very first page, the new Constitution, as José Alvaro Moisés reminds us, specifies that social rights are to be realised 'directly' (Moisés 1990: 1). In Articles 14, 29, 194, 204 and 227, the Constitution sanctions citizen participation in a variety of governance domains (Avritzer 2009: 48). For certain policy areas, such as welfare, health and education, management policy councils – a type of participatory institution to be further detailed in the case of Santo André – are mandatory for the release of federal funds, a requirement in force since 1996. Although management policy councils existed prior to this legislative enforcement, these areas have predictably experienced the highest growth in numbers. Maria Gohn (2001: 88) notes that in 1998, of the 1167 councils operating in the areas of health, education and social assistance, 488 had been created after 1997, with 305 between 1994 and 1996, and only 73 prior to 1991. However, there has also been a significant growth of these councils in other policy sectors such as work, the environment and tourism, which were, by 2001, present in over 20 per cent of Brazil's 5500 municipalities (IBGE 2003: 58). More recent survey data shows the general tendency seems to be one of unrelenting growth (IBGE 2010).

Management policy councils are becoming an ever more pervasive feature of local governance in Brazil. Yet, as they are products of local law (*lei orgánica*), they can vary significantly from one municipality to the other. Some common features are nonetheless observable. Membership of a management policy council is generally based on the parity principle, requiring half of the total number of councillors to issue from civil society while the other half are frequently nominated from the relevant department secretariat.[1] At times, employees from other departments will be invited to represent other functional areas in the hope of ensuring cross-departmental coherence in the council's decisions and deliberations. While in key areas these councils require a deliberative status – that is, one which vests them with decision-making authority – others can be consultative, merely intended to inform the Executive's own internal decisions (Gohn 2000: 179). Beyond the formal outlines provided by the Constitution and several other legal texts, such as the Statute of the City (introduced in the next section), Organic Health Law and Organic Welfare Law, the actual features of the different councils vary enormously. Research has shown great diversity in council functioning, with Leonardo Avritzer noting that some councils do not hold regular meetings, or even effectively exist (Avritzer 2006: 40).

The new Constitution provided not only the legal provisions for localised citizen participation projects; together with associated legislation, such as the Statute of the City, it at times directly shaped their format, for example by requiring the design and application of Planos Diretores (City Master Plans). In this emergent body of legislation, a new legal-bureaucratic vocabulary was elaborated that was employed in the grounded manifestations of participatory institutions examined in later chapters. However, not all participatory institutions had such important features prefigured by federal legislative negotiations. The participatory budget (PB) emerged in Santo André based both on localised attempts to democratise budgetary decision-making and, seemingly, on the replication of structures developed by other Workers' Party administrations. In the following section I give a brief history and summary of the urban reform content of the Constitution, since it bears directly on the management councils of urban development and housing in Santo André.

The Movement for Urban Reform and Legislative Formalisation

Urban reform became a salient demand for a number of social and political actors throughout the democratisation process. The disorderly and discriminatory patterns of urban development, plainly evident in Brazil's major cities by the mid 1980s, prompted various actors to struggle for a more egalitarian distribution of basic services and infrastructure and the full incorporation of *favela* settlements into the formal city. A number of these actors joined together in 1982 under the banner of the Movimento Nacional de Reforma Urbana (MNRU, Movement for Urban Reform) to intervene in the negotiations for the new Constitution. The MNRU rejected the tenets of modernist urbanism, which advocated an ordering of the urban territory based on functional separation (for instance, between living, work and leisure activities) and aligned the spatial organisation of the city with the exigencies of capitalist accumulation; instead, it favoured an alternative approach to planning that reasserted the primacy of the social (Friendly 2013: 158–9; Souza 1999: 278). Inspired by the concept of the 'right to the city' coined by French Marxist Henri Lefebvre (1968), the MNRU sought increased investment in public infrastructure throughout the city so as to minimise class segregation and improve access to services for the most disadvantaged sectors of society, and demanded that property and the city serve a 'social function'. The democratisation of urban planning and governance functions was another of the MNRU's foremost demands, seeking to redistribute power away from the political class that had overseen the creation of cities marked by stark, socio-spatial inequality. These demands were written into the 'Emenda Popular de Reforma Urbana' (Popular Amendment for Urban Reform) that was signed by over 100,000 citizens from around the country and presented to the Constituent Assembly, which was convened in 1986 (Avritzer 2009: 144; Cardoso 2003).

The MNRU was partially successful in realising its goals. Two of its main demands, the social function of land and the right to the city, were included in Brazil's first constitutional urban charter in 1988.[2] But these guiding postulates were subordinated to a requirement inserted by a conservative group (Centrão) in the Constituent Assembly: cities with a population in excess of 20,000 would require a City Master Plan (Avritzer 2009: 143), which would be the sole means for implementing, at a municipal level, legal powers specified in the Constitution that gave local governments greater control over urban development (Carvalho 2001: 131). Enabling legislation for the constitutional articles on urban policy (Articles 182 and 183) was only passed thirteen years after the promulgation of the Constitution, when congressional lobbying by the MNRU, renamed the Fórum Nacional da Reforma Urbana (FNRU, National Forum for Urban Reform), was largely successful in including most of its stipulations – including public participation, the social function of private property and progressive land taxation powers – in the law known as the Statute of the City.[3] The passage of the Statute of the City was a landmark in urban policy and municipal law, creating together with the new Constitution a new 'juridico-urbanistic order' that was premised on the development and implementation of City Master Plans (Cymbalista & Santoro 2009: 6).

The decentralisation of federal authority and the mandating of citizen participation throughout the political system provided, as Baiocchi (2006) argues, propitious administrative conditions for progressive forces to create programmes of participatory democracy at the local level. But the Constitution did more than re-index the rights and responsibilities between the political units of the new republic. Two further features need to be highlighted here. First, the Constitution and associated legislation specified many of the types of participatory institutions that governments could and in some cases were required to create. Many of the possible forms of participatory initiatives were enumerated in the classificatory texts of the new democracy, providing sets of legally sanctioned activities and organisational requirements for participatory institutions developed at the local level. Second, the Constitution and associated legislation not only specified the types of participatory initiatives governments ought to develop, they elaborated a technical vocabulary that would be deployed throughout the state system and attendant participatory institutions. At times the development of this vocabulary was extensive. For instance, in the case of City Master Plans a whole array of legal and administrative instruments were formulated that would be employed in the participatory institution, such as the UDC, created to oversee the implementation of the plan. The composition of City Master Plans complements and elaborates the technical discourse used by urban planning professionals, since what Marilena Chauí might call 'competent discourse' (Chauí 2000: 3) in the institution would depend on knowledge of the whole body of relevant legislation and how it bore on specific processes of public administration.

Yet not all participatory institutions were created to satisfy statutory requirements, and not all were shot through by discourse set out in legislation. In fact, of the three institutions examined here, only the UDC was required by law. The other management policy council, the HC, was created by an act of law, but it was not required by federal legislation. Nonetheless, the relevant legislation at the federal level, and urban planning laws at the local level, figured quite prominently in the deliberations of the HC, and influenced the way in which problems were framed. In the section above, I sketched out the legislative heritage of the UDC in the context of disputes over the juridical and political form of the new democracy. While similar, supra-local histories could be mapped out for the HC, and indeed the PB, their features were not so prefigured by such legislative negotiations at the federal level. Their development in Santo André is thus better located within the context of the local projects implemented by Workers' Party administrations.

Santo André: Its Growth, Politics and Urban Development

Santo André is a municipality of some 675,000 inhabitants in the southeast of Greater São Paulo, and part of the ABC industrial region. The name derives from a small encampment-village, Santo André da Borda do Campo, founded in 1553 by the Portuguese explorer João Ramalho. Although the title of Octavio Gaiarsa's book enjoins us to think of Santo André as 'a city that slept for three centuries' (Gaiarsa 1968), the existence of the colonial outpost, which lasted only seven years, has little more than nominal relevance to the modern municipality bearing its name. In the modern era, Santo André first emerged in 1910 as a district surrounding the railway station on the line linking central São Paulo to the port of Santos, and finally became recognised as an independent municipality when São Bernardo was partitioned in 1938 (Gaiarsa 1991: 54, 62). Some years before then, however, important features of what would become the modern city had already emerged.

Over the last forty-odd years of the nineteenth century, a railway was constructed linking the interior of São Paulo with the port city Santos. The São Paulo Railway, which became the most profitable British railway investment anywhere in Latin America (Rippy 1966: 154), was fundamental to the commercial growth and urban development that took place in the region. Construction of the railway was driven in good measure by high international coffee prices, which provided incentives for the establishment of plantations further inland and placed attendant demands on transportation to international markets (PMSA 1991: 22). There was no motorised transport at the time, and so the technically complex matter of designing and building a rail link to the sea was initiated. This link negotiated the precipitous inclines of the *serra*, allowing, over time, a more expeditious and reliable transmission of people and goods than was possible by road. The railway connected nodes of transport (the port city of Santos/São Vincente) and production and commercialisation, initially located in Jundiaí. Although the railway commonly went by the name *Inglesa* (or English), after the source of its capital and the nationality of its engineers and planners, manual labour was provided by immigrants from Portugal, Italy and Spain, in addition to rented slaves (ibid.: 26).

Many of the immigrants who settled in what is today's Santo André were Italian, a good number of whom started small viticultural enterprises and made charcoal for the region by felling and burning trees (Gaiarsa 1991: 45–47). Their progeny were already less disposed to such work, and increasingly went into many of the small artisanal workshops, craft and other commercial establishments that were then emerging. By the end of the nineteenth century three large textile and furnishings factories were established: Kowarick, Ipiranguinha and Streiff Chairs. Their owners became influential figures in the political and economic life of the city.

Italian migrants had a large ideological and practical influence on the early labour movement, as they brought with them anarchism and a direct action strategy that would leave a lasting influence on the Brazilian Left (Angell 1998: 92; Dulles 1973; French 1992). It did not take long for the anarchist-inspired labour movement to make its influence felt: the first large-scale strike occurred in the Ipiranguinha textile factory in 1906, only years after the first manufacturing plants appeared. This strike set the stage for the following decades: though there would be ebbs and flows, industrial development brought with it what Colin Gordon might call 'spaces of industrial sociability' (Gordon 1991: 31) that allowed working-class identities to form and struggle for interests common to their colleagues.

The history of the labour movement in the ABC over the decades to follow was discontinuous. Its ability to secure benefits for those on the shop floor depended, among other things, on the employment of different mobilising strategies, economic conditions, external allies, global politics and, perhaps most significantly, the at times brutal reaction of conservatives and co-optive paternalism of populists (French 1992). Nonetheless, it was activity on the factory floor and the management of the new, autonomous unions that gave some impetus to the end of the authoritarian era in the great strikes of the late 1970s (Sader 1988). The unions were also instrumental in the formation of a new political party, the Workers' Party that would compete for power in the new democracy (Keck 1992).

Celso Daniel and the Workers' Party Project in Santo André

In Santo André, the Workers' Party became the most successful political force following the return of full and free elections in 1988, and Celso Daniel, a civil engineer turned politician, was its principal figure until his brutal murder in 2002. Celso Daniel came from a 'traditional family', as elites are euphemistically called. His father Bruno José Daniel was a significant political figure in the city, winning three consecutive terms in the Câmara Municipal (Legislative Chamber), between 1952 and 1964, where he also served for a time as president. He was even made the city's interim mayor, albeit very briefly, in the 1950s. Two of his sons were, however, engaged in causes and issues seldom associated with 'traditional families'. Celso's brother Bruno was an advisor to the popular movement, and wrote his doctoral thesis on Santo André's participatory budget (Daniel 2003). Celso Daniel, as many of the city's inhabitants and his former colleagues informed me, was charismatic; his publications showed him to be erudite, and the policies he introduced demonstrated a commitment to remedying the social conditions of the city's disadvantaged. Particularly in the early years of his first mayoral term, both in his published academic work and in the documentation issuing from the administration, socialism was an explicit goal (see Daniel 1988, 1990, 1996; PMSA 1992a, 1992b).

Celso Daniel's first administration adopted the motto employed by the urban reform movement and originally coined by Henri Lefebvre (1968): 'right to the city'. This became a catchphrase to integrate the urban poor into the formal city. But it was not just a bricks-and-mortar project. It was part of a much more ambitious attempt to remake and remodel elitist political culture. The new Daniel administration saw itself as engaged in 'a struggle for hegemony', which implied a dismantling of 'the political culture of the privileged', an 'inversion of priorities' and a new state–society relationship based on a culture of citizen rights (PMSA 1992a: 36). The ideological stamp of democratic socialism seemed especially pronounced when the administration outlined how this socio-political transformation would be brought about:

> The culture of rights is only going to come about by defeating the political culture of the privileged, which helps to reinforce the control of the state over society. This dominant culture legitimates itself through an ensemble of values and practices that is associated with traditional social and political elites and has a distinctive presence in Brazilian life. (ibid.: 20)

Against this long-developed heritage, the administration under Celso Daniel issued a familiar rejoinder: 'Combating the political culture of the privileged is necessary in order to cultivate the political culture of rights – in which the state is subordinated to the aspirations and necessities of society and is controlled by it' (ibid.: 21). A 'culture of rights' was not something to be merely cultivated in the realm of values and ideas, but through 'putting into practice, in day-to-day practices ... a new relationship between the local political power and the local population' (Daniel 1988: 2; see also Daniel 1990).

The dream of effecting cultural renewal through citizen participation met with early hurdles, and some might say was hamstrung from the beginning, for it was a goal and strategy that, according to available data, had largely passive rather than active support in civil society. Even in its first term of office, members of the Workers' Party administration saw what they perceived to be the narrow, and rather less than strategic, aims of many of the organised popular actors in Santo André. The following is worth quoting in full:

> Our first year of government was marked by the enormous expectation the *andreense* [residents of Santo André] population had for us to solve its problems. Public works and urgent services were demanded, which were ignored by past administrations, and activist party members and social

movements demanded the rapid implementation of our programme. In sum, the multiple problems we had to confront, the precarious capacity of the administrative 'machine' and our inexperience in public administration made it difficult to establish priorities and to quickly meet expectations ... Self-criticism is important, but the responsibility for popular participation is not the local government's alone. The population has little experience in this area ... It is not in the habit of *informing itself, to be educated or to manage. It only wants that the public administration attends to its demands*, without considering the limitations and concrete difficulties that this entails. The organised movements do not understand costs, technical variables, or the processes and implications that are involved in realising their demands. Often they dispute among themselves to determine the service priorities in their area of activity, *demonstrating a segmented vision that is disengaged from the population of the city as a whole.* (PMSA 1992b: 30–32, emphasis added)

In other words, the Workers' Party administration found itself having to mediate between competing claimants and in a role that had complex technical considerations which were unappreciated by the mobilised public. But perhaps more fundamentally, organised civil society did not seem to share so wholeheartedly the administration's vision of a new, socialist political culture. Rather, it was more concerned with the provision of basic services (see Vigevani 1989). Active civic associations and urban popular movements were receptive to the participatory overtures of the administration, but they were too narrowly self-interested and divided for the revolutionary planners then in office.

Nonetheless, the dream of radical cultural renewal died hard. In 1996, socialism was still firmly on the horizon, or at least the horizon Daniel envisaged when in dialogue with his Workers' Party colleagues (Daniel 1996). And in 1998, Pedro Pontual, director of the PB, was still underscoring the potential of participatory praxis:

the limits and the possibilities of the process of Participatory Budgeting depend also on the manner in which we conduct this process. On the one hand, it needs to be understood that all these experiences, including the Participatory Budget, are *contributions towards a new political culture*. It is very important to take account of this. However, it is also important to be very clear that the time it will take to construct a new political culture will be much greater than our time in government, particularly taking into account the time it has taken for the dominant political culture to emerge, and which generated the clientelism and patronage politics that we know well. (Pontual 1998: 34, emphasis added)

Socio-cultural transformation remained, ostensibly, the aim of the Workers' Party's participatory institutions. But it became a project of the *longue durée*, so long in fact that attaining its ultimate goals would require 'much more' than the party's limited time in office. Speaking some nine years after the Workers' Party first won office, Pontual was aware of the entrenched nature of extant socio-political relations and the deep roots of older styles of governance. The postponement of radical goals and the concomitant de radicalisation of government rhetoric were perhaps hardly surprising, in light of broader changes the Worker's Party experienced through the 1990s and the historical experience of socialist parties in systems of representative democracy (see Amaral 2003; Samuels 2004; Singer 2012). Values that were compatible with the party's more visionary aims were emphasised in government communications – such as social inclusion, equality, human rights, citizenship and so on (see PMSA 1999) – just as the administration became more technically adept. However, administrative pragmatism did not dampen the participatory reform effort. In fact, it was from the late 1990s onwards that the participatory reform effort gathered steam. Most of the city's 24 management councils for public policy were created after the late 1990s – a diversity of participatory options that Daniel staunchly defended (Daniel 2000: 133).

Here it is worth briefly reflecting on how an appreciation of the limitations recognised by the Workers' Party administration in the mid to late 1990s might have figured in the development of Santo André's participatory institutions. For, given that organised civil society was, according to the citations above, too narrowly self-focused, too internally divided and lacking the expansive vision required for the party's radical plans, what role should be accorded to it in the participatory institutions? It would have been ill-advised to devolve power under such conditions – that is, where the government is alone in maintaining a 'universal vision' (ibid.: 132), unfettered by the corporative and particular interests of other social and political actors. To put it simply, the radicals were, according to senior administrative staff, those in office rather than the attendees of the participatory forums. In such a context, maintaining a significant government presence in participatory institutions was not only necessary in order to mediate between competing social interests, it was vital to help cultivate a new political culture and attain the goals of the radical reformers. While this presence may not have been motivated by a cynical desire to maintain control, later chapters demonstrate that the strong government role in the participatory institutions was to become highly problematic.

In the following sections, I introduce the UDC, the HC and the PB, and locate their emergence in the context of the urban development challenges faced by the new progressive administrators.

The Building of Participatory Institutions: Housing and Urban Planning

The type of housing and urban development reform undertaken by the Workers' Party administration on taking office in 1989 was influenced by an appreciation of the city's changing socio-economic conditions. First, economic restructuring – in particular the reduction of tariffs and other protectionist measures heralding the end of industrialisation based on import substitution – had a very direct impact on Santo André and the ABC region more generally, as it did on many Latin American cities (Rogers et al. 2011: 554). The once thriving industrial park known as the Tamanduateí axis, which ran along the central stretch of the city's main railway, became a graveyard of empty factories and warehouses, as large industrial interests moved to other states or abroad in search of lower operating costs, or permanently closed their doors (Souza 2007). Industrial employment dropped precipitously as a result: from 1984 to January 2002 industrial employment in San André fell by 50.68 per cent (Passarelli & Denaldi 2006: 31). An increase in services employment and a boom in the precarious informal market did not compensate for the secure and well-remunerated employment that industry had previously provided (Acioly et al. 2003: 10). Thus, while population growth, which had boomed between 1960 and 1980, had largely levelled out in the following two decades, the city's *favelas* grew in number and density, as many lower-class workers found formal housing costs impossible to bear. Between 1991 and 1996, the *favela* population increased 3.78 per cent annually, while the growth rate for the entire city was 0.31 per cent. This growth was particularly intense in the wetlands macro-zone, concentrating informal development in the region furthest from basic services; in an area with poor amenities, this put the local ecology and the quality of the water supply at risk.

A number of interrelated administrative reforms were pursued that enabled the government to respond to the housing and urban development issues the city faced. For instance, a swathe of legislative measures was passed that established directives for the construction of low income housing. In 1991, a zoning framework was introduced called Áreas de Especial Interesse Social (AEIS, Areas of Special Social Interest). Drawn from the landmark ZEIS legislation (Zonas Especiais de Interesse Social, Special Social Interest Zones) originally developed in Recife, north-east Brazil, AEIS were designed to facilitate land-title regularisation and urbanisation, and to provide incentives for developers to invest in housing projects for low-income families by, among other things, indirectly lowering land prices that had risen dramatically alongside population growth.

It was in a context of administrative reform, in which newly employed progressive public servants confronted an old bureaucratic culture (Denaldi & Dias 2003: 319), that the Housing Council (HC) was created in 1999 and effectively began the following year with the principal aim of guaranteeing popular participation in the elaboration and administration of municipal housing policy (PMSA 2006: 34). However, its specific duties suggest a fairly limited remit. Beyond the organisation of the annual housing conference, and ensuring the directives determined therein were adhered to, the HC was responsible for managing the fund for housing, determining its criteria and the projects for which it would be used, and for holding public assemblies and meetings to debate housing issues in the city. Half of the HC's sixteen members were to be representatives of civil society and were elected in assemblies. Three of these members were to be representatives of *favela* associations, three to be representatives housing associations or popular cooperatives, and two had to be representatives of disadvantaged social groups or of social segments who worked in the area of housing. The other members were made up of public servants and political appointees. The civil society portion of the HC membership thus largely derived from organisations representing popular interests.

The Creation of the City Master Plan and the Urban Development Council

Attempts to establish a new City Master Plan in 2004 were a culmination of the legislative and policy reforms outlined above (PMSA 2004). The plan merged urban development and housing policy, and established a new Urban Development Council (UDC) in a number of legislative amendments that were passed as a single law. Though Santo André's City Master Plan grew out of a local meeting stream that sought to develop a 20-year plan for the city, entitled Cidade Futuro (Future City), many of its provisions were made possible by the ratification of the federal Statute of the City in 2001 and the new legal instruments that it introduced (see Carvalho 2001; L. Pires 2007: 133–44; Rezende & Ultramari 2007). Several of the plan's specifications sought to decrease land prices, a long-standing goal of past Workers' Party administrations, through, for example, establishing new zoning districts called ZEIS. The zoning components of the legislation were more complex and comprehensive than the AEIS. A host of other formal instruments were also included that strengthened the government's hand in matters of urban development.

The City Master Plan provided a conceptual framework for the UDC, divided the municipal territory into purpose-specific zones and delineated the administration's powers in matters of urban planning and governance. Like the HC, the UDC was responsible for holding public assemblies and meetings on urban development matters and for the management of a municipal fund for urban development. But the UDC was also charged with oversight of the application of the plan's provisions and policies. It was to debate proposed changes to the City Master Plan law, to propose changes to relevant legislation and to initiate and manage technical and working groups. It was also responsible for the enactment of one of the plan's urban planning instruments, the 'Outorga Onerosa do Direito de Construir' (a tax on the sale of building rights), which enabled the taxing of constructions whose height exceeded a pre-determined floor area ratio, typically of 1:1.[4] The UDC was composed of 38 titular members, 19 to be sourced from the government and 19 from civil society. Of these, five were representatives of businesses, five from social movements, four from NGOs and five from other management councils. Like the HC, it ordinarily convened once per month, but would also assemble quite frequently for extraordinary meetings. Unlike the HC, however, its membership included representatives of business interests – an odd interpretation of 'civil society'. It also had a more extensive remit, which included the review of legislative projects before their submission to the Legislative Chamber, and its membership was twice that of the HC.

Participatory Budgeting

Unlike the UDC and the HC, whose design and functioning drew on legislative and policy negotiations that were made at federal and local levels, the PB in Santo André has a history particular to the Workers' Party. In Santo André it began as a consultative exercise in Celso Daniel's first government (1989 to 1992), consisting of four stages, all of which were organised by the administration. First, a draft proposal was composed by the governing secretariat and other departments. Second, the draft was discussed with the public in assemblies held around the city. Third, the budget proposal was reconciled with available resources by the secretariat and the mayor. Fourth, the budget was presented to the legislature for approval. The population was not accountably involved in investment decision-making in this first foray into participatory budgeting. The Workers' Party lost the 1992 elections, and during the intervening years there was no public mobilisation to demand participation in prioritising the budgetary outlay. Acioly et al. (2003: 18) interpret this as a demonstration of the superficiality of the initial consultations. But it was also an indication that there was at that stage demonstrably little popular demand for the PB, and that unlike the case in Porto Alegre, the democratisation of the budget was not a long-standing demand of local community actors (Pontual 2000; Wampler 2007: 201–14).

The second Workers' Party administration (1993 to 1996), after analysing the party's previous term in office, installed a more complex participatory structure, ostensibly based on the Porto Alegre model. Two plenary streams were thus initiated, the first of which was regionally based. The municipal territory was divided into 18 regions, in which assemblies were held that would both elect local and city-wide investment priorities and regional representatives for a mandate on the Conselho Municipal de Orçamento (Municipal Budget Council, MBC), which was the chief representative body of the PB and consisted of regional lay and state representatives.[5] The members elected to represent their regions would then attend the monthly meetings of the MBC, and during the negotiating phase would debate with members of the administration and fellow councillors to formulate demands that would figure in the presentation of the budget to the Legislative Chamber, which would receive for approval the annual budget from the Executive. Like the HC and the UDC, half of the MBC's members were public employees, while the other half consisted of community representatives elected by regional assemblies. The other plenary stream was thematically based, and one where participants would debate and discuss issues related to one of eight topics: economic development; social inclusion; housing; public-sector reform; education; health; environmental quality; and culture. This followed a yearly cycle. In March, preparatory meetings would be held in the lead up to the assemblies of June and July. Investment priorities would then be determined in each of the 18 regions, and local representative candidates were elected to seats on the MBC.

The newly elected councillors for the MBC would then negotiate with each other and the administration in a series of meetings leading up to the presentation of the budget to the Legislative Chamber.

Unlike the HC and the UDC, the PB was not part of a technical and legislative reform project, and no specialised terminology was used in its assemblies. It drew less explicitly from the internal operations of government, from policies, procedures and the particulars of legislation. Rather, one of its merits was that it engaged with the lived, local knowledge of community needs, and enabled those needs to be expressed in a way that could easily garner social support. I outline this process in Chapter 3, where the process of demand-making and negotiation is analysed in some depth. However, it must be noted that the above programme structure, seemingly adopted from Porto Alegre, had changed significantly by 2007. In 2004 the cycle was made biennial after the administration claimed that it was unable to implement all of the citizens' demands in a single year. The annual structure was to be stretched over two years, rather than one, with holding-to-account assemblies to be held in year one, and the demand-making regional assemblies and budget formulation plenaries to be held in year two. This halved the number of possible demands that could be made in a single year. In addition, the thematic assemblies were disbanded, also in 2004, after participation rates in them dwindled. Attempts were made to keep them alive by bringing together similar themes. The original eight themes became six, then four, and were finally discontinued altogether in 2004. That is, the PB I encountered during fieldwork had been 'rationalised' and reduced to its essential parts. Regional assemblies would be followed by the negotiation phase and holding-to-account assemblies, and the whole process would occur across two years rather than one, in effect freeing the administrative apparatus somewhat from the intervention of the public in its budgetary determinations.

Conclusion

The years that followed Brazil's transition to democratic rule gave rise to a series of contestations, as existing elites and actors new to the political scene sought to have their interests inscribed in the form of government that was being negotiated. The decentralisation of federal power introduced by the 'Citizens' Constitution' that was finally promulgated in 1988 bolstered the role of states and municipalities in the federation through the devolution of new responsibilities and resources. This complemented some of the participatory reforms that were prefigured in the new Constitution, since meaningful citizen participation at the local level is predicated on the existence of empowered political units that can respond to citizens' demands. Indeed, the decentralisation of state power and the constitutional provisions for citizen participation were at times intimately connected. For instance, the disbursement of federal funds to municipalities in certain governance domains was predicated on the creation of management policy councils, ensuring a proliferation of this type of participatory institutions throughout Brazil's 5500 municipalities.

The participatory project pursued by the Workers' Party in Santo André in the early 1990s was far more ambitious than the accommodations made for citizen participation in the Constitution. Celso Daniel and many of his progressive colleagues sought to transform local politics along democratic socialist lines – that is, through instituting radical, participatory democracy. However, even at an early stage there appeared to be grave doubts about whether organised civil society in Santo André was willing or capable of assuming the kind of active role envisaged for it in this radical transformation. The state of local civil society, or at least as it was perceived by senior Workers' Party officials, provided some justification for maintaining a strong governmental presence in the city's burgeoning participatory institutions. But burgeon they did: during Daniel's terms in office, scores of participatory institutions were developed that deliberated on virtually every aspect of local governance, including the built environment, which is the primary focus of the three participatory institutions examined in this book.

Santo André's participatory institutions have been influenced by the Constitution and associated legislation, and perhaps also by the local government's only qualified commitment to sharing power with civil society. However, the prospects for participatory democratisation depend not only on such overt instances of statecraft and governmental decision-making. The grounded manifestations of participatory institutions are also crafted out of organising practices that are often tacit and unquestioned because they are pervasive, buried in the complex layers of the everyday, or because they fall within the accepted purview of authority-bearing organisations. Yet these practices, I argue, can shape in important ways the capacity of citizens to influence the actions of state officials in participatory institutions. While these practices are largely banal and would thus be familiar to new participants, there is still a teleological structure of tenure in Santo André's participatory institutions that serves to reproduce them. In the following chapter, I examine the first events experienced by new participants: elections in which they vie with peers to win a place on the institution; and the induction ceremony, which formally symbolises the acquisition of member status in the institution. These are the first instances of a chain of inter-connected events that will be examined further in Chapters 3 and 4.

2
Rituals and Ritualisation

First moments of contact are often founding moments. In Santo André's participatory institutions, the initial encounters between political appointees, public servants and members of the public are freighted with strategic importance and are thus heavily ritualised affairs. In this chapter I chart and analyse two rituals in particular: the electoral contests that are the means of gaining membership to a participatory institution; and the induction ceremonies that are held for the victors. Here I aim to show how such everyday rituals, which are largely taken for granted in studies of participatory democracy, condition and help to prefigure the configurations of practices in future assemblies. By examining how relationships between lay participants and state officials are ritually initiated, the analysis is able to show how participants begin their tenure in a participatory institution in a way that is shaped by representations of the socio-political order.

The chapter comprises three parts. First, it introduces into the analysis a basic and recurring social construct in many of Santo André's participatory assemblies. Referred to in Portuguese simply as *a mesa* ('the table'), it is a construct that bears much in common with what Erving Goffman termed the 'front region' (Goffman 1957: 78) and designates a social space normally occupied by high status government officers. We see in an example from a participatory assembly how the process of 'composing the table' serves to differentiate state officers from members of the public in a way that ascribes the social space of 'the table' with power and authority. Repeated at the beginning of many public assemblies, this process helps to legitimise the power of the presiding state actors and the roles they will play in coordinating the participation of the public.

Second, the chapter analyses an election process from the participatory budget (PB) and the induction ceremonies of two participatory institutions. Elections are important practical events that decide who among aspiring candidates from the lay public will secure a mandate on a participatory institution. But they are also, like the induction ceremonies that follow them, important rituals that dramatise certain features of political society and provide normative cues for cognition and future behaviour in assemblies. Not all participation is prescribed or controlled by government officers, however. An example from one election in the PB shows how candidates from civil society carve out a space in a state-organised assembly and orchestrate their own dramatic performance in a choreographed public contest between two popular candidates. The induction ceremony is a ritual of status transition and formally symbolises the commencement of membership in one of Santo André's participatory institutions. In this chapter I examine two induction ceremonies and argue that practical political considerations also help to shape the pageantry and organisation of such rituals.

Third, the chapter also introduces the executive structures of the Urban Development Council (UDC) and the PB, while the Housing Council (HC), given its unique makeup and organisational culture, will be examined separately in Chapter 4. Election to the participatory institution secures membership, but each institution also has a small number of executive positions for state and civil society representatives. These provide special titles and privileges for some participants and will feature in future chapters.

Before examining the ritual processes in elections and induction ceremonies, I first explain how such rituals contribute to the ritualisation of practices seen in later chapters.

Ritual and Ritualisation

Ritual, despite its canonical place in the social sciences, still yields fresh insights and theoretical innovations. Debate continues over the constituent elements of ritual, over the efficacy of ritual in structuring human relations, and in cognitively and culturally connecting the participants and publics of ritual performance to broader social structures and patterns of social conduct (Bell 1992, 2009; Collins 2004; Handelman & Lindquist 2005). Both the interpretation of ritual and the mode of analysis I adopt here are shaped by the explicit purpose of the institutions. As institutions of participatory democracy, it is vital to examine the kinds of power relations that are revealed, dramatised and legitimised in the structure of these rituals, and how those power relations are spatially and temporally mapped out in orchestrated interactions between social groups. The spatial and temporal mapping out of the ritual process has significance not only for the structure or form of the ceremony, but because there is often consonance between the formations expressed in the ritual structure and the forms of participation in the subsequent assemblies of the institution. That is, the induction ceremonies of participatory institutions can be viewed as one instantiation of a more extensive process of ritualisation, or as it is otherwise termed in the lexicon of some practice theorists, 'time-space extension' (Schatzki 1997: 290).

Ritualisation, for Catherine Bell, is a 'strategy for the constitution of power relationships that appears to be "instinctive" to the socialised agent' and involves two principal dimensions (Bell 1992: 206). The first is the projection and constitution of a structured environment that 'produces and objectifies constructions of power' (ibid.: 206). In the participatory institutions examined here, this consists in the spatial and normative structures that differentiate between particular classifications of actors – and thus helps to symbolically represent and socially constitute, for example, civil society and the state as distinct social groups – who have differing roles and potentialities within a particular assembly format. In this way, these rituals represent participants as subordinate members of a dyadic order. Relations of domination and subordination are reproduced 'simply by participating' in often taken-for-granted ways that normalise certain forms of conduct and prohibit and censure others (ibid.: 207).

The second dimension concerns the appropriation of possibilities opened up through the process of ritualisation. A counterpart to the reproduction of power relationships, this dimension of ritualisation allows for the opportunity of resistance, and of negotiating efforts to secure the consent of the dominated (ibid.: 207). Though it may play a less evident role in some participatory institutions, this dimension of ritualisation is particularly evident in the case of the PB, an innovation famed for its exceptional ability to provoke robust forms of participation. However, the capacity to generate resistance is only partially provided for in an analysis of the elections and induction ceremonies. They may help to codify reciprocal social norms and generate the 'emotional energy' of collective expectation (Collins 2004: 38), but the manner in which this expectation is expressed, and the norms obeyed or contravened, depends on the interactions and tactical manoeuvres of different actors in the negotiations analysed in Chapter 3. For now, let us turn to the process that foregrounds many public meetings in Santo André.

'Composing the Table'

At almost every major public event that I attended, the chairs at the front of the gathering were initially empty. The audience would enter and take their seats and there would be, normally, only one individual facing them. At induction ceremonies or city-wide conferences, this person would be a specifically employed master of ceremonies – a role taken up, in the PB assemblies, by Mauricio, the director of the Department of Participatory Budgeting and Planning.[1] The master of ceremonies who moderated the non-PB ceremonies looked to be in his mid to late fifties, with golden brown skin, a high forehead and bald scalp. The dark hair from his temples and sides was always pomaded back, and his upright posture, combined with his formal attire and steady enunciation, gave the occasions over which he presided a stately feel. Both the master of ceremonies and Mauricio, when he took up the role, proceeded with an almost identical practice of composing the table: they would call chosen members of the audience to take up the vacant seats at the front.

In conferences and other public audiences, the table would be made up of the executive team, normally featuring specialists from specific administrative departments that correspond to the nature of the gathering. In the case of the city housing conference, for example, the front table was occupied by senior staff from the Department of Urban Development, with the occasional appearance of other government officials, civil society or NGO representatives. Where notables present at the event were not invited to occupy a chair at the table, they were frequently recognised by those who were. For example, at a relaunch of the Future City programme, upon being invited onto the stage, the mayor proceeded to thank the vice-rector of the regional university for his attendance, as well as representatives from a local business consortium, among others, all of which were given to him on prompt cards.

At these large, ceremonious events, the mayor is normally first to be invited to assume his place at the table, followed by the deputy mayor, when she attended, and then the heads of the different secretariats. On such formal occasions, the master of ceremonies would use the honorific prefixes for the mayor and their deputy, *excellentissimo* or *excellentissima* ('His/Her Most Excellent') – prefixes which were originally royal epithets.

The mayor would then walk from his place in the audience and take his seat, often behind a table on a stage, thus occupying a position in relation to the audience that is both central and elevated. The second-rung directors, managers and city councillors would in like fashion take their place on either side of the mayor, followed by their subordinates.

'Composing the table' begins with undifferentiated members of the audience. However, the slow, ritualised calling forth of municipal officials into centralised and often elevated positions pronounces their distinguished status; they are shown to be not mere audience members, but officials of high standing. For most of those present, the positions of the officials would be well known. 'Composing the table' thus reiterates their differentiated status vis-à-vis the audience and symbolises the structure of power (Goffman 1957: 103; Kertzer 1988: 30; McComas et al. 2010: 123). Once the table is composed, the master of ceremonies, normally corresponding to the attendant hierarchy, initiates an oratory sequence. The mayor, as symbolic head, speaks in the most general terms, demonstrating the oversight and assurance typical of an authority (Sennett 1980: 16). Department secretaries delve more deeply into the technical matters, while departmental specialists talk of specific processes and case studies. There are reasonably specific but still quite flexible expectations relating to the technical competency, subject matter and timing of the different orators. The relationships of graded power are thereby demonstrated not only through their formal titles or physical organisation in the front region, but also through the content of their speeches.

While 'composing the table' symbolised the relations of graded authority between the government officers, the table itself is given an identity as a whole. For example, when audience members are invited to ask questions they are invited to approach and address the table. Whereas 'composing the table' indicated a process of drawing out and separation from the audience, the subsequent use of the term 'the table' suggests the formed social construct, employed to demonstrate their unity as members of government. Questions or demands would subsequently be made to the table, and the mayor or at times Mauricio in the PB assemblies would determine who best to respond to them. It was what Erving Goffman called the 'front region', and is similar to what Arlei Damo, in his ethnographic study of Porto Alegre's PB, termed the *espaço nobre*, or 'noble space' (Damo 2006: 168) – a 'space' that is, to borrow a Durkheimian expression, sacralised at the most important assemblies.

The designation of this 'noble space' also has a preparatory role in the organisation of the event that helps to legitimise and prefigure certain patterns of interactive practices. Following the introductory speeches, the master of ceremonies normally retires from the stage, and often does not return to speak until the formal close of the occasion. The front region is thereafter charged with managing and regulating the assembly. In the case of the PB assemblies, Mauricio, the director of the PB, of course remained at the front table following its composition and, wherever necessary, served as a go-between, passing the microphone to relevant persons, making introductions, providing clarifications and quieting the crowd. Part of this role implied the management of intercourse with the crowd. Mauricio informed the audience of where to speak and time limitations, and at times threatened the crowd when it did not comply with his directions.

'Composing the table' confers on the front region both prestige and power in a way that presages its role in managing the event. The ritualised calling forth of officials, which reifies the social construct of the table, also serves as an important function for future members of the participatory institutions. That is, the front table will serve a similar role in the meetings of many of the participatory institutions that it does in the conferences and induction ceremonies: it is a space from which individuals, who are normally senior government officers, regulate and coordinate, to varying degrees, the participation of attendees in the participatory meetings and assemblies.

The ritual process of composing the table is also found in the gatherings of many other organisations in Brazil. However, the process examined here may be distinguished from those found in non-government organisations – for example, that might precede the meetings of social movements – through the symbols of state that are on show, through the formality of the assembly and forms of speech that are used, and through the use of honorific labels for high status representatives of the state. It is a common process that is in this case distinguished by markers of state power. While the process of 'composing the table' might be enacted somewhat differently in different organisational milieu, its common form is an important ingredient in the strategy of ritualisation analysed here, since it aids in configuring the practices of future assemblies. Now let us turn to the elections of civil society participants, since they provide the means by which regular citizens and representatives of organised civil society become members of the city's participatory institutions.

Elections

Elections are generally the first event for any civil society representative in a participatory institution. Different institutions arrange them differently. For the management policy councils (the UDC and the HC), special gatherings are generally convened in which individuals and groups are invited to attend, nominate and vote for representatives to take up a position on the institution for a fixed period of time. These gatherings take place on local government property, the votes are tallied and those candidates who garner the most votes are then awarded with a biennial term as a member of a participatory institution. Since the biennial terms of the institutions are asynchronous, my fieldwork did not coincide with the voting periods or induction ceremonies of all of the institutions. However, I was present for the election of civil society representatives to the Municipal Budget Council (MBC), the peak representative body of the PB, and can relate some of the ways in which the election process, while practically deciding the issue of regional representation, are also ritual events that help to prefigure the practices of later assemblies. It should be noted that the following took place after a process of 'composing the table' examined earlier, and after the prioritisation process that is examined in Chapter 3.[2]

Articulations of Power and Performance: Scenes from an Election

Each of the 19 regions of the PB is assigned an alphabetical identifier. In region S, this regional assembly was held in a Centro Educacional de Santo André (CESA) – a multi-purpose education and recreation centre – in Cata Preta, a neighbourhood in the city's south-east. It is part of the second poorest region of the city, the most populous, and is also located quite far from the city centre. One must take a bus from Centro to Vila Luzita, and from there a second bus to Cata Preta. Centro to Vila Luzita is the only route of the entire city to have articulated buses, and functions as an express conveyor belt between the two transport hubs. Centro is Santo André's central bus and train terminal, linking Santo André to São Paulo proper and to numerous bus lines that extend throughout São Paulo's urban territory. Vila Luzita functions as a secondary transport hub for the poorer south-eastern parts of Santo André. From there, small bus lines spread throughout neighbourhoods that extend into the large hills that border and traverse the wetlands area. In the morning, workers can be seen draining out of these communities and taking the express bus route to their jobs in the other urban centres to which it connects. Similarly, at the end of a working day, an enormous line snakes around the platform of the bus terminal at Centro to return them home.

I arrived at the CESA a little after 9 AM on the day of the regional assembly. Outside, crowds of people were milling about. Some fieldwork colleagues I knew were seated on a rise that overlooked the entrance of the CESA.[3] 'So, do you know who it's going to be today?' asked one. 'I think it's between Edu and Ronaldo', the other responded. Soon the crowd that had formed at the entrance, lining up for registration, gave way to two new black cars with government plates that had pulled up close to the entrance. The mayor, João Avamileno, emerged from one of the rear passenger seats, flanked by a department secretary and a personal aide. A state deputy, Wanderlei Siraque, arrived in the other. The cars remained there as the crowd of about two hundred people traipsed into the large hall.

In order to enter, one had to be a resident of the region. Just inside the entrance, the queue was directed into a couple of streams where each participant could confirm their place of residence. Registration was important since it aimed to prevent the undue influence on a region's decisions of neighbouring populations or other groups who, for whatever reason, may desire the prioritisation of particular investments or the election of particular representatives to the MBC. After confirming their residency, participants dispersed from the queues to enter the large, breezy hall that had already been set up with flat-screen television monitors, a projector screen, signage, audio equipment and an arrangement of chairs for the audience and for state representatives. Entrances to other areas of the complex and to the upper levels of the CESA, which encircled the hall, were all blocked off.

When I arrived, the executive team was already assembled in front of the audience. After a lengthy prioritisation process, one case of which is analysed in the following chapter, Mauricio broaches the topic of nomination. He stands in the centre of the hall, his diminutive figure framed by a large red sign, erected against the back wall which reads, 'Participatory Budgeting: You Have Been Making a Difference for the Past 12 Years'. His dress is casual, perhaps more so than the other senior, local administrative staff. He holds a microphone and stands in front of the table, now missing the local dignitaries who had opened proceedings. He calls for nominations. Every couple of seconds voices issue from the crowd, 'I nominate Zé Roberto'. And another: 'I second him'. 'I nominate

Dona Carla'; 'I second her'. The crowd are all on their feet. They had been sitting for up to two hours during the prioritisation process and are now able to move more freely. There is quite a bit of movement in the crowd. Some shuffle in what resemble small whirls of people who seem to know each other. A few restless kids, freed by the relaxing of protocol, are darting through the crowd.

Mauricio calls all of the nominees to assemble on either side of him. They are each given a number on a large cardboard square which is hung round their neck on a piece of string. Each nominee is given two minutes to make their case. Each states their credentials as a community organiser. 'I have been involved in the Pastoral de Saúde [an arm of the Catholic Church active in the health sector] for 20 years', argues one, emphasising the importance of improving local health services. Another recounts his history as a strike leader, a historical opponent of government who is well-equipped to hold the powerful to account, while also being able to negotiate and compromise for the good of the community. Some of the nominees are obviously practised in public speaking. Their voices are louder, clearer, more purposeful. Others are not so sure, mumble a little, stutter, but are still given generous applause by the audience.

Some nominees receive a far more emphatic reception from the audience, however. Two, in particular, receive lasting chants that extend into the time allotted to the next nominee. They are Ronaldo and Edu. If it were not for the microphone, the cries of 'Ro-Nal-Do' would have made the next speaker's voice inaudible. Every once in a while small pockets of the audience emit the same chant, unprovoked, but it is muffled and dies quickly. It is following the candidates' speeches, however, that the entire complexion of the event changes. The nominee standing on the far left of Mauricio asks for the microphone and says, 'I am withdrawing my nomination in favour of Ronaldo'. The crowd erupts once more with chants of 'Ro-Nal-Do, Ro-Nal-Do'. Another nominee asks for the microphone, this time withdrawing her nomination for Edu, 'who is best suited to represent the region'. Cries break out of 'E-Du, E-Du'. It becomes obvious that the support from the assembled crowd is principally divided between the two main nominees. One by one, each of the nominees withdraws their nomination in favour of one or the other rival, each time to a building crescendo of support from the crowd.

Finally, only the two rivals remain. Mauricio summarises the options before the crowd before they queue for the voting machines. The line is long, disorganised, and the bustling and chatty crowd take some time to pass through. As the queue snakes past the assembled machines towards the exit, many take their leave before the results are tallied. Those who remain reassemble in the main hall. After perhaps twenty or so minutes, Mauricio, microphone in hand, informs the crowd: 'The results are in!' He reads out the number of votes which slightly favours Edu. His supporters had earlier seemed the less vocal, but are now almost euphoric in their celebrations. 'E-Du, E-Du' rings out around the hall. Even with a diminished crowd, the noise is as loud as it has been all morning. Two children have long plastic horns, often used at football games, and are blowing into them in what sounds like shrill elephant cries. Edu is taken onto the shoulders of his supporters, who uncomfortably jump up and down with Edu's sizeable body teetering uncomfortably and threatening to tumble. Ronaldo, now visibly deflated, disappears in silence with his colleagues. Another civil society representative of the MBC standing by my side leans towards me confidingly: 'We aren't like this in my area', he says, 'we take things much more seriously'.

Following the election of the councillors to the MBC, the government also sought the nomination of neighbourhood representatives. But this was a much more informal practice, with the government workers spreading out into the audience to elicit and record the names of individuals who would be used to distribute information to other citizens in their area, and with whom the elected councillors of the MBC could cooperate.

The two fieldwork colleagues who were sitting on the rise outside the CESA had known and indeed predicted the contest between the two opponents in the election assembly. But they did not mention the depth of community support the candidates had garnered for their nominations in the assembly, nor its careful elaboration in public displays. As each of the nominees stated their credentials, and outlined their experience in combating the government, or working in welfare or health, they were in fact preparing for a forthcoming withdrawal for their favoured candidate. The cascading support for the two principal candidates gave the sense that, even though each of the nominees had excellent qualifications to be a regional representative, they were no match for either Edu or Ronaldo. Whatever support each candidate's speech might have garnered from the audience was, they urged, to be transferred to their favoured colleague. It was, as Edu later confirmed in an informal conversation, a meticulously planned event, rehearsed well in advance.

The dramatic performance that was choreographed in concert with other nominees, and accompanied by the waves of chanting from supporters in the crowd, helped to charge the atmosphere with expectation. When the ballot results where finally announced, expectant mood gave way to euphoric celebration, at least for one group of supporters, as the denouement of the choreographed 'sociodrama' came into view (Kertzer 1988: 108). The release of 'emotional energy' (Collins 2004: 38) was not only the result of the climactic performance, but a culmination of much prior mobilising work by Edu. Success here gave Edu a symbolic victory over a fellow community leader and earned him considerable social recognition – an important function of administrative rituals, another example of which we see later in an even more visceral commemoration in the induction ceremony. We also encounter Edu several times throughout the book as he becomes an important actor in the MBC. In one instance he is accused of being the client of a member of the Legislative Chamber in a public assembly, a suggestion that almost erupts into a physical altercation. Indeed, it is possible that the city councillor had put his weight behind Edu's nomination in the assembly we have just analysed. But it is worth indicating that although this election relied on substantial prior mobilisation, others were not always so prefigured by intricate preparations.[4]

Edu's electoral victory secured him a position on the MBC as a titular representative. Despite Ronaldo's ignominious departure after coming so close to victory, he was awarded, as the second-most popular regional candidate, a place on the MBC as Edu's *suplente* or 'second', who was authorised to attend meetings but not vote, and who could if necessary stand in for the titular representative. This grading of participants as titular or second is not unique to participatory institutions. Members of the local Legislative Chamber or the Senate, for example, also have seconds. Edu's appointment to the MBC was thus secured in a way that assigned him a place in a hierarchical order that drew from the nomenclature and labelling of other political institutions (Wood 1985).

Edu's victory illustrates the creative stagecraft of community actors that was employed in order to appoint a favoured candidate to the MBC. But it is also important to note the social norms and spatial patterns to which this performance conforms. You will recall that government officers, such as the mayor, occupy a space in the front region that is designated for high-status government officers through the process of 'composing the table'. In the case recounted above, we also saw how Mauricio coordinated the participation of audience members, informed them when and for how long they could speak, and also requested nominees and announced the victor. It should be noted that the electoral candidates gave their speeches in what was effectively part of the audience space set off to the left. They did not encroach upon the 'noble space' of state officials, and Mauricio maintained his centrality between the regional candidates throughout. Civil society exhibited its own capacity to plan and perform, but unlike some spectacular performances of popular identity (see Damo 2006; Daniel Goldstein 2003: 18–20) it did so in ways that did not challenge or impinge on the symbolic expressions of state sponsorship. As an isolated event, perhaps not too much should be read into Mauricio's positionality, the sacralisation of the front region, or the predominance of government officers in managing the participation of the audience. Yet we see near identical socio-spatial formations in the next ritual for participants like Edu, the induction ceremony.

From Election to Induction

The second ritual in store for newly elected representatives is an induction ceremony. In Portuguese this is known as *ceremonia de posse*, which translates as either 'induction' or 'initiation ceremony', though occasionally it is called simply *tomando posse*, which literally translates as 'taking control' or 'taking possession'. For example, when there is a company takeover on the stock market, the buying party will later take control (*tomar posse*) of that company's resources. A similar ceremony is carried out for the president of the republic who, on receiving a mandate via the ballot box, receives the presidential sash, makes or renews an oath to the republic, and so on (DaMatta 1986: 22–30). In the key moment of symbolic recognition, the president-to-be receives the presidential sash from the current incumbent in a lateral exchange: there are no expressions of senior status between them. Presumably this is to indicate the pre-eminence of the presidential office, one which, as befitting a secular republic, does not require the benedictory rites of a higher authority. This is quite different from the induction ceremonies we will see shortly.

Here I examine two induction ceremonies. The first belongs to the Conselho Municipal de Assistência Social (Welfare Management Council, WMC), whose induction ceremony was very similar to that of the UDC and the HC, which occurred before my fieldwork took place.[5] The second is that of the MBC, and is the ceremony in which Edu, the victor of the electoral contest just examined, participates. The first was smaller than the second and was held on the ninth floor of the town hall in the Paço Municipal.

The *ceremonia de posse* for the WMC was advertised on the local government website. The time and location was given for all interested parties; the general public was also invited to attend. It was a participatory institution that is not further examined in this book, but the induction ceremonies of the HC and the UDC occurred prior to my arrival in Santo André. I thus attended the induction ceremony of the WMC to observe the kinds of introductory rituals that civil society representatives on the HC and UDC had experienced, and to provide some means by which the induction ceremony of the MBC might be compared.

The hall, the largest available in the government building, was established in a familiar manner. A row of tables was assembled at the far end of the hall – the front 'table' – seating a handful of people with microphones for each of them. Two blocks of brown plastic chairs faced them. At the far end of the hall a table provided two types of coffee – sweetened and unsweetened – and stacks of small, espresso-size cups for attendees. The front table was occupied by four individuals. Two were representatives of the government: the secretary for social inclusion and the mayor, João Avamileno. The third was the state deputy, Wanderlei Siraque, and the fourth, a representative of civil society, came from the Black Women's Movement.

The master of ceremonies introduced each of the representatives who sat before the audience, starting from the person closest to him (on the left of stage from the perspective of the audience), which included the mayor. The secretary spoke first, indicating his hope that the council could 'create a consensus, which isn't in any way saying it means satisfaction – but rather means the reasonable agreement of the collective'. Sr. Avamileno, the mayor, followed in a declarative mode: 'This is participation. This is democracy. It is a conquest of civil society – a partnership [of the local government] with civil society'.

These declarations from the mayor were some of the most emphatically concise acts of signification during my fieldwork period. 'This' – that is, the current assembly and the process of inducting members of civil society to the WMC – was 'participation' and 'democracy' realised. Such rhetorical practices, that sought to ascribe particular social structures and processes with values of 'democracy' and 'participation', were themselves acts of power. Signification is, for John Scott, an elementary form of power (Scott 2001: 15); and in this case it is one exercised by a figure, the mayor, with singular authority to make such profound definitions of social reality. These passages from the mayor and a government secretary underscore one of the principal strategies of the exercise of power in Santo André's participatory institutions, and indeed in democratic and socialist politics more generally: a rhetoric of democracy and participation is imputed, through ritual action, to social patterns that are marked by power asymmetries – in this case, between the high-status officials in the front region and the inductees who sit before them. While the signifying acts of high-status officials are, of course, not necessarily effective – that is, come to be shared by the multiple publics of the ritual performance – our attention is drawn to the situated relations of power which ensure that some interpretations are heard and some are not.

After the government secretary and mayor had spoken, the state deputy, Sr. Siraque, and the representative of the Black Women's Movement spoke briefly to the crowd in a much less declarative and more congenial way. After sequentially addressing the audience, all four speakers stepped down from the elevated platform and lined up in front of the table. The earlier passage of the event – in which the speakers' prestige was made clear, and in which the secretary presaged a collaborative working relationship with the councillors-to-be – also served to underscore the importance of the new roles of the inductees. The master of ceremonies then called each of the elected representatives to the front of the room. One by one, the elected councillors approached the front of the room from the left and, from left to right, shook hands with each of the four members of the table. At the last, the civil society representative received a small framed certificate in official recognition of their position.

This recognition of the titular councillors was the key phase of the induction ritual. Representatives of civic and neighbourhood associations thereby engaged with a higher power through the metaphoric practice of shaking hands with the group of notables assembled before them. After the significance of their new roles had been made clear in the speeches, their changed status was indicated through their recognition by the table and the bestowal of official certificates as a lasting material representation of their new positions in the WMC. This marked the completion of their induction into the institution, their entry into an organisational hierarchy, as titulars or seconds who occupied largely subordinate positions to the executive committee and a celebration of their new status.

The induction ceremony is part of an interconnected ritual system that evokes aspects of the cosmology of the Brazilian state and is oriented by it (Peirano 2002: 28). Like other elected officials, civil society representatives must first win at the ballot box, or in an assembly contest; they are then labelled with titles (titular and seconds) that are drawn from other political positions, and undergo an induction ceremony that is procedurally and symbolically akin to those of elected politicians. Inductees begin tenure on a participatory institution in Santo André in a way that is steeped in the structuring logic and nomenclature of the state, though in this case the symbolic expressions of state power were marbled by representations of corporate forms of governance and by the pragmatic interests of party politics.

The configuration of the front region in this ceremony, however, was not simply a symbolic expression of the local administration's command structure. A civil society representative occupied a place alongside the government officials as the vice-president of the institution, as did a state deputy, Sr. Siraque. The symbolism here, then, is one of governance rather than administrative structures narrowly defined. The mayor still occupied the pre-eminent, central position in the front region, but there he and his subordinate, the secretary of social inclusion, was also joined by a civil society representative, perhaps demonstrating the corporate nature of governance in Santo André. In this respect, attendance at the table by the mayor, the government secretary and the Black Women's Movement representative were understandable, since they were all more or less directly involved in the work of the participatory institution and the administration in realising its determinations.

The state deputy, Sr. Siraque, seated between the mayor and the Black Women's Movement representative, however, was a curious presence at the event. In the early stages of my fieldwork, Sr. Siraque did not attend any of the administration's public assemblies. His appearances, from the first months of 2008 onwards, were ostensibly part of a push first for mayoral pre-selection within the party – a fractious contest that would eventually divide the party and arguably lose them government – and then for the mayoral race itself. (Sr. Avamileno, mayor at this time, had already served two terms and was ineligible for a third.) The significance of Sr. Siraque's presence at the front table concerned the arbitrary capacity of the administration to appoint members to positions of status that others must acquire through unremunerated public service (the Black Women's Movement representative), or as employed public officials of Santo André (the mayor and the secretary for social inclusion). Other participatory institutions did extend invitations to other bureaucrats and government officials to speak at events and to present at the table, but in the case of the state deputy there were was little differentiation made between him and the other presenters. Sr. Siraque spoke at length in general terms about the democratic significance of the various participatory 'channels', thanked the crowd and congratulated successful candidates – all as if he were part of the governing collective, a role he was grooming himself for in the public imaginary.

Induction Ceremony of the Municipal Budget Council

The MBC had, like the management policy councils, a membership that was composed of both titular and seconds. But its executive body was quite different, insofar as it did not have an executive committee that ascribed the labels of president and vice-president to certain members, and consequently the MBC was not folded into the formal functional hierarchy of the local administration. Rather, the chief executive body was the Parity Commission, composed of equal numbers of government and civil society members – five of each. That does not imply that the commission managed the assemblies of the MBC or that its decision-making processes were necessarily more egalitarian than those of the WMC. Throughout my major stint of fieldwork in 2007/8 it was the director of the Department of Participatory Budgeting and Planning who managed the monthly assemblies of the MBC and led and directed its deliberations – though I was excluded from the closed meetings of the Parity Commission. The induction ceremony, to which we now turn, was thus a moment in which the authority of the director of participatory planning was recognised in the ritual structure in a way that contradicted the institution's formally egalitarian design.

Whereas the induction ceremony for the WMC was a small affair, that of the MBC required a more accommodating space. The MBC had 19 titular – rather than nine – civil society representatives, was a more heavily publicised programme, and thus required the use of the municipal theatre. The theatre is made up of three stages that, when all used together, wrap around much of the audience. The rows of seats were arranged in a hexagonal manner, split up into three blocks and fanned-out in greater numbers towards the back – a large block in the centre and one each on the wings. In total the theatre could seat 429, with an additional 46 available on a balcony which ran along the back wall.

The induction ceremony for the MBC was held in the evening. Each of the visitors had to register at a booth before entering, specifying whether they were a titular or second or otherwise invited. At the start of the evening, a young musical duo stationed on the stage to the left welcomed the trickle of early arrivals that started spreading throughout the space. The male performer engaged enthusiastically with the audience and managed to get quite a few to sing along to some familiar tunes. As the audience began to fill out, the usual master of ceremonies returned to take his place at the left of the front stage and open proceedings by 'composing the table'. He invited the secretary for finance; the deputy mayor, Ivete Garcia; Mauricio, the department director; the mayor, João Avamileno; a city councillor, Antonio Leite; and a member of the Executive Committee from civil society, Adalberto. Sr. Leite, the city councillor, was the first to speak, indicating how the municipal budget is at the disposal of the mayor:

> The budget is given to the mayor by the Constitution ... Sometimes this is divided between the local executive and the city council, but never has it been shared with the people. This is precisely what the PB is: [it] shares power with the people.

Adalberto, the social representative, then spoke briefly at the stand, followed by Sr. Avamileno. The mayor began by giving thanks to a number of people from a set of cards. He then observed that the whole process involved approximately 5000 people, that citizen participation had become a central concept of government, and that it was very different to the clientelism and 'exchange of favours' (*troca de favores*) that characterised the governance practices of past administrations.

The opening remarks by a city councillor showed the overlapping, and formally contradictory, narratives of government power and citizen participation that are typical of participatory institutions. However, we can perhaps even see in the organisation of the front region, which featured the mayor most prominently in the centre and the civil society representative to one side, how these narratives are interpreted by the political and administrative elite.

The master of ceremonies returned to speak at the lectern emblazoned with Santo Andre's insignia. After similarly thanking a number of people, he introduced Paulinho, a member of the PB department. Paulinho had long had an activist role in the city. Everyone knew and was unanimous in their praise of him. Paulinho had been fighting against cancer. Four earlier periods had been quelled by chemotherapy, but this time it had spread uncontrollably. The figure that crossed the stage was certainly more diminutive than the animated person I had met in the administration. But his thick, almost Nietzschean moustache and flat cap – which both conspired to obscure his face – made him recognisable, even from the rear balcony. As Paulinho was announced and began crossing the stage to sit at the table, the place erupted. Everyone – and I mean everyone – stood, hooted, hollered and cheered in a visceral unison of empathy and support. Sr. Avamileno was wiping away tears, as were many others. After the raucousness subsided, a number of photographers gathered at the front of the stage and took photos: Paulinho and Avamileno, Paulinho and the team from the table and so on. This induction ceremony was thus not merely about dramatising the transition to councillorship or of ritualising patterns of power among the inductees and government officials, it also contained an element of another common organisational ritual, such as birthday and retirement commemorations, in celebrating a life of public service.

But even this emotional passage gave way to time and to routine. Paulinho joined the other dignitaries who had all lined up in front of the table. The master of ceremonies had the microphone once again and began calling out the names of the civil society representatives. The titular was called up first to receive their certificate, and, from left to right, would shake hands, hug and/or kiss each of the assembled dignitaries. Many would stop at the last, with Sr. Avamileno, to have a picture taken. The second followed, and the master of ceremonies progressed through the various regions, from A to S, with each councillor vigorously embracing all – and particularly Paulinho – before slowly moving along and then descending from the stage. Once again, this new phase of the event – perhaps initiated by Paulinho's entrance, by the dissolution of formality brought about by the end of the speeches, and by the standing position of those up front and a fluid movement of audience members onto the stage – created an informal atmosphere. Conversation in the crowd was more relaxed and people felt more at ease to stand and move around.

Despite similarities between the induction ceremonies of the MBC and the WMC, there were also notable differences. There was, of course, a significant size difference between the two: MBC membership was a little over twice that of the WMC. But there were also significant differences in terms of the organisation and aesthetics of the events. The induction ritual of the MBC, like the regional assemblies of the PB, was more professional and much more richly adorned by symbols of the state. There were musicians, one had to register for attendance at the event and signage was more prominent. The induction ceremony of the WMC, however, was more austere, brief and informal, lasting only about half the time of that of the MBC.

These differences might have been partly due to the publicity and political opportunity afforded by the PB. It granted access, both in the prioritisation assemblies and the induction ceremonies, to thousands of the voting public, a fact which accounts, perhaps, for the prominence of city councillors at the front table. (The state deputy, Sr. Siraque, nonetheless attended both events.) With so many citizens attending PB assemblies, their pageantry was essential to the administration's techniques of 'impression management', and also to attracting and maintaining public interest in a key government programme (Goffman 1957: 116).

In terms of ritual form, however, and particularly in the key passages in which the transition to membership was formalised, both induction ceremonies were cut from the same cloth. The front region was sacralised, the differentiated statuses of its attendees were made clear, and it was through engagement with state officials that admission to the institution was symbolised. It was a ritual process that symbolically bound the participant to the institution, enjoining solidarity and communal bonds on government and civil society members (Durkheim 1965; Turner 1969); but in doing, it cast senior state officials as the gatekeepers of those institutions. This gatekeeping role was more than a transitional expression of power, for the inductees were granted their certificate by the political appointee who would be, if not formally then in effect, the president of the institution in which they would participate over a biennial term. In many of Santo André's participatory meetings, the front table remained the 'noble space' from which the institution's president would direct proceedings, introduce the agenda and manage the order of speaking. The induction ceremonies thus served a key role in preparing a normative framework for behaviour in future assemblies, and in prefiguring socially and spatially ordered relations between state officials and community representatives.

Formal Hierarchies and Their Enactments

Santo André's participatory institutions are organised on the principle of equality. For every representative of civil society, a government representative is similarly assigned a place. If, for whatever reason, the full complement of civil society seats cannot be filled, then the number of government representatives will be reduced accordingly. This is important, not so much because of the practicalities of council functioning, but because it allows equality to be symbolically maintained.

The induction ceremonies introduced us to a first instance of formal hierarchisation: the ritualised grading of civil society councillors as titulars and seconds. But there were other formal hierarchies that structured the participatory institutions and assigned responsibilities and special titles to some of its members. Each of the participatory institutions had an executive group made up of a small number of its state and civil society members that was formally charged with organisational responsibilities. In the case of the management policy councils (the UDC and the HC), it was called the Executive Committee, while in the case of the MBC, it was the Parity Commission. These executive committees augmented the status of certain members and provided (near) symbolic equality between government and civil society representatives in the institutional hierarchy. Yet such formal structures were often subverted by the practice of informal power.

The Executive Committee of the UDC was elected in an expeditious manner. The council president, director of the Department of Urban Development, Fernando da Silva, outlined what the committee's duties would be: establish the daily meeting schedule; organise 'extraordinary meetings', that is, meetings that were required in addition to the scheduled, monthly meeting; administer the works that issue from the technical and working groups; and complete urgently required administrative tasks, as required.

The assignment of government places on the executive committee replicated the hierarchy of the secretariat: Sr. da Silva, as secretary of urban development would assume the position of council president, while Ruth Motta, director of the City Master Plan department, and ex-director of the secretariat, would take up the role of (government) secretary. A member representing the social movements segment in the UDC informed Sr. da Silva that there was consensus among the civil society delegates for their nominations to the executive committee: Claudio, a representative of Santo André's metalworkers' union, would be the vice-president; and Roberta, an architect and founder of an NGO, Instituto Ambiente, would be the (civil society) secretary. The roles played by each of these representatives in managing the meetings of the UDC tell much about the cultural embeddedness of existing power relations among its participants.

Since Sr. da Silva (state) occupied the highest ranking position in the UDC, it was little surprise that he, when present, ran the meetings, confirmed the minutes of the previous meeting, introduced the event programme, mediated between speakers and responded to questions. But when he was absent, his role was not passed to the vice-president, a post held by a civil society representative; it was assumed by Sra. Motta, the government secretary. This, in fact, contravened the internal regulations of the council. The internal regulations of the UDC specify that 'the vice-president is responsible for substituting the president when she is absent or impeded'.[6] Not only was it expected that management of the UDC would pass to the vice-president, the second-most senior member of the institution; it was mandated by the formal regulations of the institution. But here there were clear expectations, and perhaps assumptions, that the coordination and management of the UDC was the rightful domain of administrative officers, even if it broke a formal rule.

There was one notable exception to the prevailing dominance of political appointees in the UDC, and it came not in the person of Claudio, as one might expect from the official hierarchy, but of Roberta. Roberta was one of the few examples that I witnessed during fieldwork of a civil society actor who played a prominent role in the deliberations and administration of a participatory institution. She often accompanied the president or vice-president at the front table, and her role became even more pronounced in the wake of Sr. da Silva's departure from the administration, when she effectively became a co-manager of the UDC.

In the past, Roberta had held a senior position in the local government, had been involved in the design and passage of the City Master Plan that formed the legal basis for the UDC, and her NGO, Instituto Ambiente, maintained a financial relationship with the local administration. It appears that her close association with the administration and her technical knowledge helped end the convention of having government chairpersons, and also helped transgress the regulations of the executive committee in assuming a role that ought to have passed to the vice-president. If the state is held to make the rules for Santo André's participatory institutions, then the above case shows that it also breaks them, in exercising discretion over who assumes roles of prominence in a participatory institution.[7]

While the UDC maintained near parity in its formal hierarchy – the only exception of which was that the council presidency was held by a state official – the MBC had absolute formal parity. Its internal regulations merely stipulate that there should be 38 titular councillors and 38 supplementary councillors, each group split evenly between representatives of the state and civil society.[8] The Parity Commission, consisting of five members from civil society and five from government, was the equivalent of the executive committee in the PB. Unlike the officious and simplistic nomination process for the UDC's Executive Committee, election to the Parity Commission was a hard-fought affair that took place following a training session for the new civil society representatives in the amphitheatre down the hall from the municipal theatre. Government representatives were present during a session on negotiating tactics run by a representative from the metalworkers' union. After the conclusion of the meeting, all of the government workers left, together with the metalworkers' trainer, leaving the civil society participants to work out the election of representatives to the Parity Commission by themselves. As the government employees left, so too did the meeting's formal atmosphere.

Previously seated in silence, the civil society representatives soon burst into life as aspiring candidates started talking animatedly, at times shouting above one another. Earlier in the evening, as I had entered the foyer of the amphitheatre, some members were earnestly cultivating support. Now was the time of quick renewals of those initial discussions, as would-be candidates headed for the stage via groups of other participants in attempts to shore up their votes. This agitation continued on the stage, where the nine candidates continued speaking loudly between themselves, and to members of the audience, in what seemed at first a vain attempt to establish some kind of order.

There was disagreement over how many votes each participant should have. Perhaps torn between competing loyalties, several councillors who remained in the audience wanted to have two votes to assign to the candidates. After some debate it was decided, in accordance with the PB's internal regulations, that each participant would have one vote only to use in support of a candidate for the Parity Commission. Nine participants had assembled on the stage. In a fashion similar to their initial candidature speeches in the regional assemblies, analysed earlier, each candidate spoke for one minute, making clear their aptitude for one of the five positions. Edu, as he walked past me heading for the stage, expressed his anxiety: 'I'm scared now I'm going to lose'. Edu's anxiety was largely unfounded, for though he seemed to have little support early on, he earned enough late votes to join Valdir, Robison, Jorge and Sonia on the Parity Commission. Nilson, a director of a local technical college, took up the post of ombudsman.

The interactions between civil society and government members of the Parity Commission largely took place in settings to which I was not privy.

The commission often convened before the regular assemblies of the MBC, but these were closed meetings. It was only during the negotiating phase of the PB (analysed in the following chapter) that both state and civil society parts of the commission had an identifiable presence in the meetings of the MBC. At times during these negotiations, when the priorities of the different regions were debated, two tables would be placed on the stage so that both civil society and administrative members of the commission were represented. However, the civil society members occasionally abandoned their place at the table midway through a meeting. Unlike the prominent role Roberta came to play in the UDC, the civil society members of the Parity Commission did not occupy a significant, mediating role in the management of the MBC's assemblies. Formal equality was maintained throughout the formal structures of the PB, yet its meetings and assemblies were almost singularly managed by the director of the Department of Participatory Budgeting and Planning. Here, there was no direct contravention of the official regulations, for no 'presidential' role was specified; the coordination of the PB's assemblies was assumed to be within the remit of the director of the department – or at least, the fulfilment of that role by the director met with no visible resistance that I observed.

The structures of both the UDC and the PB helped undergird a number of rhetorical claims made by the administration. An egalitarian design gave substance to the declarations of participation, democracy and partnership made by the mayor at the induction ceremonies just examined. The official structures of the institutions did, of course, have patently observable effects, such as the physical presence of equal numbers of civil society and government representatives, and many others. Yet we also saw how existing power relationships, and the attitudes and assumptions they afforded, shaped the way formal structures were interpreted and enacted.

Conclusion

The induction ceremonies of participatory institutions are normally ignored in the scholarly literature, perhaps because they are considered extraneous to the main business of demand-making and negotiation. Here, by contrast, the first events of Santo André's participatory institutions have been cast as integral parts of a much larger process of ritualisation that initiates civil society representatives into a spatially ordered and socially hierarchical relationship with government officials. The elections and induction ceremonies examined above are entirely banal and bear much in common with a suite of other organisational and political rituals. However, the mundane should not be mistaken for the analytically unimportant. Rather, it is the banality of such rituals that makes them so effective at weaving together the grounded manifestations of projects of participatory democracy with existing structures of political authority, and of normalising relations of unequal power between state officials and lay participants. Continuity of form, among and between government and attendant participatory bodies, serves to reproduce predictable and enduring patterns of status, authority and prestige – and to create the image of the state as fixed and immutable (Tambiah 1979: 122–3) – while more practically often confounding the formal goals of participatory reform.

The front region of the assembly space was, on stately occasions, sacralised by a ritual process – 'composing the table' – in a way that foreshadowed its pre-eminent role in that same assembly, and also in the future assemblies in which lay participants would take part. In this process, the status distinction between senior government officials and other participant members was dramatised in a way that prefigured and legitimised a differential allocation of rights and responsibilities in the meeting format. If certain spaces of the assembly hall were largely designated for high-status officials, the election contest in the PB showed that the opportunities for public performances could be seized with some creativity by social actors, as rival community leaders orchestrated a minutely choreographed 'sociodrama' in the hope of gaining a seat on the MBC. Edu came out the victor on this occasion, earning a place on the MBC as the titular representative of the region. This very public triumph also imparted significant responsibility: Edu would be charged with representing his supporters, other members of the community and perhaps other political interests in the negotiations that will be analysed in Chapter 3.

Induction ceremonies are the second event for participants-to-be. They are rituals in which lay participants are formally granted admission to the participatory body by government officials who often then assume similar, coordinating roles in future participatory assemblies. The symbolisations of state power in these rituals are not always directly borrowed from the government command structure – for instance, in both induction ceremonies a civil society representative also attended the front region. But the command structure of government was nonetheless broadly expressed through the structures of the ritual performance, in which the categories 'state' and 'civil society' were mobilised, projected onto sections of the organisers and attendees and cast in hierarchical relation to one another, thus modelling interactions in the participatory forums on an image of the socio-political order (Geertz 1973: 93; Handelman 1990; Shore and Wright 2003). The induction rituals are also shown to be somewhat flexible arrangements, which serve multiple purposes: they are moments in which elected politicians gain access to the voting public, and they are moments also for celebration, as we saw in the case of the PB.

Participants may compete for membership and be inducted into a participatory institution in a way shaped by expressions of state power, but that does not mean that elections and induction ceremonies would have the effect of dissuading participants from robust forms of participation. Indeed, the recognition, proximity and validation provided by the sponsorship of the rituals by the political and administrative elite, underpinned by a discourse of democratic participation, might inspire participants to take government to task and to demand that they live up to their participatory rhetoric. This is what Catherine Bell calls the 'second dimension' of ritualisation (Bell 1992: 207), a dimension that becomes highly visible in the following chapter. The rituals would, nonetheless, have the effect, I argue, of ritualising the social configurations through which combative performances would take place. In the following two chapters I examine how participatory institutions might cultivate different patterns of participation, despite similar ritual initiations.

3
Participatory Budgeting: Ritualisations of Petitioning and Power

In the previous chapter I examined elections and induction ceremonies as instances of a more extensive process of ritualisation. They introduced elements of the form of future assemblies, just as they accomplished practical tasks, such as determining membership. Yet despite similar introductory encounters, the three participatory institutions examined here cultivated very different kinds of interactive cultures. This chapter analyses the most dynamic and contentious of the three: the participatory budget.

Where countless other projects of participatory democracy in effect become merely presentational spaces for state agencies, participatory budgeting has gained notoriety for the purchase on government decision-making it affords the participating public. The direct petitioning of government actors with concrete demands, a defining feature of participatory budgets, gives participants identifiable objectives around which to rally. Moreover, the participatory rhetoric and the acceptance of demands by state officials generates powerful expectations of reciprocity: through the receipt of demands, a tacit promise is made that at least some of the proposed works nominated in assemblies will be realised. The lifeless formality found in many studies of public meetings (see Adams 2004) was, in the case of Santo André's participatory budget (PB), almost inevitably broken: citizens were expected to articulate their demands, and once recorded, the administration was beholden to respond to them. This created a pattern of interactive practices quite different from the management policy councils I will examine in Chapter 4. On the one hand, regional representatives had identifiable demands which they were elected to the Municipal Budget Council (MBC) to defend; on the other, the government had a swathe of different demands, issued from across its territory, which either needed to be implemented, refused on technical or other grounds, or had to be accommodated in some other way. Given the administration's limited funds and human resources, some form of confrontation was almost inevitable. The claim-making, negotiations and the varied responses from the administration would all transpire in a series of interactions between civil society and their state counterparts over a number of meetings.

In contrast to the routine meetings of the management policy councils, the PB might be called a campaign-based institution, where, at least in the first year of the biennial cycle, each assembly furnishes something on which subsequent meetings depend. Each instantiation of the PB's constituent bodies contributes to the goal of including in the next year's budget some combination of the demands gathered in the various regions of the city. Its campaign-based structure fostered expectations and built a kind of momentum that advances towards a decisive, heated and emotionally charged climax. In this chapter I continue the diachronic approach applied to the examination of the PB's introductory rituals, and focus on a series of meetings that lead from the preparatory to the regional assembly, and then into the negotiating phase — a sequence of meetings in which the final priorities are determined. In the interactions between state and civil society participants we can see the interplay between the two dimensions of ritualisation, as conceived by Bell (1992). On the one hand, the petitions are made in situations clearly shaped by state power, which shows how larger structures of the political order help to configure face-to-face interactions between state and community actors in participatory forums; on the other, the reactions of civil society members in the negotiating phase demonstrate how the process of demand-making over a series of interconnected meetings codifies norms and generates reciprocal expectations between the participants and presiding state officials in such a way that provokes resistance and contestation. In this analysis of the intertwining dimensions of ritualisation, I pay attention to the spatial and temporal organisation of practices, a focus that is maintained in the analysis of management policy councils in the next chapter. In this chapter, however, the analysis diachronically follows the tactical interactions and contentious performances that are distinguishing features of PB.

Table 3.1 gives an overview of the PB process that was in force during my first period of fieldwork. For the purposes of the PB, the territory of Santo André is divided into 19 regions. Initial meetings are organised in each of the regions to inform local residents that a larger, regional assembly is forthcoming, where they will be able to elect demands – three regional demands and one demand for the city – which may be included in the following year's budget. They are also notified that they will be able to elect regional representatives (a titular and a second) who will become members on the chief decision-making organisation of the PB, the MBC, which is made up of 19 members of civil society and 19 members from the government. Regional assemblies are then held in which local residents select demands and elect regional representatives, after which the regional representatives go through a series of training seminars and are taken on a tour of the city (the so-called 'caravan of priorities') so as to better visualise the effect of the prospective works that were nominated in the regional assemblies. Subsequently, the regional representatives meet, as part of

Table 3.1 Biennial cycle of the participatory budget.

First Year			
Preparatory meetings	Regional assemblies	Induction ceremony, training seminars and priority caravan	Negotiating assemblies
9 to 30 April	5 to 31 May	9 to 21 June	25 June to 21 July
Government organises initial meetings in each of the 19 regions to mobilise participation for the prioritisation assemblies.	Assemblies are organised in each of the 19 regions, where registered citizens can elect three regional priorities and one city-wide priority. Participants also elect representatives to the MBC as well as neighbourhood representatives.	Councillors elected in the prioritisation assemblies undergo an induction ceremony and four training seminars. A 'priority caravan' is also held, where, over the course of a day, civil society representatives tour the city by bus to visit the sites where the investments elected in the prioritisation meetings would be carried out.	Civil society and government councillors meet, in the first meetings of the MBC, to negotiate which priorities, elected in the regional assemblies, are to be submitted to the Legislative Chamber as part of the municipal budget for the following year.
Second Year			
Evaluation/holding-to-account assemblies		Monthly meetings of the MBC	
May		First Monday of every month	
Government organises initial meetings in each of the 19 regions to report back to the local population on the works they selected the previous year. Citizens may also pose questions to the government regarding the progress on investments.		The MBC meets once per month over the course of the year to hear regular presentations from different government departments on the progress of work that had been committed to in the previous year.	

the MBC, in the negotiating phase with the aim of determining which demands will be entered in the following year's budget. In the second year of the biennial cycle of the PB, the government has a round of 'holding-to-account' assemblies throughout the 19 regions of the city in order to report back to the population on the progress that had been achieved on their chosen demands the previous year.

The structure of the PB is complex and the analysis presented here is therefore necessarily pared down. I thus examine the decisive series of meetings in year one, when the demands are registered and debated, prior to the finalisation of the budget. Continuing the diachronic approach of the previous chapter, I examine the regional assemblies of a single region, the wetlands area, before following the demands collected there into the negotiations. But first I examine what is called a preparatory meeting. Like the rituals examined in Chapter 2, this informal gathering, held in the lead up to the full regional meeting in the wetlands region, is part of what might be called 'an ecology of public events', events that help shape the practices evidenced later in the chapter.

A Preparatory Meeting in Chácara Carreiras

The preparatory meeting for the regional assembly of the wetlands region was held in Chácara Carreiras, part of the municipality farthest from the urban centre of Santo André. I had been in the wetlands area several times before this meeting. In fact, I attended my first official event, the opening of a water-treatment station in Jardim Santo André, which bordered the large water reserve that was named after the American engineer Asa Billings. I had also returned on a couple of other occasions, once on a guided motor-cycle tour with the husband of one of the civil society representatives on the MBC, and on a trip to the mountainous railway station of Paranapiacaba. I accompanied three government employees to the preparatory meeting, including Mauricio, director of the Department of Participatory Budgeting and Planning. I met them at 5 PM on the second floor of the town hall, where even though staff from the other departments were in the throes of concluding the working day, the PB office was abuzz: piles of bright red brochures, ready for the regional assemblies, filled out the normally more sparsely occupied workspace, and the staff had an intensity written into their demeanour. This was the busiest and most stressful part of the year for them: all 19 of the regional assemblies had to be meticulously planned and catered for in advance. Lucia, a new employee in her early 20s, accompanied us on the journey.

The four of us piled into a VW Beetle and began the trip to Chácara Carreiras, in the Paranapiacaba region. Because the heavily urbanised area of Santo André is separated from much of the municipality's wetlands by an arm of the Billings reservoir, one has to traverse four different municipalities to reach it by car. Predictably, the roads worsen the further one gets from the city centre. Shortly after we left, the heavens opened. We arrived amid torrents of rain and cracks of thunder a little after 6.30 PM at the house of Renato, a regular face at the participatory assemblies. Renato welcomed us, but the meeting itself wasn't to be held in his house, but rather in a detached, but covered, concreted landing near its entrance. The air was damp from the rain and made cool from the altitude and surrounding greenery. Concern that no one would attend because of the weather was partially merited, as only six people arrived, and only after the worst of it had passed, one visibly inebriated and there for socialising. This distraction did not help the new employee, Lucia, who was tasked with giving the presentation; unused to speaking in public, she was a little nervy and apprehensive, and deferred most questions to Mauricio. Lucia gave a broad introduction to the process, specified that three priorities for the region could be registered, along with one for the city, in the upcoming prioritisation assembly. In response, Renato outlined his idea for surfacing his road with paving stones (*paralelapipedo*). As it was currently unpaved, and important to the area, he said the government had a ready-made excuse for denying him and his neighbours basic services, such as refuse collection and policing. After we returned to the Beetle and started the journey back to the administration, one of the other public servants asked Mauricio: 'What do you think about the paving? Is it possible?' 'No', replied Mauricio, 'I don't think that will happen'.

The preparatory assembly, though fairly unsuccessful as an event aimed at mobilising attendance for the regional meeting – in part due to the inclement weather – did show how the larger, more stately events of the PB also have local, diminutive equivalents where quite different norms and behaviour obtain. A junior member of staff was able to practise her presentational skills on this less stressful, less important occasion. The small numbers and the lack of any consequential decision-making meant that it felt more like a neighbourhood meeting than a formal government event. No formal titles were used; no formal seating arrangements were employed, and indeed would have been impossible on the small, concrete landing. Nonetheless, the meeting did serve to shape expectations about what attendees could hope to achieve from the regional assembly, and they were introduced to the prominent, organising role of state officials in it. Moreover, the discussion between the government employees on the return car journey shows how informal discussions concerning investment decisions circulate within the administration, and how some already seem to be decided. Renato would never get to know if the government would surface his road since it was not supported in the regional assembly, to which we now turn.

The Prioritisation Assembly in the Wetlands

I returned to the wetlands area some weeks later for the prioritisation assembly in the Clube do Campo, Parque Andreense. It was again damp and cool, and the hall, so high-ceilinged, felt empty despite the 151 participants in attendance. Mauricio 'composed the table', as usual, including this time a representative from the sub-prefecture of Paranapiacaba, an administrative body installed to address the particular problems of the wetlands area, who spoke after the city councillor, Motorinho, and emphasised what a great honour it was to receive the mayor, João Avamileno, in the region. When he spoke, the mayor thanked both Renato and Robison – the civil society representatives from the region – before the video played on the two projector screens that had been set up. The video presented a litany of the works undertaken due to decisions made in the PB, paying special attention to the attraction of the region – the steam-powered Paranapiacaba railway – which had seen the annual number of visiting tourists rise from 30,000 to 200,000. The audience clapped after the conclusion of the multimedia production.

The mayor sat at the centre of the table at the front of the hall, with a large group of senior administrative officers arrayed behind him. Political actors – mostly members of the Legislative Chamber – were seated to either side of him. Participants were invited by Mauricio to form a queue along the left-hand side of the audience so as to wait their turn to take the microphone and voice their demands. The microphone was facing the table of the mayor, so that those lining up were facing away from the audience and towards the front table. This spatial arrangement served to break down the audience into individuals making individual demands. Indeed, the operative interaction of the assembly was not an engagement between the audience and the table, which would accord with the state–civil society discourse of the institution, but between individual participants from the audience, who could, one after the other, make their demands known to the mayor and other notables.

Figure 3.1 Participants making demands during the Parque Andreense assembly.

The assembled political and administrative elite were seated around the mayor, symbolising the relations of power within and among the branches of government. This everyday symbolisation of state power was not just expressive of the station of the notables at the front table; it provided cues for the petitioners who were lining up to address them. In contrast with the robust rhetoric of the institution, which casts petitions as 'demands', most of the participants who made proposals at the microphone (seen in Figure 3.1) initiated their petition, which generally consisted of a public work for their neighbourhood followed by a justification of why it was needed, with a show of appreciation towards the mayor and the other assembled notables. The most common phrase used to thank the mayor mirrored the sentiments of the government representative mentioned above, who lauded the mayor for travelling out into the regions: 'Firstly, I would like to thank the mayor and the city councillors for taking the time to come out here today'. Here the social status of the notables at the table, and pronouncements which exemplified that status – for instance, through the use of honorific prefixes in the composition of the table – evokes deferential forms of petitioning. While a few used the opportunity at the microphone to criticise the government, a far greater number voiced their proposal in a courteous and respectful manner that recognised the prestige of those occupying the front table through expressions of gratitude and humility (Futrell 1999: 511). In this way, petitioning the political and administrative elite in the assembly becomes a supplication to state representatives (see Fassin 2000), and bears a family resemblance to the submissions made to medieval kings and dignitaries (see Koziol 1992: 24).

The assembly was held in the wetlands region, which is, measured from its geographic centre, the farthest officially habitable part of the city. By thanking the mayor for 'taking the time to come out' to this part of the city, the petitioners recognised that it was the mayor who had travelled to their region to receive the petitions. Mayors in Santo André have historically only seldom visited the peripheral regions of the city. But while the mayor was perhaps more engaged and peripatetic than many of his predecessors when discharging his other duties, during the voicing of petitions he maintained the immobility that is typical of an authority figure who receives a supplicant, meaning to suggest that he is not obliged to give favours; the participants are rather obliged to ask favours of him (see ibid.: 27). Although the behaviour of the petitioners was generally deferential, direct interactions with the mayor were still managed carefully by the officials. State officials manned the queue in order to regulate the amount of time each participant spoke and to ensure that the petitions took place at regular intervals, and also to guarantee that anyone who used the opportunity at the microphone to take the mayor to task could be quickly and quietly dealt with. From the front table, it was Mauricio who managed proceedings, and was responsible for passing the microphone to relevant persons, making introductions, providing clarifications and quietening the assembled participants. He was the overseer of all exchanges between the table and the floor. Mauricio informed the audience of where to speak, time limitations, and occasionally threatened the crowd when it did not comply with his directions, making explicit the behavioural norms expected by the organisers.

Even without a large, dissenting audience, the rudimentary nature of many of the demands were likely to be discomforting for the mayor and other public officials. The first demand was for running water. Robison, a civil society representative on the MBC who was ending his term, and attached to the PCdoB, the Brazilian communist party, pointed out that residents needed to 'be able to drink, wash clothes and so on'. The next

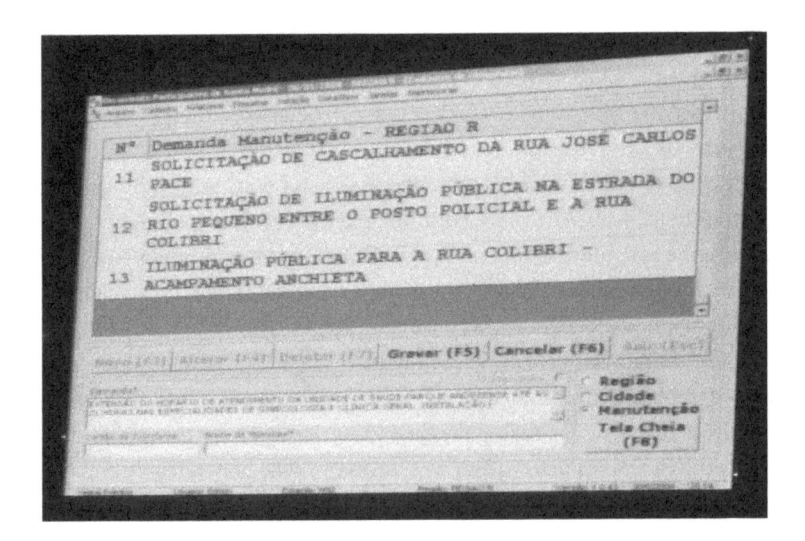

Figure 3.2 Demands displayed on a projector screen.

request was for an X-ray machine at the local health centre, for at the time, local residents had to travel to central Santo André to have one done. Another resident requested an extension of the power network: 'It is silly to ask', she said, 'but we need lighting and other similar services, for the love of God'. Renato, at whose home the preparatory meeting was held, was an often irreverent personality at public events, and he boldly asked for a commission to visit Chácara Carreiras: 'You should not just come at election time', he said, directly taking aim at the mayor. 'Bring your secretaries [to have a look at the conditions there] because we are sick of living in the ugly part of the city'.

The many basic requests betrayed the fact that this was the poorest, least well-serviced region of the city. The mayor felt impelled to respond to the elementary nature of these demands, and did so employing a recurrent trope of his speeches, his working-class background:

> I don't have fear or shame of poverty; we have it in the periphery and in the centre of the city. I grew up in Bertioga and got here through the [political] struggle; or I had luck, or God helped me ... Unfortunately this can't happen to everyone ... and it takes a long time, many budgets, to take care of the periphery.

This was the mayor's one, placatory response. He was not obliged to respond to individual criticisms and requests, or to Renato's implied charge of electioneering. Power very often, as Richard Sennett (1980: 100) notes, means the power to ignore, to practise indifference in the face of multiple, specific claims and criticisms. Yet, whether in approval of the mayor's humble beginnings, or due to an appreciation of the public work that had already been carried out in the wetlands region, he was keenly applauded by the audience.

The criticisms aired were largely ignored, and the demands that were voiced at the microphones were registered electronically on the ballot machines for the attendees to vote on. Renato's suggestion, that a commission come to visit his region, was similarly omitted from his request. Thus, while some studies of Brazil's participatory budgets have emphasised their deliberative elements and potential (see Avritzer 2002b; Baiocchi 2005), the regional assembly described here shows another, quite different interactive and organisational dynamic. It is one shaped by the status and authority of occupants of the front table who, as evidenced in many of the proposals voiced by members of the lay public, evoke deferential forms of petitioning and participation. The tightly focused organisation of the assembly ensured that the demands would be registered with maximum efficiency, but it also determined that the assembly merely served 'a small number of objectives', in the manner noted by James Scott (1998: 23) as a general tendency of the state.

Following the registering of demands, collated and displayed on a projector (see Figure 3.2), and after the mayor's brief response, Mauricio requested nominations for participants to represent the region on the MBC (here the assembly turned to the election process analysed in more depth in Chapter 2). Renato, Juliana, Robison and Rosa were all nominated. The audience then filed out of the hall to register their voting preferences for both the nominated investment priorities and the candidates for the MBC, using the electronic ballot machines set up near the entrance (see Figure 3.3). About half of them returned to assemble in the main hall to hear the results. Mauricio took the microphone again and began his summary of the voting outcomes: Juliana had received the most votes and was thus to become the titular representative of the region, while Renato, who came second, was able to maintain an attachment to the institution as her second. Juliana then participated in the induction ceremony, and together with Edu from Region S, became a titular representative on the MBC.

The interactive patterns in the regional assembly may have occurred in a structured environment which signalled and ritualised the superordinate status of state officials, who acted as convenors and coordinators. But at the

Figure 3.3 Attendees vote for investment priorities and regional representatives using electronic ballot machines.

same time, the assembly produced very specific sets of expectations about what would occur in the following encounters. The civil society representatives elected during the assemblies had a definite set of demands that they would be carrying through to the negotiating assemblies. Deferent or not, the participating citizens expected the good faith of their participation to be reciprocated. Bolstered by their electoral victories, and in possession of a number of discrete demands, the newly elected civil society representatives had specific objectives to pursue in the negotiations with state officials. Through holding regional assemblies in which local citizens select and prioritise demands, government becomes ensnared in a petitionary formula, which opens up possibilities for resistance and confrontation, and that lent strength to what Bell calls the second dimension of ritualisation (Bell 1992: 207). The negotiating assemblies were indeed a complex and tempestuous set of meetings, and so I concentrate on some of the key tactical features of the exchanges between governmental and civil society representatives.

The Municipal Budget Council and Negotiation

A small theatre was used for the negotiation assemblies, just down the hall from the larger municipal theatre where the induction ceremonies were held. Its spatial organisation was very similar to that of the induction ceremony, with the exception that in most of the negotiation assemblies a second table was placed on the front stage for two civil society representatives. It was the first time that civil society had a separate, identifiable presence in the front region of an assembly during my fieldwork, and suggested that government consciously recognised the importance of symbolic representation. Nonetheless, interactions were still largely mediated through the government chairperson, Mauricio, seated at the right-hand side of the stage. In the negotiating phase, however, there was much greater behavioural and communicative turbulence – mutterings between participants, heckling from the back, and in one or two cases, raging diatribes. These were created by the confrontational negotiations, if that is the right word, between the two camps of representatives of the MBC, symbolised by the two separate tables on the stage, and each steeled by different processes of ritualisation.

In the prioritisation assemblies, an example of which was described in the previous section, the government went to some length to foster an interpretation of the participatory budget, and of the government itself, as collaborative and participatory (Futrell 1999). Across different types of media – in signage, print advertising, pamphlets, video presentations and, indeed, in the speeches of senior officials – the government identified citizens as a driving force behind the participatory budget and its outcomes, and celebrated a history of productive cooperation between government and the local citizenry. There was the occasional summary intervention by Mauricio in the proposals of the participants in the prioritisation assemblies. But for the most part, in the regional assemblies the high-status officials were welcoming, receptive to the chosen demands and diplomatic in responses to complaints of past government performance. Mauricio and the mayor were a little concerned to manage expectations, and on more than one occasion urged audience members not to expect too much. The administration had human and financial resource limitations, they cautioned. Indeed, at the end of the regional assembly in the wetlands area, Mauricio concluded proceedings by adding that: 'It's not 100 per cent [certain] that these [demands] will be implemented. They will first have to go to the MBC'.

The high-status officials did not, however, maintain such cordial dispositions in the negotiating assemblies. For the much larger audiences in the regional meetings, great effort was put into managing public opinion about the participatory budget, in part through the use of promotional media, media that were absent during the negotiating phase that followed. This was a decisive series of meetings for the chosen demands. Here, government officials were sterner and more determined, and would, through deliberation or by decree, have to discard a great number of the previously collected demands in front of a much smaller audience. The administration thus avoided denying voting participants of their demands directly; that would take place, at some remove, in the meetings of the MBC.

Erving Goffman uses the term 'audience segregation' (Goffman 1957: 57) for just this kind of performative differentiation, and draws our attention to the way that different sets of actors tactically tailor their performances for different audiences. Such differentiation was vital, for had the negotiations of the MBC taken place in front of a much wider audience, it is likely that the government would have suffered far greater criticism, and the participatory budget a loss of popular legitimacy and support.

The negotiating assemblies of the MBC followed the conclusion of the stream of prioritisation meetings and the induction ceremony. They were also preceded by a series of four training seminars and a 'priority caravan', in which elected representatives spent a day touring the city by bus, being shown where the demands made in the prioritisation assemblies would be carried out.

Government Responses to Demands

The demands that had been chosen in the regional assemblies were passed on to the relevant government department for analysis. The first two meetings of the negotiating phase of the participatory budget thus consisted of reports back from departmental representatives. Various departmental representatives, from SEMASA (Serviço Municipal de Saneamento Ambiental de Santo André), the urban sanitation and management organ of the local government, and education, gave presentations on the sewage and drainage requests, and on the crèches, teaching education centres and municipal schools that had been nominated. The second reporting meeting was held two days later to resume the department-by-department analysis of the chosen priorities. At the end of the second meeting, a 29-page summary of these evaluations was provided for the civil society councillors. For each demand, the responsible department was listed, the demand stated and an evaluation of its technical feasibility was given. Over the course of these two meetings, the municipal staff seemed to give earnest and thorough reports on the chosen demands. There was no indication, that is, that the report or their presentations were doctored to make certain demands seem less feasible than they were.

Following the conclusion of the departmental analyses, the civil society representatives were to convene their own meeting in the absence of any government representatives to re-evaluate and resubmit the demands of their regions. This seemed strange, for it meant that despite the arduous process of voting for the priorities in the regions, the civil society representatives of the MBC were able to arbitrarily re-prioritise or voluntarily retract demands before submitting them to government, perhaps in light of the evaluations made by government representatives in the previous two meetings. It was no matter, for despite an extraordinarily disorderly meeting with much wrangling and arguing, the group of civil society representatives largely held firm in submitting all of their demands to the government, though some regions altered their priorities. The determination of the civil society councillors here is evidence of another kind of ritual and emotional involvement – or what Randall Collins terms 'emotional entrainment' – for group members (Collins 2004: 25). Their solidarity and the collective expectation generated through the voting practices examined earlier impelled them to reject the opportunity to pursue their own favoured priorities and to return to negotiations with a largely unaltered array of demands. The ritualisation of government power and authority in the participatory budgeting assemblies was caught up with another kind of ritualisation based on the unity and collective expectation of civil society councillors.

Governmental Counter-Proposal and Intransigence

The first negotiating assembly was held after the government departments had submitted their reports, and after the civil society representatives resubmitted their demands to the government. Mauricio was joined by the mayor, João Avamileno, over to the right, in one of the very few occasions that the mayor had a more than ceremonial role in one of the city's participatory institutions. In response to the resubmission of the regional demands, Mauricio remarked that 'there have been discussions in the different secretariats and there are some very obvious limitations'. He then read what was termed a government 'counter-proposal', which specified the demands the government was willing to implement, and explained that some regions could not have their demands realised. Many of the civil society representatives, visibly indignant, began criticising both the selection of individual demands without any prior consultation, and the reticence of the government to explain why one demand had been chosen over another. Given that the previous meetings were largely presentational, this was the first meeting that the civil society representatives on the left-hand side of the stage had something concrete to respond to. Yet both of the representatives seemed a little ill at ease on the stage, and in fact abandoned it for long periods of the meeting to rejoin their civil society colleagues in the audience. Perhaps this was to confer with their peers and determine what kind of stance the civil society representatives should be taking in response to the counter-proposal, but perhaps it was also because they were a little unsure of how to act in front of the audience.

The criticism from the other civil society attendees was vociferous, irrespective of the performance of their representatives on the front stage. Mauricio, appearing to want to avoid verbal attacks, suggested: 'It would be a better idea to close the meeting early, rather than go point-by-point, which would take too long. And perhaps civil society could meet afterwards to reach some consensus and reply to government'. Luana, from the Department of Health, argued that some of the demands simply could not be met: 'We want to do it but just cannot due to financial constraints'. Diego, an until now reserved civil society representative, retorted: 'It is absurd to prioritise the demands one, two, three, when the government just selects number three. It delegitimises the whole process'.

The mayor, who had attended very few such assemblies, suggested that the counter-proposal could go to a vote. Rather than a means of democratic resolution, this was interpreted by civil society attendees as a threat, for should the vote be split along government and civil society lines, it was possible that none of the demands would be included in the budget for that region. From the 19 assemblies that had been held around the city, involving thousands of participants, 57 priorities had been nominated. The government had selected 28 of them and, rather than giving detailed case-by-case justifications, was trying to close the meeting early. Many regions now only had one listed in the counter-proposal, rather than the three that were selected. It seemed that the regional assemblies had provided an array of investment options from which the administration had cherry-picked those it favoured. No rationale was given for the choice of one demand over another, or how much money was available for capital investments, taking year-on-year renewal and human service costs into account. Indeed, a detailed explanation of why one demand was chosen over another was what the administration seemed determined to avoid. The attempt by government representatives to push through their favoured suite of demands disrupted the 'impression of committed governance' (Futrell 1999: 502) earlier cultivated by the administration, and signalled a more concerted effort to exert the governmental authority that had been constantly paraded over a sequence of meetings.

Another meeting of the MBC was convened the following week, after the government had received a resubmission from the civil society representatives, which set out the items of the counter-proposal they were willing to accept. In response, government submitted a second counter-proposal and civil society did win several concessions, based on its resubmitted demands. In the three following meetings, the government increased its calls for going to a vote. This would be a vote by the entire MBC on each region's demands. The civil society representatives felt that the government would 'vote in block', as they put it, and that the two-thirds of the assembly necessary for pushing through a demand would be impossible. If the cohesive performance of the governmental representatives in the previous assemblies was any indication of their voting tendencies, then the sentiments of the civil society group seemed justified. Voting, so often cast as the defining practice of democracy, here threatened even the investments that government had committed to in the second counter-proposal.

In the final two meetings, Mauricio's superior, the secretary of finance, assumed the job of moderator and became more blunt and threatening. During his opening speech in one of the final meetings of civil society representatives, he declared: 'It is a privilege of yours [to participate]. Many municipalities don't allow the population to have a say in the budget'. After numerous meetings, and perhaps under strain, another discourse began to surface. Participation was, according to the secretary of finance, not a right but a privilege that was electively bestowed upon the civil society representatives.

This intervention by the secretary of finance was significant on two counts. First, it was largely effective at quelling criticisms made by the civil society participants. Many of the civil society representatives seemed fatigued by the unwillingness of the state representatives to enter into meaningful dialogue over the demands, and also apprehensive about the threat of voting – which may have meant, in the event of an impasse, that none of their demands would have been implemented by the government. Second, the rhetoric used by the secretary of finance was a reminder of status: he reminded the lay participants of their only contingent role in municipal decision-making. It was an intercession from on high to definitively resolve the impasse in negotiations that was legitimised by the ritualisation of state authority throughout the regional prioritisation meetings, the induction ceremony and much of the negotiating phase. The intervention of the secretary was largely effective, and the second government counter-proposal was approved without significant changes by the MBC.

Conclusion

In this chapter I have taken a diachronic approach to participatory budgeting that demonstrates how the performance of power, over a series of interconnected meetings, shapes the manner in which petitions are made and how final investment decisions are reached. Building on the findings of the previous chapter, this approach helps to explain why members of the lay public petitioned the assembled political and administrative elite in an often deferential manner. Further, the observance of ritual protocol in tandem with situated expressions of state authority and power eased civil society representatives towards the adoption of government proposals and away from the determinations of civil society consultations.

Yet the analysis also revealed a second dimension of ritualisation that mobilised the expectations of civil society representatives and ensured a combative series of meetings in the negotiating phase. However, the attempt of civil society representatives to maintain the original set of demands chosen in the regions met with a series of decisive manoeuvres by state officials. The government seemed unwilling to deliberate and instead distributed their own counter-proposal, which contained a list of preferred demands. When there were deadlocks in the negotiations, voting was used, in the view of civil society representatives, as a threat which could jeopardise even the diminished number of works listed in the counter-proposal. Several concessions were won by civil society, though their more ambitious demands were met by government intransigence. In a final series of interventions by the government, the secretary of finance assumed control of the process and sought to remind civil society of their contingent role in matters of local governance, a kind of imposition of government priorities that prompted Brian Wampler's description of Santo André's PB as 'cooptative' (Wampler 2007: 261–2). I will examine in more detail the portrayal of citizen participation as a kind of contingent interference in Chapter 4, where Mauricio, other state officials and their civil society counterparts reflect on the PB and citizen participation more broadly.

An important consequence of the argument presented here is that the intervention of the secretary of finance was enabled by patterns of performed political power that legitimised the status and pre-eminence of state officials. It was somewhat surprising, however, that his use of the term 'privilege' did not directly provoke any criticism, for it directly contravenes the participatory rhetoric of the institution, not to mention 'the discourse of rights' that has undergirded demands for democratic citizenship in Brazil (Cornwall et al. 2008: 33). It is therefore apposite here to reflect briefly on how these the ritualisations of state power were perceived by the civil society participants. Did they help to make the affordances of state power 'instinctive' to the social agent as suggested by Bell (1992: 206)? Were these situations, with their spatial and social hierarchies, simply perceived to be 'the way that things are' (see Bourdieu 1977: 164)? In the interviews I conducted with social activists, participants and public functionaries, it was indeed very difficult to elicit reflection on the form of participation and the everyday ritualisations of power examined in earlier sections. My questions concerning the spatial organisation of assemblies and the procedures of participatory meetings were normally met with a quizzical look or, in the case of social activists, provoked a recounting of specific demands that had been made by community representatives and consequent government responses. The form of participation was either seen as a kind of presumed knowledge, or it was assumed to be within the right of government to determine it. This was succinctly expressed by one participant, Luana, who was an outgoing titular member of the MBC for the wetlands region. After a long discussion about the organising procedures in the assemblies just observed, she summarised her perspective thus: 'It is the government that organises. We just participate'. Luana's distinction between organisation and participation describes the normative reach of government authority in prescribing and delimiting the possible forms of interaction in Santo André's PB.

Yet there were one or two examples from the ethnographic and interview data that suggest that other actors and participants had insights into the symbolic structuring of social relations. The only fieldwork colleague who explicitly spoke about the symbolic structuring of space in participatory forums was Claudio, a regional representative on the MBC and a small businessman. Claudio told me about a regional PB assembly in which he gave, in his words, 'the speech of my life'. Claudio observed that he was not normally a gifted orator, yet on this occasion his speech was met with rousing applause from neighbours and fellow community members in the audience. After he concluded his speech, rather than returning to the audience, he was invited by the mayor to join him in the front region with the government representatives. This invitation into what Arlei Damo has called the 'noble space' (Damo 2006: 168) was meant to suggest, in Claudio's words, that 'This little fish is mine'. The invitation for Claudio to join the mayor at the front table was, according to Claudio, an attempt to make some sort of claim over him by admitting him into government space.

A similar episode was recounted by another fieldwork colleague, Camila, who once had to give a speech in the Legislative Chamber. Unaccustomed to speaking in such venues, Camila felt evidently honoured by the experience, which was mentioned to me years later and on a barely related topic. Camila used a similar term to that employed by Damo above, and described the Legislative Chamber as a 'noble place' (*lugar nobre*) and her speech in it an extraordinary event that made her feel a little out of place. In these examples, the ritualisation of spaces of state power become the subject of (rare) conscious interrogation when there are transgressions of normal use. Claudio and Camila show us that it is only in the relatively rare instances when the patterns of everyday practice are transgressed that the real power embedded in the situated structures of public life are revealed.

These rare cases refer to the form of political authority, and they do not of course imply that the actions of state officials are somehow accepted by members of the lay public. In fact I knew very few participants who approved of the conduct of the high-status officials during the entire negotiating phase. But Camila's and Claudio's examples do provide evidence of how state power is embedded in the complex layers of the everyday, which are often only rarely consciously interrogated. Participants may not have agreed with state representatives, or with the secretary of finance, but their performances were largely accepted expressions of institutionalised power. If this power is not simply an immutable historical given, then it is important that the everyday social practices that ritualise power relations be constantly monitored and examined. It is a theme I address more explicitly in the conclusion to the book. For now we turn to two quite different participatory institutions, the Urban Development Council and the Housing Council.

4
Embedded Participatory Institutions: The Urban Development Council and the Housing Council

In this chapter I examine two management policy councils, the Urban Development Council (UDC) and the Housing Council (HC). The UDC is the larger of the two and represents a more concerted and technically sophisticated attempt to address Santo André's urban planning and development challenges. It provides oversight and was itself enacted by the passage of the City Master Plan. City Master Plans, at the municipal level, consist of a catalogue of legal stipulations that outline the capacity of local government to intervene in matters of urban governance. They are, that is, instruments that establish abstract models of the municipal territory that demarcate purpose-specific zones and specify the legally sanctioned means through which local government can intervene in planning, construction and the use of land. As a legal entity which deliberates on urban planning regulations that derive from federal legislation, the UDC is far more embedded in the language and operational conventions of the Brazilian state than the participatory budget (PB).

City Master Plans emerged out of a much lauded urban charter, which consists of provisions in the 'Citizen's Constitution' of 1988 and enacting legislation, the Statute of the City, passed thirteen years later. However, the quality of citizen participation in enacting City Master Plans – a key tenet of the new 'juridico-urbanistic order' (Cymbalista & Santoro 2009: 6) – has received critical attention, with several analysts noting the significant practical challenges that are encountered when lay citizens participate in the planning process (Avritzer 2009; Friendly 2013; Villaça 2005). In one prominent study that establishes a typography of participatory institutions in Brazil, Leonardo Avritzer characterises City Master Plans as having a design based on 'public ratification', given the prerogative of government to initially author the plans and to use the attendant participatory forum (in this case the UDC) as a space for vetting the administration's policy proposals (Avritzer 2009: 141). Even Teresa Caldeira and James Holston, who are comparatively optimistic about the potential for participation in City Master Plans, have also observed the preponderance of members of the affluent classes at key moments in the development of São Paulo's own City Master Plan (Caldeira & Holston 2014: 11). The high threshold for technical competency set by the regulatory provisions of City Master Plans, and state control of the passage of amendments through the attendant participatory forum, are thus key issues to be explored.

Santo André is a propitious case with which to examine the challenges to participation in City Master Plans because the UDC and the HC deliberated on similar urban and housing planning policies and issues. This enables some comparative purchase on the conditions under which the City Master Plan is discussed and debated, in a similar governance environment, and some reflection on the challenges faced by those who wish to realise more participatory forms of urban planning in Brazil and indeed further afield. I begin this chapter by examining how City Master Plans are discussed and deliberated in practice in the face-to-face meetings of the UDC. While it is important to examine the effects of City Master Plans on patterns of socio-spatial segregation in the city (Holston 2008; Irazábal 2005; Klink and Denaldi 2011; Souza 1999), I am concerned here with the manner in which the plan, as part of a larger architecture of state power, figures in shaping the patterns of participation in the UDC. This analysis might be considered a response to the 'how question' (see Gordon 1991: 7); that is, how is it that social and political factors, such as the power of high-status officials and the technical complexity of City Master Plans, help to cultivate certain patterns of interactive conduct and engagement. But it also moves beyond the 'how' question to also reflect on 'why', on why it is that state power is selectively deployed in some institutional spaces and not others. This question is pursued initially through contrasting features of the UDC and the HC, and then in a more expansive comparative analysis of the UDC, the HC and the PB in the conclusion of the chapter.

The management policy councils are quite different from the PB. In the UDC and the HC there were no campaigns that gathered pace over time, generated emotional energy and laid the groundwork for tactical manoeuvres. There were, of course, issues discussed in their meetings that provoked discord and that were suggestive of the different political and economic interests at play. But these arose intermittently and were addressed in the course of routine gatherings, rather than months-long campaigns. For this reason, and also for reasons of space, the diachronic approach taken in the previous chapter that examined the flow of (inter)action over a series of interconnected meetings is impractical to pursue here. The repetitious nature of many of the meetings of the UDC, and to a lesser extent the HC, makes it more amenable to some form of synchronic analysis, though this is also supplemented with ethnographic data. There was less spatial and performative variability in their gatherings, and the organisation of their meetings was more explicitly prescribed. Despite these differences, there are basic thematic continuities of spatial and temporal organisation that enable comparison between the three institutions.

Time and space are not empty contexts in which citizen participation takes place; rather, they are fundamental to the constitution and manifestation of power in participatory institutions. Here I distinguish between time and space analytically only to emphasise certain patterns, which can then be contrasted and compared. Spatial organisation is a basic element of the configuration of practices in participatory forums, since how individuals are arranged in relation to one another prefigures certain patterns of speech and interaction and discourages others (see Giddens 1984: 66–68; Hall 1963, 1966; Lincoln 1994). Patterns of bodily positioning are intimately caught up with the exercise of power, for as we have already seen in the preceding two chapters, sequences of ritual action can demarcate and sacralise certain spaces for high-status officials that can legitimise highly unequal structures of interaction. In the UDC and the HC these physical arrangements were almost invariably followed over the entire fieldwork period and are thus susceptible to quite simple characterisations that I use, borrowing from Edward Hall (1963, 1966).

Control over the timing of participation is another crucial dimension of power in participatory institutions. As we have already seen in the PB, Mauricio was able to regulate the length of time that petitioners in the regional assemblies got to speak, cutting short many of those who sought to criticise the administration. In UDC and HC meetings, the sequencing of orations was codified in agendas, creating a formal schedule that the meeting should adhere to. This formal regulation of the meeting format was mandated in law by the internal regulations of the UDC.[1] Meeting agendas emerged as instruments for structuring and regulating the gatherings of first ancient and then more modern parliamentary bodies (Van Vree 1999: 324–5). The legal mandating of a meeting agenda here continues this historical practice and anchors it in the legislative conventions that underwrite the Brazilian state. But such formal regulations, as many practice theorists have argued, are only intelligible because of existing practical knowledge of normative conduct (Bourdieu 1977; Giddens 1984; Schatzki 1996, 1997, 2001). In this chapter I examine how similar formal regulations that are designed to govern the sequencing of participation are enacted quite differently in the UDC and the HC, and how they draw on existing practical understandings of normative behaviour and interaction that differ depending on the situation. Within the analysis of timing I also summarise the content of the meetings of the two management policy councils over a twelve month period, in order to give a sense of the content of meetings – content that helps to illustrate the principal policy concerns of the two institutions and their diverse members.

Spatial Organisation in the Urban Development Council

Every meeting of the UDC is preceded by periods of social interaction. Outside function rooms, coffee and sometimes other snacks are provided. Before the official start of the meeting, members of the institution gather around, to drink, eat and talk. Often the subjects broached will be personal in nature. The government and civil society representatives often talk of the well-being of their children and family members, and about the performance of football teams (especially the declining fortunes of the São Paulo's Corinthians Football Club!), and work and life in the city. Senior staff of the local administration mingle genially with civil society counterparts. In spite of what are at times fairly obvious disparities in language, clothing and appearance – that is, in social class – between members of the UDC, the mood that precedes its meetings is quite informal and egalitarian. But as the scheduled beginning of the meeting approaches, conversations dwindle in anticipation of a more serious type of activity. The arrival of other members, who pass the small groups of people conversing, indicate that the start of the meeting is at hand, and the small groups break up. Some take this final opportunity to visit the toilet. Others join the file entering the seminar room. The doorway seemed to partition the informal from the formal. Once in the seminar room, conversation becomes muted and the animation that accompanied earlier conversation is replaced, among the seated council members, by an earnest and respectful silence.

For those UDC meetings held in the SEMASA seminar room, the division between the front table and audience analysed in previous chapters was written into its physical structure: seats were affixed to the ground, cinema-style, while the projector screen had a computer to its right where a government employee would often sit to change slides for the presenter. In the UDC meetings held on the eighth and ninth floors of the town hall, removable chairs were arranged in the same format. This seating arrangement helped restructure the informal groups that gathered prior to assemblies in a spatial format that anticipated a small number of orators.

Edward Hall published a series of influential contributions to the study of the spatial facets of human interaction called 'proxemics' (Hall 1963, 1966). His calculative approach is complex, and I borrow only two analytical distinctions he uses. As part of his categorical framework, Hall distinguishes between 'sociopetal' and 'sociofugal' spatial orientations. Hall originally called this a 'sociofugal–sociopetal axis' (Hall 1963: 1008), hypothesising that the greater the face-to-face orientation of the actors, the more amenable, or sociopetal, it was to communication between them. As the angle between the actors widens, the more difficult communication becomes. When shoulder-to-shoulder, though still able to communicate, the two individuals normally have another spectacle occupying their attention. Further than this, the actors are disengaged or disengaging from social interaction, thereby assuming increasingly sociofugal positions to one another. Differentiating between sociofugal and sociopetal seating arrangements may be simplistic, but it does help to explain how certain patterns of interaction are reproduced and reified through patterns of spatial ordering.

Spatial Configuration and Meeting Format in the UDC

The meetings of the UDC took place in what might be called a typical class- or seminar-room format. The table was always located at the front of the room, and the audience was seated, in a grid-like formation, in front of it (see Figure 4.1). There was little variation in the seating arrangements over the course of my fieldwork, even when its location changed.

This seating arrangement gives maximal face-to-face contact between the table and the audience without curving the angle of the rows of chairs

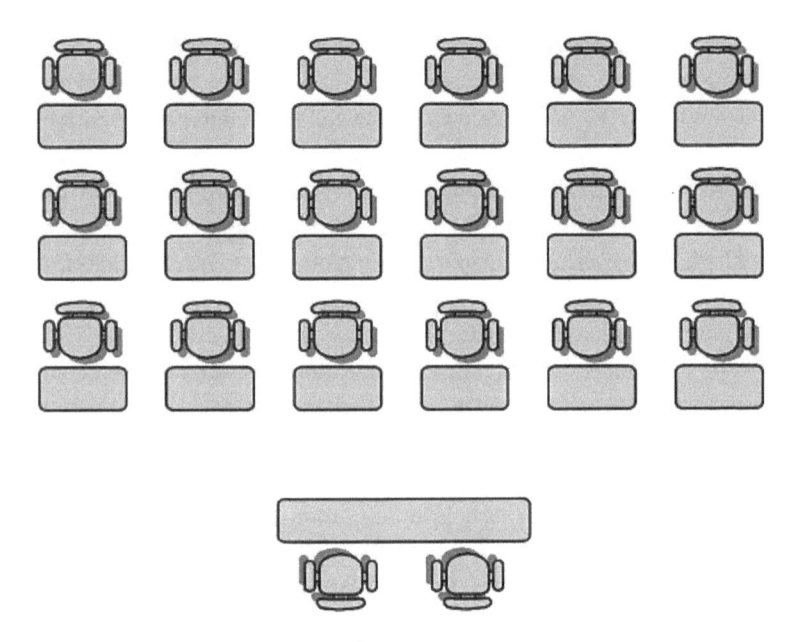

Figure 4.1 Spatial organisation in the UDC.

to face the table absolutely. In the SEMASA seminar room, there may have been a slight curvature of the rows and a small space through the middle, to permit entry and exit; however, the above arrangement held throughout the course of fieldwork, even when the location of the meeting changed. When meetings were held in the town hall, and the seating manually arranged rather than fixed to the ground, the chairs would often be assembled to directly face the table. This grid-like design is sociofugal inasmuch as it discourages communication between audience members, and foreshadows bilateral interaction between the audience and the table. It is an arrangement that is suitable for what Ronald Toseland and Robert Rivas call the 'maypole' interaction pattern, 'when the leader is the central figure and communication occurs from the leader to the member and from the member to the leader' (Toseland & Rivas 2005: 70). After outlining the formal schedule that regulates interaction in the UDC, we return to examine how tacit understandings of normative conduct undergird the exchanges between the front table and the assembled participants.

Temporal Organisation at the Meeting Level

UDC meetings followed a format that is common to the meetings of many other modern organisations. This format or structure is explicitly realised, among other things, through the use of a meeting agenda. A banal feature of many, if not most, organisational meetings, an agenda, when strictly applied and adhered to, becomes a framing instrument that orders and sequences participation and interaction, establishes and fixes expectations, and crucially includes and excludes certain kinds of claims and issues (see Tatagiba 2002: 77–79). The meeting agenda (*pauta*) was used in both the UDC and the HC, and was structured into three separate parts.

First, the approval of minutes: The first act of most UDC assemblies was the approval of the previous meeting's minutes. Following the entry and seating of the attendees, at times with the agenda already displayed on the projector screen, the UDC president would, after brief greetings, ask the audience if the minutes of the previous meeting met with their approval. For the UDC the minutes are posted to council members a week in advance, enabling some time for the examination of the drafted minutes before approval. Where, however, the president was unavailable to assume the role of chairperson, the second most senior government representative informed those present of the reason for his absence and assumed the role themselves. The announcement of this change of convention normally preceded all other agenda items.

Second, a briefing: The second agenda item of almost every meeting is a briefing session. It is an opportunity for both civil society and state representatives to inform the council of relevant news. Administrative representatives, who speak first, often use this time to promote other events, such as conferences, or to bring up developments in the local press. Often, possessed of much of this kind of news, the UDC president (and director of the urban development department) will themselves brief the UDC from the front table. Occasionally awards received by the administration will also be presented to the council. Civil society representatives, for their part, tell of developments in their locales, the outcomes of social-movement conferences and so on. Quite frequently, neither party has very much to contribute.

Third, general agenda items: This section primarily consists of presentations organised by the Department of Urban Development. Often, these were presentations of legal projects designed by the Executive that aimed at amending existing or passing entirely new legislation to the Legislative Chamber for ratification. The UDC received legislation-in-making on patrimonial protection, on laws for the parcelling and occupation of land, zoning laws and much more. These presentations sought to rework sections of the City Master Plan or associated legislation, and derived from ongoing work within the local administration, presented by those charged with and involved in their development. In the passage of these works and projects through the state bureaucracy, they acquire processing numbers, make established circuits through various departments, are measured against pertinent legislation and may or may not be legally required to be approved by the UDC before they are submitted to the Legislative Chamber for ratification. At times, representatives from NGOs, universities or other state agents will make presentations during this section.

Structure of the Agenda

Meeting minutes are normally treated, somewhat derisorily, as irrelevant to the realpolitik of citizen participation. Indeed, I was told by one civil society representative on the UDC that they have 'nothing to do with the actual decisions of the government'. But minutes are more than mere bureaucratic adornment: authorship of the public record is an essential strand – and legislative requirement – of the reiterative webs that, in the quotidian work of state actors, tie together the past, present and future into a coherent, institutional narrative. The minutes of the UDC recount the content of meetings in a formal Portuguese that reflects the legislative basis of the institution. Granted, there is little evidence to suggest that the recorded minutes are carefully analysed by different representatives on the council. During my fieldwork, the official minutes were challenged only once, when Roberta, at the front table, suggested a minor amendment. It was, for the most part, a ritualised approval of the official narrative that encoded the proceedings of the institution into a legal-bureaucratic idiom (Goodwin 2009: 454–5).

The briefing section was a part of the meeting in which civil society and government representatives could notify the UDC of 'news' and 'newsworthy' developments relevant to urban development that may interest other councillors. In analysing this kind of institutional aperture, which permits the spread of notifications among different social actors, it is also important to consider what is also proscribed and concealed. Eric Wolf uses the term 'organisational power' to denote the ability of actors to 'circumscribe the actions of others within determinate settings' (Wolf 2001: 384). In a similar vein, Steven Lukes, drawing on a short, influential article by Peter Bachrach and Morton Baratz (1962), labels this proscriptive ability 'non-decision making power' (Lukes 2005: 22). Lukes thus calls attention to the way that those who wield power can often restrict access to issues that might be incompatible with elite interests through, in this case, quite literally controlling the agenda. The briefing section was the only regular opportunity for civil society representatives to offer new material to the council, but it was not an occasion for submitting before the UDC substantive issues experienced in the neighbourhoods of the representatives. Civil society representatives were not invited to speak about the state of public infrastructure, the servicing of one region compared with the next or how provisions in the City Master Plan might influence their communities, but only to notify those present of changed circumstances or recent events. More often than not, the news referred to other public conferences or assemblies, or to goings on in the Legislative Chamber. The agenda therefore helped restrict the type of information aired by non-governmental councillors to recent, newsworthy developments.

The fact that the meeting agenda invites and engages certain kinds of information and restricts others is even more salient in the final agenda item. This became the section in which state employees gave presentations and reviews on all manner of work associated with urban development. In the first agenda item, the minutes, UDC members were asked to confirm the official record of the meetings, penned by public servants. It was but the first, minor instance of what was to be a much more pervasive pattern of knowledge production and dissemination, chiefly controlled by state officers. In the final, general section(s) of the agenda, new projects were announced and analysed, administrative processes were examined and policies that related to the City Master Plan, such as the Patrimonial Protection Plan and the Special Social Interest Zones (ZEIS) were examined. Legislative amendments were also brought before the UDC before their submission to the Legislative Chamber. After the presentation and analysis of administrative processes, legal amendments and plans and policies, the organisational tasks required to maintain the bureaucratic structure of the UDC was the third most common agenda item (see Table 4.1); these concerned the filling of council membership positions when they were vacated, establishing preparatory commissions for upcoming events, and the management of the general bureaucratic upkeep of the UDC and its ancillary bodies.

Agendas are order-making instruments that make explicit the generally more informal practice of advance planning that precedes many social occasions (Goffman 1963: 19). They prescribe what is to take place in the course of a meeting to ensure that predetermined aims are attended to. The predetermination of those aims – what is written into, and out of, the agenda – is one of the less obvious expressions of power in organisational gatherings. The intentionality and rationality that are an immutable part of the design of agendas are cast as impersonal, bureaucratic procedure. Agency becomes obscured through objectification. Participation can then be shaped by what is 'on the agenda' (*o que está na pauta*), as if it were something tangible, 'out there', rather than a product of conscious and purposive design.

Nonetheless, the structure provided by the agenda is far from comprehensive. Little else is specified beyond the agenda items in three different sections. The agenda provides a set of formal rules that are, as Giddens observes, 'codified interpretations of rules' (Giddens 1984: 21), insofar as the information provided in such sparse formulations becomes intelligible only on the basis of a more profound practical understanding of normative behaviour. Of particular relevance here is the question of who determines the issues to be brought before the council, and the unspoken rules of interaction that govern the discussions and deliberations that take place. We have already considered the exclusion of particular matters in the preceding section.

To examine the tacitly accepted rules for deliberation in the UDC, it is useful to consider a commonly used expression, *dar a palavra*, which has direct correlates in other Romance languages, but roughly translates as to 'have the floor' or to 'have the right to speak'. In public assemblies its use refers to the bestowal of the right to speak and is routinely used in meetings of Brazil's political institutions. The granting of permission to speak in the UDC was a prerogative of the chairperson, that is, the president, who confers it on different actors who are either orators who give a presentation at the front table or respondents in the audience. No signalling was needed for the right to speak to return to the meeting leader in this maypole pattern of communication. It was presumed that the chair 'has the floor' in the absence of indications to the contrary. The chair also does the 'semantic policing' (Morton 2014: 739): sanctions responses, interrupts the speakers who go on for too long, stray off-topic or contravene the professional norms of the meeting. Silent receptiveness, rather than robust participation, thus appeared to be the expected norm for the civil society participants of the UDC.

Another formal rule specified in the UDC's internal regulations, and one that was realised in practice, helped to prevent spontaneous discussions in the UDC of material that was not included in the agenda.[2] This stipulates that any material for discussion in the UDC not included in the pre-distributed agenda would first require a majority vote of members, and would thus require that a case be made to the assembled members before the start of the meeting. It is little surprise, then, that this occurred only once during my fieldwork. Table 4.1 is based on a summary of the meeting minutes which took place during fieldwork, and reveals the technocratic character of the issues presented to the UDC. The fact that new material was seldom proffered for inclusion in UDC meetings means that it is an accurate representation of the kinds of issues discussed in its meetings, though each of the items consumed varying amounts of time.

Table 4.1 General agenda items for the UDC

	Admin. processes	Legislative analysis	External presentations	Civil issues	Funding deliberations	Org. functions
19 Apr 2007	1	1				
10 May 2007			1			3
17 May 2007	1				1	1
31 May 2007	1					1
19 July 2007	1	1				2
30 Aug 2007	1		1			1
16 Aug 2007	1	1				1
13 Sep 2007		2	1			
18 Oct 2007		2				
20 Nov 2007	2	1				
13 Dec 2007		1		1		1
14 Feb 2008	2		3			
13 Mar 2008	2	1				
Total	15	10	6	1	1	10

Note: This table presents a summary of the official minutes of the UDC for the period April 2007 to March 2008. 'Administrative processes' refer to proposed or existing procedures and projects undertaken by the Department of Housing; 'legislative analysis' refers to the examination of existing or proposed changes to local, municipal laws; 'external presentations' are presentations that are delivered by other departmental staff members or NGOs; 'civil issues' refer to the analysis of government processes and how they related to the work of civic associations and local residents; 'funding deliberations' here refer to the analysis and decision making for the municipal housing fund, which is managed by the HC; 'organisational functions' of the HC are those agenda items concerned with the routine administrative procedures of the council, such as the management of attendance records of its members and the organisation of the municipal housing conference

Source: Urban Development Council, meeting minutes of the UDC, meetings 1 to 9 (including extraordinary meetings), 19 April 2007 to 13 March 2008.

According to the formal minutes, the most frequent agenda item was administrative processes and projects. The most popular of these processes were requests from developers to be exempt from tax on the sale of building rights for proposed construction projects whose height exceeded a floor area ratio of 1:1. The examination of existing or proposed legislation recorded the second highest number of entries. In fact, apart from two exceptions, one funding decision and an issue raised by a civil society representative, the UDC dealt almost exclusively with administrative projects and processes, and legislative change. That is to say, the meetings of the council became largely a presentational space for the existing work of the administration and the policies that guided its activity. There were seldom open-ended discussions over how to implement the 'social function' provisions within the plan, which, for instance, enable the government to apply progressive taxes on properties that do not serve collective interests, or indeed how to respond to the needs of disadvantaged social groups.

The influence of government officers over the sequencing and substance of the meetings of the UDC seemed to extend to the decision-making practices of its members, which were mediated by a show of hands. According to my analysis of the minutes for the above meetings, voting took place on 25 different occasions. Sixteen of those decisions were unanimous. Moreover, of the remaining nine decisions, in only three instances were any votes registered that contradicted the vote of the president. In the six other instances, several representatives merely abstained from voting. In effect, the voting preferences of the council president went unopposed in 22 of the 25 occasions that decisions were made by a show of hands in the UDC. As we have seen, selective control over the timing and content of meetings, exercised by senior government officials, also appeared to contribute to their effective control over the voting practices of UDC members. This control was embedded in what Bob Smith and Aaron Stewart have called a 'regime of routine' (Smith & Stewart 2011: 119) that largely excluded the effective input and participation from the civil society representatives who represented disadvantaged social sectors.

City Master Plans: The Partial Fiction of Technical Complexity

Technical complexity is widely thought to be a barrier to citizen participation in government decision-making and is often advanced as a justifiable impediment to interference by non-specialists. Democratic theorists have, at least since John Stuart Mill, identified the manifold differentiations and constantly changing nature of modern society as a significant challenge for participatory reform. Public administration has become correspondingly complex, as it must meet the diverse economic, service and mobility needs of the population. As a heavily professionalised domain, the complexity of urban planning processes and laws in the UDC was thus, perhaps unsurprisingly, a common complaint made to me by lay participants in Santo André, and I explore their perspectives further in the next chapter. Acceptance that certain domains of governance require specialised training forms part of what Michael Herzfeld calls the belief system of bureaucracy, or what he otherwise terms 'secular theodicy' (Herzfeld 1992: 5; see also Hilbert 1987). While some urban-planning processes are undoubtedly complex, the belief that complexity is prohibitive for citizen participation is at least partially due to the language that is mobilised in the course of framing and analysing the problems. City Master Plans are an excellent example of how complex and non-complex matters are encoded into a legal-bureaucratic idiom that functions as a 'type of power' (Apthorpe 1997: 43).

City Master Plans are a bundle of legislative stipulations and zoning regulations, and an impressive example of the state's ability to create sprawling taxonomies. Legislative taxonomies, of the kind enumerated in City Master Plans, illustrate well how substantively complex and non-complex issues can be encoded in a way that can exclude non-specialists. Take, for example, the following, from Santo André's City Master Plan.

Law No. 8.696,

Of 17 December 2004

Project of Law No. 13, of 30.03.2004

Process no. 8.082/2004-9

I instituted the new City Master Plan of the Municipality of Santo André, in the terms of Article 182 of the Federal Constitution, from Chapter III of Law No. 10.257, of 10 July 2001 – Statute of the City – and from Title V, Chapter II, of the Organic Law of the Municipality of Santo André.

João Avamileno, Mayor of the Municipality of Santo André, State of São Paulo, in the use and enjoyment of its legal capacities,

Let it be known that the Municipal Council approved and it sanctions and promulgates the following law:

> Article 1. In the service of the dispositions of Article 182 of the Federal Constitution, from Chapter III of Law no. 10.257, of 10 July 2001 – Statute of the City – and of Title V, Chapter III of the Organic Law of the Municipality of Santo André, the City Master Plan of the Municipality of Santo André has been approved, in the terms of this law.[3]

Note the numeric identifiers referencing federal and local legislation and attendant administrative processes. These represent the interlocking legislative and bureaucratic conventions shared by all the federal governments of the Brazilian state. The numeric identifiers for federal laws would be known to applied and academic specialists. But referencing for Santo André's municipal laws are unique and would be routinely used by a more restricted group of locally based public servants, political appointees and elected officials in the local branches of government. The use of numerals to identify laws and administrative processes avoids an unnecessary jumble of phrases and enables easy cataloguing. However, it also functions as a 'coding scheme' (Goodwin 2009: 454) that references directives and provisions in a shorthand routinely used by public servants, and it was pervasive in the assemblies of the UDC.

An intense use of this referencing system can be seen in the establishment of new regulatory proposals. I cite, for example, from the internal regulations for the Third Municipal Conference of the Cities:

> The 3rd Municipal Conference of the Cities – Santo André, convoked by Municipal Decree No. 15.561, of 30 May 2007, altered by Municipal Decree No. 15577, of 10 July 2007, in the terms specified by Federal Decree No. 5790, 25 May 2006; of Normative Resolution No. 4 of the Ministry of the Cities, and of State Decree No. 51.762, of 18 April 2007, will be realised on the days 27 and 28 July 2007 and will have as its aims:
>
> To advance the construction of National Urban Development Policy;
>
> To indicate priorities for the actions of the Ministry of the Cities;
>
> To elect 60 delegates of the Municipality of Santo André for the third State Conference of the Cities, as established in article 17 of the Regulations for the Third State Conference of the Cities.[4]

Such references to legislative classifications were part of a 'complexity', to be sure; but it was not a substantive complexity, insofar as it referred to the enabling chain of references, given by the constitutional basis of the state, rather than to some concrete modification to or evaluation of the built environment. The purpose of the law above was, in fact, to organise a conference! Legislative taxonomies, often combined with locally applied urban-planning categories and calculations, helped encode substantive issues of urban development in an esoteric idiom. Town planners, architects and their managers were thus what might in Saussurean terms be called 'members of a speech community'. The unreflective presentation of legislative amendments, or evaluations of proposed developments, or discussions of the legality of extant dwellings according to the referential system are all presentations by members of a speech community for other constituent members. Use of the esoteric idiom in participatory meetings can establish a self-contained dialogue based upon privileged knowledge of the referential system that insulates itself against public interrogation. It therefore operates as part the authority of public employees by restricting the judgement of their performance to expert peers (see Sennett 1980: 173).

Claims about efficiency are thus often claims about the maintenance of discourse in the esoteric idiom. And the maintenance of discourse in the esoteric idiom serves to undergird power, insofar as it excludes the uninitiated and creates exclusive circuits of dialogue and deliberation. This also means that there need be no contrivances on the part of public employees for a hierarchical culture to emerge, nor for lay participants to become marginalised from debates and discussions – at least, that is, when formal modes of speech are combined with formal patterns of social organisation (Bloch 1989: 28). Just as exclusion from governmental affairs has been problematic for members of Brazil's popular classes, so too, perhaps frustratingly, is the unmediated access to its processes. Of course, there is also a substantive complexity to urban planning and infrastructural management – something perhaps underappreciated in anthropological approaches to bureaucracy. To evaluate the capacity of drainage systems, establish predictive models for overflow and flood management or forecast traffic impact from population density estimates are all substantively complex matters. However, esoteric referencing adds to these complexities a further layer of abstraction. In the UDC, internal processes and legislative amendments were presented with little accompanying effort to evaluate their substantive effects in lay terms, thus contributing to the reproduction of hierarchical relations. In the following section, however, we see, in a quite different participatory institution, how other forms of language can be employed, and other, less hierarchical relations can obtain, when discussing similar urban policy and planning issues.

Another Kind of Institution: Deliberation in the Housing Council

Thaisa was a civil society member of the HC. At times during its meetings, Thaisa's eyes, after blinking heavily, would close completely. Her head would tilt forward, or much more uncomfortably, backward, triggering a metronomic nod between sleep and a bleary wakefulness. 'Hey', the council president, Vanessa, joked more than once, 'are we boring you?' Thaisa's attention would be drawn back, at least momentarily, to the content of the meeting, which normally numbered between ten and twelve of us in one of the town hall's smaller meeting rooms. Others, too, after a hard day at work, would fight off fatigue – sometimes a losing battle – in an attempt to concentrate on the issues of the council. It was strange that, perhaps excepting the largest public audiences, I had never seen anyone else fall asleep in a participatory meeting. True, the meetings were late; beginning at 7.15 PM, they would sometimes extend beyond 10 PM if there was a complex issue that elicited debate and discussion. But I do not believe that it was the late hour alone that had participants yielding to sleep. It was part of the informality of the council.

The language employed in the HC also attests to its informality. For example, the council president called the state meeting for the Conference of the Cities held in central São Paulo – the great countrywide participatory scheme organised by the new Ministry of the Cities – the 'biggest farce (*palhaçada*) I have ever seen' – referring to the often chaotic atmosphere among the 1500 participants in the conference theatre. Others called it 'nonsense' (*bobagem*), poorly organised and an event in which voting did not matter. It was not only frank, colloquial speech that distinguished the HC, however. In the same meeting, one of the civil society representatives recounted the way voting in the Conference of the Cities assembly was manipulated by politically attached social-movement organisations. The subject, taboo in most state-organised assemblies, was here taken up by the participants who initiated a searching and critical discussion about social movements and co-optation.

Such candour contrasted starkly with the caution and circumspection displayed in the meetings of the UDC and the PB. Co-optation, clientelism and other features of the political culture, dissonant with predominant political ideals, inevitably surfaced in the meetings of the two institutions. However, often resulting from gaffes, or from emotionally charged personal confrontations, these intrusions of political reality were normally promptly silenced. At other times, such matters were tactfully presented to both maintain the respectable veneer of liberal government while also intimating more subtly, say, the influence of developers on elected officials. In the official meetings of the UDC and the PB, as in most formal events in Santo André, practices of patronage, co-optation and the exchange relationships endemic in Brazilian politics were rarely openly discussed. I explore the relationship between these publicly disavowed yet pervasive features of politics and the performative expectations of public assemblies in Chapter 6.

The following section examines how it is that the HC was able to develop a more freely deliberative culture, for the informal and open modes of communication noted above were indicative of a relatively stable set of permissive behavioural norms rather than exceptional cases. The analysis follows the same structure that applied to the UDC. To this end I examine: the formal hierarchy and membership composition of the HC (something which was carried out in the cases of the PB and the UDC in Chapter 2); the forms of spatial organisation that obtained in the institution's meetings; how interaction and dialogue were coordinated and managed; and the HC's policy interests and priorities as revealed in the minutes of the institution over a twelve-month period.

Formal Hierarchy in the HC

According to its president, Vanessa, the HC was the only participatory institution in Santo André that had a civil society representative as its president. This had not always been the case. In the institution's first mandate, the presidency was held by the erstwhile secretary for housing, Fernando. Vanessa explains:

> We had a discussion with the government representatives at the time … In the second council [mandate] we already had a president from the workers union … In the third mandate it was me, and this is the fourth mandate and the second in which I am president … This is good because it ends up bringing representatives of the population closer to the government. It is easy for associations to reach me by phone to discuss the problems they are facing in their *favelas*. This access also contributes greatly to the discussion within the HC. There is great respect on all sides for this, and we will continue to maintain that representatives of the population should occupy the presidency.

Although Vanessa had a great influence on the HC, and was an irreverent and energetic spokesperson, her position as a representative of civil society was problematic. She qualified as a civil society representative for her attachment to the Cooperativa Habitacional dos Servidores Públicos de Santo André (SERVCOOP, Santo André Municipal Public Servants' Housing Cooperative). But she was also a tenured public servant in charge of data administration and archiving in the Department of Urban Development. She thus might have qualified for both a civil society and a government position on the HC. Had she proved more subject to pressures from above or less driven or receptive to popular concerns, a civil society presidency, a unique asset among Santo André's participatory institutions, might not have had the significance it did.

The position of vice-president was occupied by Rafael, a government employee. Charged normally with minute-taking and other organisational tasks, Rafael also moderated the meetings in Vanessa's absence. Even in these cases, the HC did not lose its deliberative character; open-ended discussions still took place, as did the forthright interrogations of the uses, and perceived abuses, of government power. Rafael was not, it must be noted, the most senior government representative on the HC. The secretaries for housing and urban development were also among its members. The secretary of housing, Luana, attended most of the meetings at the beginning of my fieldwork. But such was the egalitarian nature of the HC, and perhaps her own personal disposition, that it was some weeks before I became aware of her position in the administration. Following her exit from the administration, however, the new secretary for housing did not attend the meetings of the HC. During my fieldwork, the secretary for urban development never attended a meeting, despite his formal membership.

With a civil society president, unlike the UDC and the PB, the HC was not cloaked by the command structure of government. This helped foster a more liberal, communicative atmosphere in its meetings. Not only were meetings less formally regulated – that is, concerning who could speak and when – but the matters discussed therein also attested to a different ideological orientation among its members. In this regard, it is important to note the makeup of the council. As described in Chapter 1, the civil society participants were representatives of associations of *favela* inhabitants, housing associations, popular cooperatives, so-called 'classist entities' or social segments whose work was related to housing – presumably the provision under which SERVCOOP and Vanessa's membership was allowed. With these formal conditions, there was a greater likelihood that civil society representatives had similar material interests, and a similar working, if not popular, class background.

This group of civil society representatives from the popular classes was paired by a unique set of individuals from the public sector. Rafael and Vanessa were not the only progressive employees among the members of the HC. Bianca, an urban planner, whose perspectives are analysed in the following chapter, and Anderson, a housing analyst, displayed a similar predilection to assist civil society councillors in understanding government policy, communicating the intentions and consequences of government practice, furthering progressive policy within the administration, and helping civil society organisations, occasionally out of working hours and off government property. I had seen Bianca, in particular, on several occasions at the meetings of a small social-movement organisation, and at the home of a social activist, giving advice and support. One or two other government representatives did not seem so disposed to work with their civil society counterparts, or to partake so wholeheartedly in the progressive deliberations of the institution, but their influence was episodic if not negligible. They also tended to miss many of the HC's meetings.

So it was here, among this ensemble of progressive public servants and popular representatives that, among all the institutions I studied, the promise of a cooperative form of participation seemed best realised. The content of discussions, though moderated by Vanessa and loosely oriented by housing issues, was not rigidly regulated, and each person could, when not dozing at a late hour, contribute and be heard. There were, of course, social inequalities among HC members. Yet, the collegiality evident in the meetings of the HC proved that 'it is possible for interlocutors … to bracket status differentials and to deliberate *as if* they were social equals' (Nancy Fraser, quoted in Goode 2005: 39, emphasis added). Deliberative forms of communication were not dependent on the absence of inequalities, but rather on the dispositions of HC members and the behavioural norms that were negotiated and established between them. Indeed, so unique were the dispositions of government representatives on the HC that I developed a quite different relationship with them than I did their counterparts involved in the PB and the UDC. We met for coffee and exchanged ideas, and it was through these relationships that I gained many insights into the inner workings of government that contradicted the official version, or the 'public transcript' (Scott 1990) that executive officers sought to advance in public performances and associated media. They were co-producers of knowledge of a more involved kind – fieldwork colleagues who were 'complicit with their institutional functions', but who were 'able nonetheless to mark a space of reflection – a space of various uses and ethical inflections' (Marcus 2000: 5). Those spaces of inquiry and discussion were spread over several physical field sites, over informal chats, during social-movement gatherings and in the meetings of the HC. The spatial organisation of these field sites also contributed to the kinds of dialogue and deliberation that were cultivated.

Spatial Configuration and Meeting Format in the HC

The HC was a smaller institution than either the PB or the UDC, but like them its 16 members were divided evenly between government and civil society representatives. However, it was only rarely that something like a full complement of its members would meet, and over the course of my fieldwork an average of ten to twelve councillors attended its assemblies. The location of these meetings changed more frequently than those of the PB and the UDC. A room would be allocated, often with little forewarning, leaving me, occasionally accompanied by other HC representatives, scurrying around the floors of the town hall, after hours, looking for the right place. Its members, who assembled around rectangular or oval desks about the size of a large dining table, had greater face-to-face contact with one another. It was more sociopetal than the formal meetings of the PB and the UDC (see Figure 4.2).

The increased proximity to one another, provided by the spatial arrangement illustrated in Figure 4.2, afforded a capacity to observe, and be observed, by a greater proportion of attendees in the course of communicative exchanges than, for example, in those assemblies of the PB and the UDC, which were formally divided into table and audience. One

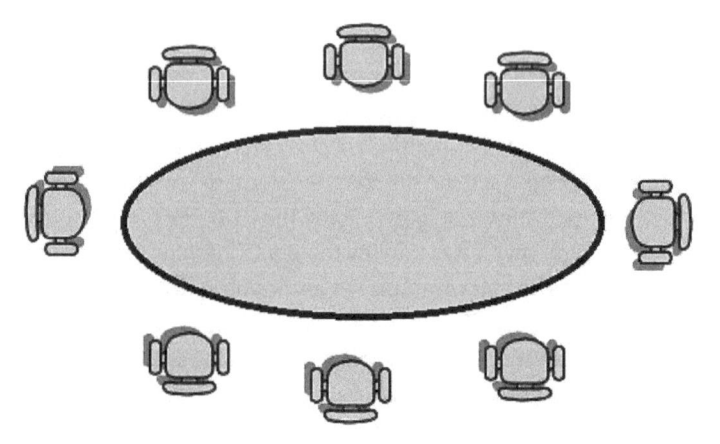

Figure 4.2 Spatial organisation in the HC.

could take in gestures that accompanied verbal communication and make eye-contact while speaking directly with each of the attendees around the table. Vanessa was identifiably the chairperson, but moderated and stimulated discussion more than managing it. The public servants – Bianca, Rafael and Anderson – were the most communicative members of the council, though their efforts were often employed to relate and translate processes and policies of the administration for the civil society participants. They were linguistic brokers of a kind, whose efforts served if not to 'de-code' then at least to re-code some of the legal-bureaucratic idiom that was employed in the City Master Plan and similar policies and put them into more colloquial language for the civil society members of the council. The informal, frank and public-spirited deliberations were helped, rather than hindered, by the role of the meeting agenda in HC meetings.

Meeting Format

The meeting format of the HC was similar to that of the UDC, though not all of its features were retained. Minutes of each meeting were kept and circulated by e-mail in advance of the following one. Yet, unlike the UDC, there was often no meeting section when participants voted to approve them, an omission of protocol that was indicative of the disregard of the council for bureaucratic procedure. The HC also maintained a briefing section at the beginning of meetings when its members could exchange information. State representatives would relate information that might be of interest to members, such as proposed legislative changes, progress on urbanisation works and upcoming conferences. According to the formal agenda of the HC, however, the briefings section was meant to be open to contributions from civil society members only. Finally, like the UDC, Vanessa, or Rafael acting in her stead, would begin the 'general items' section of the meeting, in which the main subjects and issues to be addressed during the meeting would be discussed.

But unlike the UDC, many of the organising instruments of the HC were treated like inconvenient bureaucratic fetters. The minutes were not exhaustively written and at times consisted of little more than a register of attendance. Indeed, the meeting agenda, used to such effect in managing and controlling the meetings of the UDC, served as an aid for the discussions of the council rather than as a device that strictly regulated and ordered its deliberations. The practical knowledge of normative conduct in the meetings of the HC was thus only very loosely related to the formal regulations of the institution. The informality of its meetings, which enabled deliberation and fostered a congenial rapport, applied not only to the relationships and interactions among the members of the HC, but also to the fulfilment of its bureaucratic tasks. There was nothing so uniform as the 'regime of routine' seen in the meetings of the UDC.

Despite the summary way in which records were kept in the HC, Table 4.2 breaks down the main agenda items of its meetings, and provides a rough indication of the kinds of issues discussed in them. While a similar breakdown of general agenda items given for the UDC (see Table 4.1) and compiled over the same twelve month period, it allows the progressive nature of deliberations in the HC to be discerned.

It is clear from Table 4.2 that the analysis of administrative processes and projects, existing or proposed legislation and presentations from other

Table 4.2 General agenda items for the HC

	Admin. processes	Legislative analysis	External presentations	Civil org. processes	Funding deliberations	Org. functions
12 Apr 2007				1	2	1
24 Apr 2007				2		1
15 May 2007						1
29 May 2007			1		1	
10 July 2007		1				2
31 July 2007						1
28 Aug 2007						1
11 Sep 2007						1
2 Oct 2007						3
30 Oct 2007					1	1
27 Nov 2007						
29 Jan 2008						
26 Feb 2008					1	3
25 Mar 2008						
Total	0	1	1	3	5	15

Note: This table presents a summary of the official minutes of the HC for the period April 2007 to March 2008. 'Administrative processes' refer to proposed or existing procedures and projects undertaken by the Department of Housing; 'legislative analysis' refers to the examination of existing or proposed changes to local, municipal laws; 'external presentations' are presentations that are delivered by other departmental staff members or NGOs; 'civil org. processes' refer to the analysis of government processes and how they related to the work of civic associations and local residents; 'funding deliberations' here refer to the analysis and decision making for the municipal housing fund, which is managed by the HC; 'organisational functions' of the HC are those agenda items concerned with the routine administrative procedures of the council, such as the management of attendance records of its members and the organisation of the municipal housing conference.

Source: Housing Council, meeting minutes of the first extraordinary meeting of the UDC, meetings 2 to 12 (including extraordinary meetings), 12 April 2007 to 25 March 2008.

organisations or departments did not figure strongly in the meetings of the HC. While the HC did not analyse any administrative processes and projects, over the same time period the UDC had analysed 15. And while the HC only analysed a piece of legislation once, the UDC analysed legislation on ten different occasions over the same time period. The HC received fewer presenters from other organisations or organisational departments than the UDC – only one was recorded over the same period the UDC had six. The next HC agenda item type did not, however, appear in Table 4.1. In Table 4.1 there was only one instance where civil society issues were specifically entered into the formal agenda of the UDC by civil society representatives, while in the HC there were, in fact, no agenda items that were identifiably sponsored by civil society members.

However, there were several agenda items of a different kind: what are labelled 'civic org. processes' in Table 4.2 did not appear in UDC meetings. These addressed the relationship between civic associations and specific government processes and programmes.[5] While only registering on the meeting agenda three times, this interest in expounding the relationship between the government and civic associations was indicative of a broader concern of the HC to render government resources and services accessible to the civil society organisations of the city. For instance, of the five agenda items addressing deliberations over the municipal housing fund, four concerned investments that were sponsored by civic associations or unions. While occasionally these discussions were seemingly inflected by self-interest,[6] three of the funding deliberations related to a civic association which did not have members on the HC but whose representatives were invited to attend relevant meetings. The other funding decision was for a request to augment an existing project in Sacadura Cabral – a project which did not, to my knowledge, benefit any of the HC members. This demonstrates some preoccupation with the welfare of civil society beyond the interests of its members.

Decision-making in the HC was even more collective than in the UDC: the votes on all of these investments were unanimous, thus confirming F.G. Bailey's hypothesis that smaller councils 'incline towards consensus' (Bailey 1965: 2). Perhaps that is a little more understandable in the case of the HC than the UDC for reasons other than size, since the HC was a participatory institution in which civil society members had similar socio-economic backgrounds, and from what I was able to glean, political leanings. Administrative tasks, according to Table 4.2, seemed to occupy the agenda of the HC more so than the UDC, which had ten items to the HC's 15. However, this figure may have been skewed somewhat by the housing conference, which was a recurrent item in the agenda of the HC, and has been considered here an 'administrative task'. Another notable feature of Table 4.2 relates to the blank spaces; that is, meetings where there were no general agenda items (the approval of the previous meeting minutes and the briefing section were not counted in the table). As mentioned earlier, the minutes of the HC were not exhaustive, unlike the UDC, and there were several meetings, particularly either side of Christmas, that were little more than informal discussions between civil society and government representatives.

Conclusion

Over this and the previous chapter I have examined how different configurations of practices were cultivated in three participatory institutions organised by the same administration. But it is important to look beyond the question of 'how' and to question 'why' participation and the structures of interaction were so different in the participatory institutions, and why state power was deployed more concertedly in some spaces than others. This analysis helps us to discern, to use an expression coined by Bob Jessop, the 'strategic selectivities' of state power in institutions of participatory democracy (Jessop 2008: 125–6). In the following section I take a step back from the situated phenomena of participation in the individual institutions, and argue that we can see patterns among the practices that are suggestive of the organisational and political interests at play.

The Participatory Budget

The PB drew widespread acclaim, as a model of good governance, for the inclusion of disenfranchised social groups in critical decision-making processes. Control over the budget is control over the lifeblood of an administration. Establishing an assembly-based system through which local citizens could lobby for local investment was seen as a means of redistributing public investment (Santos 1998) and of correcting a governance tradition that had patently failed to provide for disadvantaged members of society. In the previous chapter, however, we saw how public servants, political appointees and elites carefully choreographed those encounters in a concrete example. Drawing on a comparison of the PBs in Belo

Horizonte and Porto Alegre, Avritzer argues that, 'participation in the PB has the role of securing a deliberative form of publicity and public access to information and to deliberation over the distribution of material goods' (Avritzer 2002b: 583). It is perhaps surprising, then, that in the public assemblies of Santo André's PB there was little deliberation concerning the 'distribution of material goods'.

While opportunities for deliberation and discussion may have been restricted, the regional assemblies of the PB, in which participants determine priorities and elect representatives, were certainly the most festive, and were replete with the sounds of football horns and chanting for electoral favourites. However, this animated component of the event related to the representative composition of the MBC rather than the distribution of material goods. The PB director, Mauricio, following the casting of votes, would read out the results for those who had not exited immediately after voting. In effect, the participatory component of the PB, in which citizens were able to address the issue of material investment, was limited to the vocalisation of priorities at the microphone.

The regional assemblies were carefully managed by government officials and municipal staff for at least two reasons. First, concrete influence over future government action was at stake, since a list of potential works would issue from these assemblies after further negotiation and prioritisation. Inter-departmental work schedules, budgetary and planning processes and human resource allocation would all be affected. The construction of new facilities, such as crèches, and the significant upgrading of existing amenities would also have ramifications for future governments, which would bear ongoing renewal costs. Second, the reputations of elected officials were on the line. Face-to-face contact with thousands of the voting public constituted a political opportunity for those able to associate themselves with a widely feted participatory institution. This opportunity was exploited not only by Workers' Party members of the Legislative Chamber. The mayoral hopeful, Wanderlei Siraque, who had won pre-selection in the Workers' Party, was also keen to appear on such a public stage. At these events, João Avamileno availed himself of the opportunity to distinguish himself, as he so often did, from mayors past who rarely ventured into the periphery, much less involved the poor in government decisions. Presence before so many of the public was, however, also problematic, since many poor residents had grievances to air with the local government. If handled incorrectly, such public audiences could be chastening for those courting the voting public only months away from municipal elections. With such matters in the balance, the careful management of public participation insured against unfavourable potentialities while associating state and political elites with the successes of a highly celebrated institution. The careful management of such assemblies perhaps also served to maintain the dignity due to high-status officials.

The regional assemblies did, of course, effectively record priorities that were sent to the negotiating assemblies of the MBC. It was there, perhaps more so than in the regional assemblies, that one would have expected robust deliberation. The regional assemblies had collated over 50 demands that were to be debated and discussed among the members of the MBC, and a number of issues, potentially, required attention. Members of the MBC might have considered the unequal investment histories of the different regions, or the requirements of businesses, or the local needs for the nominated demands. To engage in such deliberations, however, would have carried risks – the risk that the mayor and the departmental secretaries would lose face when challenged on past performance, or perhaps that political patrons could, acting through their clients in civil society, unduly influence deliberations, or indeed that demands, favoured by certain government officers, would simply be argued down 'by the force of what one says' (Pellizzoni 2001: 62). Open-ended deliberation does carry risk, and it was against such potentialities and others that the government tactics in the negotiating phase effectively safeguarded.

Here, state representatives, rather than evaluating one demand against another, attempted to influence the outcome of negotiations by submitting a complete list, in the form of a counter-proposal, of 'what was possible' and to reduce criticism by attempting to close the meeting early. By remaining united behind the counter-proposal, and by forestalling calls to discuss its selection of demands, the presiding political and state appointees avoided the possibility of persuasive argument against it – though there were several minor concessions which stemmed from the protests of the civil society group. In this way, the state officials drew on the understanding that the city budget was, in the last instance, theirs to control. 'Power over communication' (ibid.: 62) was, in this case, a means of retaining control over most of the next year's investments.

The Urban Development Council

With 38 members, the UDC had a large membership – twice that of the HC – that included representatives of high-status organisations in addition to those representing the popular classes. That is to say, representatives from powerful groups in the city were among its members. There were representatives from the commercial and industrial association of Santo André; the federal university of the ABC region; the association of engineers and architects of the ABC; the metalworkers' and civil construction unions; and the lawyers' association of the ABC, in addition to representatives of the civic associations and social-movements segments. With a membership drawn from such diverse professional and social groups, the political appointees administratively responsible for the UDC had an interest in managing its assemblies with tact and diplomacy.

The UDC was also charged with overseeing the implementation of the City Master Plan and of vetting urban development policy before its submission to the Legislative Chamber. One of the key criticisms of the City Master Plan has been that it is comprised of 'generalities – directives, objectives, concepts, etc. – that do not oblige anyone to do, or to stop doing, anything' (Villaça 2005: 23). Yet, urban planning policies do create taxonomies that affect the work of government employees, who, among other things, use them to check the legality of proposed and existing construction. Legislation also creates legally sanctioned possibilities, where in the past there were none. With progressive land taxes, the government has the power, even if rarely applied, to fine and potentially dispossess property speculators who under-utilise the land. The sale of building rights gives the government new controls over urban density and the height of buildings, and the ZEIS zoning classifications can be used to reserve land – a precious commodity in Santo André – for low-income housing. Despite the fact that the enactment of the provisions in the City Master Plan are dependent on, in the words of Erminia Maricato, 'the correlation of forces' in the city (Maricato 2010: 6; see also Maricato 2011: 23, 30), the decisions taken by the UDC potentially affected the interests of a number of important actors in the city, including the local administration. Like the PB, decisions of some consequence were at stake in its meetings – meetings in which powerful associations were represented. The regulatory techniques seen in the meetings of the UDC – the presence of the government hierarchy, the formal coordination of meetings and the use of a technically esoteric idiom – can thus be conceived as structuring effects of political power (Maricato 2010: 6), which were selectively enacted because of the administrative, commercial and reputational interests that were at play. We can see similar correlations between the

The Housing Council

In contrast with the UDC, and many of the assemblies of the PB, the HC had, as indicated earlier in the chapter, an egalitarian culture, proving that the hurdles presented to popular participation by technically specialised subject matter were not insurmountable. It had a smaller membership, which allowed seating around a single table, virtually all the non-state participants were from the popular classes, and it was the only participatory institution in the city, as far as Vanessa and I were aware, that had a president that was a representative of civil society. While the meetings of the HC were not dominated by the terminology of the City Master Plan, many of its concepts, directives and specifications were discussed at length. But here the combination of council size and sympathetic public servants allowed the otherwise esoteric elements of the plan to be unpacked and discussed at length by its members. Individual councillors were also given the opportunity to discuss their own issues – often in the kind of interminably protracted land-titling disputes analysed by James Holston (2008: 203–64) – and offer candid assessments of government policies, new legislation, the effectiveness of conferences and so on. The more formal enactments of state power in the PB and the UDC were patently absent and replaced by a cordial collegiality that, although at times inflected by individual interests, also encouraged open-ended deliberation.

The collegiate culture of the HC may have been, however, at least partly due to its relative lack of influence over consequential policy and decision-making, and the absence of powerful actors in its membership. Several of its properties point to such a hypothesis. First, the most senior government member on the HC, the director of the Department of Urban Development, was absent from its meetings, although he attended other engagements with regularity. Even the director of housing that replaced Luana, the second-most senior government employee, attended infrequently, leaving it to an advisor from their department to help coordinate the sessions. Second, while both the PB and the UDC had assigned, institutional responsibilities – in the case of the former, the establishment of demands to be implemented the following year; in the latter, the vetting of urban policy destined for the Legislative Chamber – the HC had little by way of official, administrative authority, apart from organising the annual conference.

Third, the municipal housing fund, its management perhaps the HC's only other responsibility of note, was, according to the HC president and the director of housing, meagrely resourced; during my fieldwork, it was only used as a supplementary fund for existing projects rather than to finance original works.[7]

Previous chapters have shown how state power figures in the different configurations of practices – practices that have cultivated quite different structures of interaction and dialogue in three of Santo André's participatory institutions. But there is also a broader logic discernible here of the 'strategically selective' enactments of state power in some participatory gatherings and not others. The status and influence of the individual participatory institution within the machinery of local government serves as something like an activator, triggering manifestations of state power in those moments of interaction where there is most at stake, in the negotiations over the budget and important urban planning legislation. It is in those moments where important decisions are to be made, where powerful organisations are represented, where the authority of the state is symbolised most strongly and where deliberation occurs according to tightly controlled parameters. Egalitarian forms of participation were indeed possible, but these tended to take place at some remove from the centres of decision making power. This suggests that should progressive public servants and local activists wish to realise the promise of participatory democracy in Santo André, then they also have to negotiate with the vested organisational and political interests that shape the conditions under which they are discussed and debated.

5
Shared Practices, Contrasting Ideologies

Over the past two chapters I have examined how state power shaped the configuration of practices in three participatory institutions. Here I turn to the participants, who critically assess and measure the conditions they encountered in the institutions against broader participatory and governance ideals. Despite the shared experience of participation, there were quite divergent interpretations about the role of state officials and the possibilities for participation. The realisation of ideals of participatory democracy was, that is, in constant and dynamic tension with other beliefs – beliefs about the exigencies of governance, the (in)competence of popular actors, and the sincerity of the administrative commitment to citizen participation. There were also points of ideological overlap, convergence and consonance, among the tensions people reported. In this chapter I chart this ideological terrain through examining the narratives of participants as they critically reflect on their practical experiences of participatory institutions. The chapter thus provides insights into the way that state structures, and the moves of state-based actors, are rationalised, supported and critiqued, both by lay participants and from within the administration itself.

The ideals of participants that are revealed in their assessments of the institutions are often contradictory and complex, and yet can be meaningfully clustered together. This clustering is provided for, but not determined by, their role in the participatory institution and, where it applies, the administration. Political appointees and public servants are socialised into roles in the state administration, an entity which has shared structures, norms and a more-or-less coherent belief system that might be called an 'organisational ideology', which serves to maintain the administration and its patterns of order (Abravanel 1983: 274; Baba 1989: 7; Starbuck 1982: 3). Many of these beliefs challenge and contradict the ideals of participatory democracy, for they often privilege the state rather than citizens, prerogatives and priorities, and institutional rather than popular forms of knowledge. In concrete interactions with the public, this can tend to produce, perhaps even unintentionally, disparaging characterisations of its participatory 'others'. Beliefs that derive from the organisational ideology are manifest in rhetorical practices that extend to a broader population the evaluative criteria that are applied internally. While there are specific beliefs that shape the behaviour of political appointees and public servants, the bonds of collegiality that bind organisational members to one another are the base materials of collective coherence. They ensure that, notwithstanding individual differences of opinion, government performances normally appear cohesive (see Goffman 1957: 36). These bonds are often expressed through metaphors of internality, which may be woven into broader 'idioms of opposition' (Edwards 2005: 192). It is important to note, of course, that such ideological structures help to ensure broad collective, rather than uniform individual, cognitive and behavioural adherence to organisational norms and strictures. As will become apparent in interviews with some public servants, other beliefs mingle in diverse ways with the ideology of the organisational order.

In the first half of this chapter I examine a patent source of ideological tension in the narratives of political appointees and public servants: the relationship between one's position in the administrative structure of graded authority, and accordingly the position of responsibility one has in the institution, and one's commitment to participatory democracy. I begin with testimony from a couple of political appointees, before turning to two, particularly outspoken, tenured public servants. By comparing and contrasting their reflections on participatory institutions, I am able to show how different administrative roles and responsibilities correlate with, and at times compromise and provoke tensions between, their ideological commitments.

Civil society participants, to which the second half of the chapter is devoted, were not bound together by anything so cohesive or materially influential as a command structure. They had different class backgrounds, and many were from different parts of the city, with often quite dissimilar aims – at times quite narrowly interested, while at others more collective and radical. There was, nonetheless, widespread adherence to the ideals of participatory democracy: a valorisation of popular knowledge and a conviction that lay citizens ought to be able to decisively influence the plans and policies of the administration. In this chapter I present the insights of some of the participants whose views typify many of the perspectives and critiques of their peers. These perspectives set in stark relief the dissonant beliefs between different actors in the institutions and also reveal important substantive insights into the practical issues of participation.

In selectively ordering and analysing the narratives, I build on the comparative practice of earlier chapters by examining how the interpretation of particular events and more enduring patterns of deliberation in the participatory budget (PB), the Urban Development Council (UDC) and the Housing Council (HC) reveal different ideological orientations in the perspectives of the participants. In this way, the interviews allow a deepening and synthesis of the analysis that has already been advanced. Previous chapters have drawn heavily on my participant observation of meetings and other gatherings, a practice that was necessary given that much of the analysis focused on structures and practices that were largely taken for granted by participants. Here, I examine some of the diverse perspectives of participants, who were also friends and co-producers of knowledge, in a way that imposes my own voice to a lesser degree upon what they say and how they say it. Space is also allocated to analysing and exploring substantive issues raised by the participants, some of which, such as technical complexity and the push by state-based actors to favour certain demands in the PB, have already surfaced in previous chapters.

Perspectives from the State

Given the importance of the PB, I begin with Mauricio. We met in his office on the fourth floor of the town hall just as the negotiating assemblies were drawing to a close. Below, Mauricio reflects on the decision-making processes of the PB, and also gives some interesting insight into the tactics seen in the negotiating phase, analysed in Chapter 3. Having already observed the PB through a series of public meetings, I began by enquiring into how it functioned within the administration:

> V.A.: Can you describe the process within the administration, after the demands are received [from the regional assemblies]?
>
> MAURICIO: We have two stages. Citizens go to the plenary and nominate the demands, and from the nominated demands which are drawn from the 19 regions, we will have three demands [per region] and one for the

city ... These demands are analysed by technocrats from the appropriate department who evaluate the technical viability, the cost, what will be needed to implement the demand, [and that will depend on] whether it is a service or whether it is an investment work. While the technocrats in the administration are working on these demands – this is why I spoke of two stages – there are also discussions between the councillors of the population and those of the government. [At the beginning of the mandate of the civil society councillors] there is a stage that we call 'education', in which we hold the induction ceremony for the MBC [Municipal Budget Council], and we also have some [training] modules where we work through the internal regulations, and discuss how the MBC functions and the rights and responsibilities of the councillors who have been elected in the regions. We also give some instruction about the public budget and public finance. We are not going to make an economist [out of any of them], but they will have some notion of how the budget is divided among the various expenses that the administration incurs ... We're accustomed to comparing the budget to their home; they have a certain income and expenses, and the expenses cannot be increased much without [a similar increase in] income, as it doesn't balance out. And it is the same in the administration ... If we have to do some [investment] work or [deliver] a service, we have to save this money in order to spend it.

The household budget analogy was a recurrent trope in speeches given by the mayor, João Avamileno, in the PB assemblies, intended to provide a readily comprehensible metaphor to temper participants' expectations. Budgetary limitations constitute both an undeniable fact of public administration and a rhetorical tactic that was used to control the expectations and claims of representatives from civil society. I also want to draw attention not only to the homely metaphors but to the conception Mauricio advances of the civil society representatives. Mauricio indicates that they cannot know everything that goes on in the administration: they are not going to be economists – that is, formally educated; they can only have a partial and fragmented understanding of how the administration really works. Unknowingness, in this context, was a reflection of the values of the organisational ideology, which privileged the official knowledge of public servants, onto the participating public. But perhaps just as important as such stock characterisations of civil society participants was the conception of limited resources as a hard reality. I do not suggest that it is invented or unreal. Rather, I am interested in the way that limited resources, as a truth claim of the organisational ideology, becomes a rationalising axis for the governmental tactics we witnessed in the negotiating assemblies of the PB, and other modifications to the PB, as I will later show. This emerged when I questioned Mauricio about some of the criticisms that had been levelled at the government by civil society representatives.

> V.A.: I would also like to broach some subjects that other councillors of civil society have raised. One is that the government is able to choose from among the demands nominated by the public that are part of the [government] programme.
>
> MAURICIO: It isn't that we choose the demands that are part of the government programme. We don't allow and nor do we approve demands that contravene the directives of the government. For example, we have a policy of social inclusion for the disabled. Whatever demand that is elected, be it in education or in housing, that contravenes this policy, we don't allow it to be voted for. In education, the policy is to include the disabled in the same classroom as so-called normal people. [There may] come a demand from a region that is, let's say, a school for the blind, or the construction of a school for those with auditory deficiency. So this isn't the policy of the secretary of education, nor of the government. It contravenes the policy of the secretary of education and of the government that was elected. So we don't even allow this to be voted for. We don't choose the demands that are made, we bar them there at the origin [in the regional assembly]. What happens is that as money is short, it isn't possible to do all the works and services [that are elected in the assemblies], so various programmes that the administration intends to implement or to do, they end up 'getting a ride' within the PB, a ride in the sense of doing this work through the PB. At times the population wants to make a demand, and the administration really has to construct a school, so the administration benefits from knowing where the population wants a school. So it [the administration] ends up making the school in the region where the population requested it, where the councillors [of civil society] voted the budgetary demand. So this is not a manipulation, it is an adaptation to reality. When we started discussing the budget in the city, we always said to the population that it was easier to make the budget in the administration and then to implement it, without the participation of the population, and that then

we would not have had the headache we do now with participation. But this is what we want, we want this participation, we want this headache, because who knows better where to install works and services than the population itself.

The first and most glaring feature of Mauricio's response concerns the negotiating phase of the PB that I recounted and analysed at the end of Chapter 3. He reveals in an understated way how existing plans and priorities within government departments are deployed through the PB structure: he essentially substantiates – albeit partially and indirectly – what was only a reasonable supposition in the negotiating phase. His verification of the hypothesis that government counter-proposals were used to push through extant government plans and priorities was embedded in a rationalising framework that reveals features of a more pervasive organisational ideology.

First, Mauricio addresses the problem of demands that contravene government policy. He gives the example of a school for the disabled as one which breaches a principle of inclusive education. This is prevented from being registered; it is stopped at the source. Mauricio justifies the exclusion of the demand by privileging governmental directives. He portrays a policy hierarchy, legitimated by electoral mandate, within the administration that conditions citizen participation. This is the belief that the policy and service determinations of the government hierarchy are paramount, and function as an arbiter, or filter, of the demands of civil society.

Second, Mauricio turns to the issue of limited funds. The government has intentions to make particular investments, and these are, in his words, 'given a ride' through the PB structure. That is, the nominations made in the regional assemblies are used, as we saw in the negotiating phase, by different departments to push through their own investment plans by selecting demands from among those nominated by the population. Mauricio suggests that this is not a case of manipulation – perhaps implicitly acknowledging its appearance – but an 'adaptation to reality'. The reality to which Mauricio refers is the reality of extant plans and priorities doing the rounds in the town hall; these are reified features of the organisational ideology that enshrine and privilege the favoured plans of state-based actors, and accordingly recast the demands of civil society, the dozens of other priorities they elected by the thousands, as malleable and dependent.

Third, and perhaps consequently, citizen participation is portrayed as a fetter – literally, in Mauricio's words, 'a headache'. This is the combination of an unknowing public and a reified administrative hierarchy. The participatory assemblies are not indispensable, Mauricio suggests, and it would be much easier to do without them. Maintaining the forums for citizen participation was therefore an elective and voluntary exercise. The consequent organisational burden and confrontations with the public were justified by the capacity of lay citizens to correct investment patterns in the city. This is the point of ideological overlap and agreement between what Mauricio described as the exigencies of governance and his commitment to participatory democracy.

Mauricio's ideological commitments were, of course, interdependent. Attendance to the dictates of the government hierarchy seemed, in his interview, to shape and influence his adherence to ideals of citizen participation, which was described as a kind of encumbrance.[1] His recognition of the pre-eminence of institutional knowledge consequently recast popular participants as comparatively ill-equipped for governance responsibilities and only partially able to comprehend the reality of public administration. The scarcity of resources is an organisational fact and one that occupies a rarefied place in governance cosmologies. In Mauricio's testimony we saw how limited resources complemented the privileging of government plans and priorities and helped relegate citizen demands to a dependent status. Elected investments cannot all be carried out, Mauricio suggested, and in any case, government plans and priorities must be attended to first, plans that refract through the participatory institutions and calibrate the nominations made by the participating public. Participants who oppose this refraction are considered burdensome. And yet, in spite of the burden, and in spite of the only contingent grasp the public has on matters of governance, the citizenry does understand better where investment and infrastructure works are required.

Balancing the plans and policies of an elected government and the specific claims of citizen groups is, in abstract terms, a fundamental problem for participatory reform. It begs a number of important normative questions. Much democratic theory has thus concerned the influence that elected leaders ought to have – particularly, whether the supposedly more expansive participation of the population in general elections is a sounder basis for political power than the more active and engaged participation of a minority. Such questions have characterised debates about democracy, both ancient and contemporary, and surfaced with renewed vigour during

Brazil's democratisation (see e.g. Barber 1984; Dahl 2000: 100–18; Dias 2001; Genro 2003). Yet, this kind of theoretical dilemma was, according to Mauricio, subject to the much more mundane workings of power within the administration. Perhaps the electoral interests of politicians, and the appointees who depend on their re-election for continued employment, helped ensure that the investments touted in the government plan were privileged over the demands of the participating citizenry. Also, perhaps money might have been found for other priorities elected in the assemblies. We do not know, and this is one of the principal problems identified by participants.

It would be easy to personally condemn Mauricio for his role in the government manipulation of the PB structure, which was used for its own ends. He gives, as far as I am aware, the most candid account by a Workers' Party official, and no such insider revelations are found in previous studies of Santo André's participatory institutions. Yet I feel compelled to provide some qualifications that, while not exonerating Mauricio of personal responsibility entirely, do provide some necessary contextual considerations. First, as will be made clear in the interviews with civil society representatives – who reflect on previous budgetary cycles – the practice of pushing through government-favoured demands antedated by some years Mauricio's term as director. In addition, you may recall that the mayor was present during negotiations, and supported the government counter-proposals, while Mauricio's boss, the secretary of finance, took over the moderating role in the final series of meetings with the civil society councillors. This suggests that the counter-proposals Mauricio supported in the assemblies were sanctioned, if not authored, by those in the highest echelons of government. Second, the values he exhibited were part of a more-or-less coherent set of beliefs held by other political appointees.

Before we turn to another political appointee, it is worthwhile indicating the immense rhetorical and justificatory utility of limited resources. The subject was again touched upon, albeit indirectly, in a discussion of institutional change:

V.A.: How has the PB has changed since your first contact with it?

MAURICIO: From 2002 until 2003, we were practically copying what was being done since 1997, which was the deliberative participatory budget; we deliberated over four demands for a region, two for the city, and we did this every year. In addition we elected a representative from each region. From 2003, 2004, it was necessary to make a change in this project, to make an improvement in attending to the demands of the public, since more demands were accumulating than the administration could implement in one year. From 2003/2004 we started this discussion together with the population ... [And from] 2004 it changes and the deliberation of demands takes place every two years. On even years we go to the population and hear the demands that they want to effect, and on the odd years we also go to the population but only account for our progress on these demands. So the PB assumed a biennial structure.

Changing from an annual to a biennial cycle more-or-less halved the demands civil society was able to make through the PB. Consequently, it also more-or-less halved the amount of money that was at stake. A yearly cycle was now stretched over two years; demands made in the assemblies were for one budget only. On the so-called 'odd years', where the government would organise the 'holding to account' assemblies, there would be no public influence on that year's budget through the receipt of new PB demands. In the above excerpt, Mauricio suggests that this was needed to better attend to the demands of the population, likely because of limited human and organisational resources. Limited resources were used to justify halving the demands that could be made through the PB, and thereby diminished its potential influence over the administration. And, if you recall, limited resources were also used to justify the way that government plans and priorities were pushed through the PB structure. A lack of resources and limited capacities were thus used to justify both effectively halving the demands that could be made in the PB and subordinating it to the prerogatives of political appointees.

My interviews with other senior public servants were quite different. They only rarely unearthed insights into the conduct of government officials which contravened so directly the ideals of participation. While Mauricio's candour – his personal disposition and our relationship – may be one reason for his frank depictions of governance exigencies, it may have also been because other government representatives, from other departments, were not privy to the kind of realpolitik he portrays. The plans and priorities of other secretariats were channelled through his institution. Many of the other government representatives I interviewed were less responsible for such processes, and therefore their perceptions of the institutions in which they took part were more critically evaluative and hence more akin to their civil society counterparts. This is an issue of the access one has to the circuits of decision-making and review within the halls of the administration and how status and responsibility for those decisions can reveal otherwise inoperative ideological tensions. It is perhaps unsurprising, then, that other employees less responsible for the oversight and implementation of government plans and policies in the institutions draw less explicitly and consistently on organisational ideology. In the following interview, we see how Matheus, another political appointee, both lauds a combative style of citizen participation and justifies the defensiveness of government representatives. His description of different institutions also allows for a line of comparative investigation that will be continued throughout the analysis of other narratives. The interview was held in Matheus's office at the Department of Urban Sanitation, where he was assistant director of planning and works.

V.A.: Can you talk a little bit about how the participatory institutions function in the administration?

MATHEUS: I haven't participated in the HC for some time, but when I did it was quite different to the councils I participate in today. It was a small council, there were few people there, the meetings were always in a small room, everyone was around the same table and it was more like a work meeting. We could better discuss and perhaps discuss things more deeply, in a more truthful way in my opinion, because there were fewer people there. There was space to discuss, to exchange [ideas]. They were small group meetings, and this enabled us to study the projects better. And then I started to participate in the MBC. That was something totally different, it has another dynamic. There, the themes are controversial, there are various government departments involved, and there are many subjects that the whole council has to analyse. The other aspect that I like and that I have also found interesting is the combative aspect of the representatives of the population, although it is in a form [that is] a little bit controlled by the government. They are really combative, they come to discuss, to debate, to really use the space to say what they came to say, to hold the government to account and to insist that the government is here to govern for 'us'. We are in this participatory space and we didn't come here to congratulate you, to say, 'How great, I'm a Workers' Party member, the government is good, you are all doing beautifully in government'. No, it's good, I am a Workers' Party member, the government is good, but hang on there, there is also this problem here, what is going to happen with that? I think that this is great, it's cool, because generally in a council people don't like it much when some people spend the whole time arguing, and holding others to account. It is true, we are here inside, we know how much we work, what we have constructed until now. And when someone from outside comes here to criticise, the natural reaction is to defend oneself. But I, honestly, with my citizen's hat on, I like it when there is criticism, when the council positions itself and applies pressure. I think that this space is for this, not to always be agreeable.

Matheus was more diplomatic than Mauricio in his responses. He did not broach in any depth issues that contravened the ideals of participation, such as practices of administrative brokering that go on behind the scenes and influence the favouring of some investments over others. But his position was likely influenced by the fact that he was not directly responsible for the institutions he describes. Diminished responsibility also diminishes the potential for ideological tension and the necessity of compromise. Matheus's participation in the HC and the PB, moreover, allows such questions to be put into comparative perspective, and recalls the analyses of the institutions made in Chapters 3 and 4. In his description of the HC there were no divisions among the councillors; it enabled more 'truthful' discussions. But in the PB, he explains, the criticism of the civil society participants triggered defensiveness. The passage is thereafter riven by a state/civil society dualism. Only then does Matheus identify himself as 'inside'. Criticism thus comes from without, but it is a desirable criticism – the penance of democratic participation mentioned by Mauricio. Matheus's comparative assessments of the two institutions show how the design logic of the PB, in which real interests and resources were at stake, revealed a sense of organisational belonging and solidarity that remained latent in his depiction of the HC. Power, as I indicated in the previous chapter, can be an activator, and in Matheus's experience it prompts and produces divisions among the councillors – divisions that can also reveal the tensions between organisational membership and a commitment to participatory democracy.

Some public servants adhered much more closely to ideals of participatory democracy. Although complicit in the functioning of the administration in their everyday work (see Marcus 2000), in interviews, and even in colloquial conversation, they often eschewed metaphors of internality and organisational belonging altogether. They were non-managerial, tenured employees, several of whom self-identified as socialists. Vanessa, the president of the HC whom we met in Chapter 4, is an interesting example. Although a government employee, she portrayed herself as a defender of popular interests, and critically and rhetorically distanced herself from the government, as the following excerpt makes clear.

> V: Have you participated in the UDC?
>
> VANESSA: I have never participated in the UDC, although I helped to develop part of the City Master Plan. I'm proud to say that for most of the zones demarcated for ZEIS [Special Social Interest Zones], it was I who walked the city and saw which were the best zones [that should be reserved for low-income housing], and I sat down and discussed them with the social movements, and I represented the social movements in the discussions with the government, with business people, universities and everyone else. But when a law was promulgated that created the UDC, there was an article that says that a paid functionary cannot participate in the UDC [that is, as a civil society participant]. As I am employed by the administration, the law prevents me from participating. Now, as you already should have observed ... there is no other councillor more present in the meetings of the UDC than I, or I would say, in some moments, more participatory. I continue defending the interests of the population within the UDC, it's just that I don't have the right to vote. But my voice, I make a point of using it all the time. I am used to always saying that when you know how to use your voice well, it is more powerful than the vote, and I consider this a lot – in this case my voice is more powerful than the vote. I'll keep using it.

Rather than as an insider, protecting herself against critical participants, Vanessa identifies with civil society, and perhaps considers herself an activist working from within. It may have been a slight exaggeration to suggest that she was the most present on the UDC, since Vanessa did miss quite a few meetings, and they were, in any case, quite rigidly coordinated by the presiding chairpersons. But she certainly was a presence, and her commanding voice was a common feature, not only of the meetings of the UDC but relevant public assemblies in Santo André in general. It is interesting to note that while the law prohibited her participation on the

UDC as a civil society participant, she did not even consider taking part as a government representative.

Vanessa's outspoken support of participatory ideals was at least partially enabled by her secure employment status. Unlike Matheus and Mauricio, Vanessa had tenured employment in the administration. She indicated to me in another section of the interview, after a lengthy reflection on co-optation, that 'if I wasn't here saying all this as a public functionary I would be putting myself at the risk of being fired'. Secure employment provided what Michael Lipsky has called 'relative autonomy from organisational authority' (Lipsky 1980: 16). Lipsky studied work in state bureaucracies, paying particular attention to the discretion workers are able to exercise over the performance of their roles. It is impossible to fully regulate the conduct of an employee, he argues, and it would likely be undesirable to do so were it possible. The liberty granted to lower-level employees may thus be used to subvert managerial directives, because they consider them illegitimate, or not in their interests, or because they do not share the organisation's goals or values (ibid.: 16). Secure employment contracts, of the type held by public employees in Brazil, grant a certain liberty to workers opposed to managerial directives. Although senior administrators do have the authority to demote employees or withhold privileges, the more distressing prospect of unemployment is virtually nullified. This decreases the perceived costs of adopting critical postures regarding the conduct of political appointees. Of course, worker conduct remains tempered by complex and context-contingent organisational and cultural norms, but it also means workers are somewhat insulated against the potentially conflicting interests of the government in power. Secure employment was likely a factor that gave another of Santo André's activist-employees, Bianca, confidence in her often vocal criticisms of the local administration, and in other expressions of participatory and socialist ideals.

Bianca was an urban planner who worked as a tenured public servant in the Department of the City Master Plan. Like Vanessa, Bianca did not self-identify with the government or use insider metaphors. The following excerpt comes from the end of our interview, and shows how different she is in her assessment of the kind of surreptitious realpolitik Mauricio defended. Bianca's responses were extraordinarily long, and so I will just give a short extract. It comes in a discussion of how the UDC spends the funds accrued from the sale of building rights, that is, funds collected from developers whose constructions exceed the established coefficient meant to control urban density and building height.

> BIANCA: If you do not take care, you know what will happen? You will go to the PB to present a demand – for example, I want a crèche here – then the guys [from the government] will grab the budget [set aside from the sale of building rights], join it together with the [general] budget [fund] and they will say: we will build the crèche with this money. You have lost out because you've taken this resource [money], coming from this fund, and put it in the general budgetary fund. This has already happened, not with resources from the sale of building rights, but with the housing fund. The people were going to demand resources for housing [in the PB], this is back in 1999, 2000. The people approved it, [but] instead of coming from the budget, it came from the housing fund. But the money was already set aside in the housing fund. If we knew that it was in the fund, we wouldn't have demanded it in the PB. The housing fund was meant to be a funding surplus that is reserved for housing.[2] We haven't had a discussion about this yet. And the government could be inconvenienced by this, because like it or not, the government loses a margin for manoeuvring. I don't know what the position of the government will be, but it should be as transparent as possible. The concept of the sale of building rights is that it is a surplus resource.

Bianca talks of 'the government', sometimes as 'the guys', guys that might 'grab' funds received from the sale of building-rights tax. She rhetorically distances herself from the determinations of the government hierarchy. She does this emphatically when recounting a behind-the-scenes episode of public finance. Rather than coming from the general budget for the following year – what the PB is generally thought to entail – the government procured the money from what Bianca suggested was an existing surplus fund that had been set aside for housing. In contrast to Mauricio, who defended a similar episode of administrative brokering through drawing on features of the organisational ideology, Bianca denounced what she perceived to be a subversion of the aims of the institution – an allocation of the forthcoming year's budget. Such critical assessments of elite conduct were characteristic of Bianca's support of participatory and socialist ideals, which she pursued in a leftist faction of the Workers' Party.

Cases such as Bianca and Vanessa suggest that distance from the top, and secure employment, permitted greater flexibility in the positions public servants were able to take concerning the conduct of political-administrative elites. It allowed a fulsome expression of support for participatory ideals, not only in our private interview, but also in public assemblies. However, diminished responsibility was also part of that flexibility, since it also diminishes the potential for ideological tension. Matheus and Mauricio tended to more closely identify with the administration, through the use of insider metaphors, and in the case of Mauricio, the explicit subordination of participatory ideals to the exigencies of the organisational order. In one sense, this is the price and effect of responsibility. Diminished status can at times also mean the capacity to criticise freely, while power and responsibility require adherence to other ideals and conformity to strictly monitored expectations. After all, a manager – particularly one occupying a highly visible position – fulfils a representative function: they are a model for behaviour and mouthpiece for the organisation (see Goffman 1957: 149). The coherent management of the organisation relies on a shared ideology, but it is also materially enforced. In Santo André, as in all branches of Brazilian local government, such enforcement is directly exercised through the influential yet tenuously employed executive positions, or *cargos de confiança*, such as those held by Mauricio and Matheus, which are appointed by and serve at the pleasure of the mayor.[3]

Perspectives from Civil Society

Organisational ideology is, perhaps by definition, most immediately an influence on its members. Most civil society participants were not, by contrast, subject to anything so cohesive as a common, organisational ideology or a command structure, though these had, as we have seen, a tenuous influence on the beliefs and actions of some employees. Where participants assess the institutions, the rhetoric and the design logic of these contribute to and shape their expectations. Individual, material interest also plays a role in influencing the more general evaluations of participatory institutions. The perspectives of civil society participants were also oriented, like some of the public employees, by the ideology of participatory democracy – a related set of beliefs and values that undergirded their own activities in participatory institutions and shaped their normative expectations. Many of the interviewees analysed here reflect on the way that the ideals of participation have been partially realised or thwarted, for differing reasons, and generally, but not always, by the administrative elite. While participants generally adhered quite strongly to these ideals, albeit in a variegated fashion, they also maintained seemingly contradictory beliefs that drew on organisational ideology. In the following section I recount and analyse a set of participants and, continuing the comparisons between the institutions already begun, I start with reflections on the HC, followed by the UDC and then the PB. But since contrasts between and references to these institutions were woven throughout the interviews, I follow the somewhat overlapping nature of the narratives. I begin with Bruno, who was a member of the MDDF (Movimento de Defesa dos Direitos de Moradores em Favela, Movement for the Defence of Favela Inhabitants' Rights) and a veteran activist in the city who had participated in several institutions.

> V.A.: In the HC ... do you think that the population has an effective voice?
>
> BRUNO: It has. It has a voice and has achievements as well ... In the HC ... it is limited, it has little [by way of] resources. When the housing fund it controls has to be divided between different sectors, it ends up that little can be done. But it helps a lot. It is better that you have the HC in Santo André than not having anything.
>
> V.A.: For each participatory institution that you've participated in, I'd like to ask about their advantages and disadvantages, and how they might be improved ... Do you think, for example, that it is easy to communicate about different subjects in the meetings?
>
> BRUNO: Look, in the HC, what happens? It is a mixed council, between the government and civil society. What is the advantage of this? If it were just the government ... if x amount of money was given to the HC, and there was the area available, and we want to make 100 houses ... if you took these 100 houses and distributed them by *favela*, and by region, then you are attending to the existing housing needs [of the city]. So this is the advantage of the HC. Civil society has more knowledge of where to invest because it lives the problem. The representatives of civil society see the problem more than the administration ... So they ensure that the funds and resources are destined for works that are really necessary. Civil society is involved in this. This is an achievement. The disadvantages? I don't see any disadvantages. Because whatever achievements can be obtained are advantages. As far as the participation

of civil society is concerned, it can only have achievements. It doesn't have much to lose; it can only win.

Bruno supports an ideal that underpins the creation of the HC and other management policy councils – that the knowledge held by the popular classes is vital for good governance and the just distribution of resources. Yet the HC did not have the resources to realise this ideal as an independent body. It may have been consulted should anything like the investment windfall, cited in Bruno's example, have come to pass. But no such grand investments were recorded in my study of the institution. Urbanisation projects were instead nominated through the PB. Bruno recognised these limitations, but was nonetheless approving of the institution. He did not identify issues or barriers to participation or denounce the undue influence of some councillors over others. In fact, he was far less critical of the HC than the other two institutions, as we shall see. Bruno was also a councillor on the UDC, however, and had a quite different opinion of it than he did of the HC.

V.A.: And in the UDC?

BRUNO: There were [disadvantages]. Because, man, it's planning. It's urban planning. That's not just a little thing that you just show up and fix it in one go. There are some benefits and some drawbacks. I have been a titular for one mandate [two years], and the first year there I just stayed [quiet], saying, 'Okay, okay'. And when voting for or against [particular motions], at times I abstained, because I didn't understand the thing, because it's complicated, because it's about urban planning, it's about the planning of the city, it's about a series of things. So it's complicated for us from civil society. So it's a draw. There are some benefits and some drawbacks. But it is good, though it is very new.

Bruno differentiates the UDC from the HC quite significantly. He argues that there were disadvantages, and cites a technical complexity that prevented his active participation in its debates and discussions. Bruno uses a footballing metaphor – a draw – to depict this ambivalence. But this, in fact, seems to contrast with his earlier assessment of the HC, where he emphasised the importance of popular knowledge: 'civil society has more knowledge because it lives the problem'. However, faced in the UDC with complex planning legislation in assemblies formally regulated by the government chairpersons, Bruno is forced to acknowledge the challenges to effective participation. Yet he is not condemnatory, and instead seems to justify its complexity through giving the sense that it is something grandiose. Bruno's position is somewhat contradictory. On the one hand he describes complexity as problematic; on the other he seems to accept it as a consequence of the grandeur of the task. Criticism and acceptance of the complexity is, in one sense, a point of ideological overlap, where his participatory ideals founder on accepted features of the organisational order.

Other civil society participants, such as Rodrigo, an administrative director of a residents and business owners association, were not so ambivalent in their evaluations of the UDC. Rodrigo had participated in the UDC but had not taken part in the initial development phase of the City Master Plan. He preferred not to be recorded, so our interview was conducted in a local café, where I took notes. In reference to the UDC, Rodrigo argued:

> Everything that comes, comes chewed. The only thing that the civil society councillors can move is a comma. It comes 'ready'. The government maintains control, makes proposals and changes them slightly only if the senior administrative officials agree. They only make concessions when they think they should. There aren't any more than six government councillors normally present in the meetings, but when they vote it's packed. The government has a pre-made bloc of support, while civil society doesn't always agree: it is separated into interest groups. The government never votes against the government, or else the offending public servants would be out of a job.

Rodrigo, unlike Bruno, is not concerned so much by the complexity of the deliberations of the UDC, but rather by the means by which the government exercises control in its assemblies. The information that is presented to the council membership for discussion and review is, in a distinctive metaphoric expression, 'already chewed'. He refers here to the extensive forethought, analysis and collective authoring that went into the material before it was given to the council. Rodrigo's frustration perhaps stems from the fact that this forethought and analysis ought, in line with participatory ideals, to have been carried out, collectively, within the council rather than beforehand. Indeed, Rodrigo identifies the collegiality and cohesiveness of the government as a key problem to realising the promise of participation. The UDC, in his view, employs the unity of a government team in rubberstamping the policies it produced – a function that is guaranteed by packing assemblies during voting times and through the command structure of the administration. That is, while in the PB the government used the counter-proposals to push through its plans and priorities, in the UDC it depended on its specialist knowledge, collective authoring and unity, especially at tactically significant moments. But although Rodrigo expresses frustration at unrealised ideals and the conduct of the high-status officials on the UDC, he was one of the few individuals I met who had remedial suggestions for the deficiencies he saw. After the above extract, Rodrigo changes tack, and makes the following qualification:

> The objective is good – I'm not criticising it to the extreme, just the way it is administered. You need to have a popular steering group that could prepare proposals without the involvement of government representatives. Once you are negotiating with government, it is already another thing.

Contact with the government, for Rodrigo, was almost polluting – a catalyst that changes the chemistry of participation. To realise the participatory ideals of the institution, greater autonomy is therefore required. In other conversations we had, Rodrigo suggested that it should be possible for citizen participants to summon government experts. It was surprising that similar propositions were not made by my other fieldwork colleagues. The only proposed changes to the city's participatory institutions featured in party platforms. For example, an affiliate of the Socialism and Liberty Party (PSOL) argued that a set amount of the municipal budget – 10 per cent – should be reserved for the PB every year, and the Workers' Party mayoral candidate who was defeated in the 2008 elections, Wanderlei Siraque, had significant changes planned for the PB. The lack of any debate, much less consensus, concerning proposed changes to the participatory institutions suggests that any modifications to the institutions would likely issue from political rather than civil society.

Alessandra was another participant who was highly critical of the UDC. As a resident of a middle-class suburb not lacking in basic services, she was more interested in participation as a civic duty than a means of providing for her neighbourhood. At the end of an interview, characterised by much colloquial conversation, Alessandra became quite serious when I asked about the different sets of members in the UDC.

> V.A.: What do you think about the different roles of the councillors of civil society and those of the government?
>
> ALESSANDRA: Look, we have to talk frankly. I believe that they feel that they have power in their hands. I go, but I will be just a number. Civil society participates, but power is with the government.

Alessandra feels that government representatives 'feel' that they ultimately have power. It is perhaps a sense of entitlement, subjectively felt by public servants and political appointees, that is cultivated through quotidian work in the administration (Scott 1990: 49) – work that is concerned with governing the urban territory, managing the yearly budget, enforcing laws and so on. Alessandra's perspective is similar to Rodrigo's; but while Rodrigo criticised the cohesiveness of the government, Alessandra alludes to the cultivated sense of entitlement that undergirds that cohesion. Alessandra, like Rodrigo, portrays civil society participation as a kind of dependent participation, depicting her own contribution in that most belittling of statistical metaphors: a mere number. Both of these assessments, in a strange way, agree with Mauricio's evaluations of participation, though from the other side of the ideological spectrum. Mauricio suggested, in reference to the PB, that citizen involvement in the budget was voluntary, an elective institutional aperture that in the last instance is subject to the determinations of the government. This was a part of his privileging of elite prerogatives, legitimised by what he felt were organisational exigencies, and his framing of citizen participation as malleable and dependent. Both Mauricio and Alessandra share the substance of his evaluation – that citizen participation is indeed dependent and ancillary to the organisational order – but have divergent interpretations, informed by their contrasting ideological commitments. For them, the imposition of government plans and policies was a contravention of participatory ideals, while for Mauricio it was a mundane governance necessity.

Another civil society participant, Edson, did not see the problem of citizen participation in this light. His criticisms were more personal in nature. Edson had been a metalworker in São Bernardo, where he first became affiliated with the Workers' Party. He only later took part in Santo André's participatory institutions when, in 1999, as a resident of Vila Luzita, he was elected as a regional representative on the MBC. Like Rodrigo, Edson noted that the City Master Plan was, as a law, somewhat fixed and inflexible. But this, for him, was a merit rather than a drawback.

> V.A.: What do you think of the deliberations over the City Master Plan? Do you think civil society has the ability to participate?
>
> EDSON: It has. In the City Master Plan, in my view, civil society is better able to discuss with the government than in the PB. For instance, we were able to bar particular specifications that arose during the development of the City Master Plan on two occasions because civil society didn't agree with the proposals. We voted against them and won in the voting. The City Master Plan doesn't have manipulation. And if all goes well, when I die I will leave a better city for my children and my grandchildren.

Manipulation was, for Edson, a ubiquitous threat when dealing with political elites and the administration. This point became clearer in the following exchanges.

> V.A.: What are some of the positive and negative aspects of the councils and programmes in which you've participated? How could you improve them, let's say.
>
> EDSON: A positive aspect is that you are heard. You have the right to speak directly with the mayor and the directors [of government departments]. We don't speak as subalterns. This is a point won. And we accompany, up to a certain point, the process. And a negative aspect? We aren't within, we aren't able to know what is happening with the work, how is it being processed, entirely, from beginning to end. The administrative representatives speak superficially. So I don't think that's right, that there. I think that the population should have more clarity about what's going on internally with the work that's discussed in the councils. And the negative? The negative is that they manipulate the councillors a lot, they manipulate the people a lot.
>
> V.A.: How?
>
> EDSON: When they see that you are pissing them off, they call you there to 'discuss'. So how is it worth getting elected by the population, thinking that you're going to do something, when at the time of voting you realise that there are civil society councillors who won't vote in favour of a proposal because they have another demand that is sponsored by a member of the Legislative Chamber (*vereador*), a demand that is sponsored by the government ... [You] understand?

Together with Bruno, Edson values the opportunity to speak with government officials – a realisation of a key participatory ideal, and what he considered, possibly also using another footballing metaphor, a point won. But he also rebuked the manipulation of civil society councillors and, perhaps drawing on personal experience, denounced the way that vociferous critics of the government would be singled out to be silenced in private audiences. As a law, the City Master Plan provided a refuge from such personal reprisals. He also cites two occasions during the formative phase of the City Master Plan in which civil society voted down proposed amendments to the plan. These exclusions created a lasting effect on the plan, one Edson hoped to pass on to future generations. However, Edson did not acknowledge that the plan was subject to legislative change that was often effected without popular consultation. And only time will tell how its provisions, should they endure, will influence Santo André's built environment.

Another frustration expressed by Edson concerned the superficiality of government presentations in PB assemblies, and his own inability to fully accompany the works the administration carried out. Indeed, the depiction of government discourse as superficial continued, using another interesting metaphor. Our discussion turned to his participation in the PB, and I questioned his description of it as 'cosmetic' (*maquiagem*).

V.A.: Why do you think it [the PB] is cosmetic?

EDSON: How can I demand a hospital, for my region, a small medical unit, if I don't even know if there is terrain owned by the government [to build it on]? So people go to the microphone and demand, then the population and other people who like the idea vote for it and it is approved. It arrives in the administration and is rejected. This, for me, is cosmetic. You [the government] need to go to the microphone at the time and say, 'Your demand is praiseworthy, congratulations, but it is unviable for the region, it is unviable for the public coffers'. Don't make promises that you can't keep. Because after the population goes to the microphone and demands something and approves the demands, it arrives in the [negotiating phase], and a discussion starts to see how the voting [will proceed], what will be done and what won't. Only that this isn't communicated to the community. So the support walls that I talked to you about, they were to be made in 1992. It has taken more than ten years for them to do this, and for God's … Isn't this a disgrace?

Understand? It's really cosmetic. In the past, in the first administration of Celso Daniel, the works were carried out rapidly ... [but now] the people are tired ... So you can't say that the people betrayed the government, much less the people from the periphery, us here.

Edson applies the term 'cosmetic' to a couple of examples from the PB. First, he uses it to describe the way the regional assemblies create the expectation that the works nominated therein will be carried out. We have seen that this was not the case. In another section of the interview, Edson bemoaned the fact that, as a regional representative, he was held personally responsible by local residents for the failure of the government to implement these priorities and was called a 'liar and a sell-out by people on the street'. Second, Edson also describes as cosmetic the way that the government failed to make good on old promises, criticising what he perceived to be a lax attitude, one that had crept into the Avamileno government's realisation of citizen demands. Edson's assessments of the institutions are complex, for they combine elements of critique (of superficiality, tardiness and manipulation – all of which impinged on the realisation of participatory ideals) with approval, of moments of citizen participation and the perceived immutability of laws. Indeed, they were complementary, as we have seen: the superficiality of government positions and performances seemed to contribute to his valorisation of the law.

Edu, like many others, began participating in government institutions as part of a broader interest in administration and politics that arose during his pursuit of land-title regularisation. It was his induction ritual that I analysed in Chapter 2. He was perhaps the most critical of all of the participants I interviewed concerning the PB.

> V.A.: How does a meeting function? And what power does a councillor of civil society have in relation to the state councillors?
>
> EDU: Very little. Extremely little (*limitadissima*). If we aren't careful, the council will end up being merely informative, and the government will end up only informing [people] what it will do. It depends a lot on the quality of the elected comrades (*companheiros*), and the vision that they have for the city.
>
> V.A.: Why don't you meet together with the other councillors and have a discussion about how you could have more influence on the MBC?

EDU: There are various reasons. The principal, I believe, is that some colleagues on the council come with a warped vision of the council [MBC]. In fact they are more preoccupied with pleasing the government than with doing their role, which is the total opposite: to hold the government to account. Each and every councillor elected by civil society, he has to represent civil society. But he ends up arriving there, looking at the government, and thinking that he can be the little buddy of the government and maybe he'll be able to receive some favours. Apart from this, the personal dispositions of the civil society councillors, there is also the fact that our democracy is very recent. Brazil has only been a democracy since the end of the '80s, so it is very recent for a country to have a mature understanding of the value and nature of democracy. Beyond this, there is the absence of information, of culture, and I would say that it's not only the scholarly or academic education you receive, but yes an education … of character.

Edu's criticism is interesting, because unlike Alessandra and Rodrigo, who directed their ire at the organisational order, he lays the blame for the power imbalance at the feet of what he considers to be feckless colleagues. Rather than targeting figures like Mauricio, who defended the privileging of government plans and policies, Edu finds fault among his peers. Participatory ideals are not thwarted by actors with management roles and contradictory beliefs, but by the participants themselves. But then again, perhaps for Edu the ideological convictions and cohesive behaviour of government employees is to be expected, and the only logical recourse is to improve the effectiveness of civil society colleagues.

Bruno, whose evaluations of the HC and the UDC we have seen earlier, was similarly frustrated that the practice of participation did not match the rhetoric. After talking about the UDC, we turned to the PB.

V.A.: And the MBC?

BRUNO: The PB? It, as well [as the UDC], causes some disillusionment.

V.A.: Why?

BRUNO: Because, what happens? Society understands the following to be true. When you take Region E – I will take my region – and you have hundreds of people who vote for the demands, and you elect a representative, full of willingness, full of expectation, society understands that when you go and vote for four demands in the plenary [it was three priorities at the time of the interview], society understood that the demands will be realised. The government says that this is not approved, it is an indication only. But society thinks, the region thinks that they will be realised the following year, which is not true. And this is where the difficulty comes in.

V.A.: So who has control over the investments after the indications are made by civil society?

BRUNO: What happens is, when you go there with four priorities, you discuss them with the other civil society representatives from the 19 regions, one by one. You go there, to the negotiating assemblies, and the government says this demand is not possible due to budgetary restrictions, and the government says each region can only have two demands and not four ... You have to indicate two demands, and not four ... At times you can only indicate one demand. And then the councillor is at a loss ... You had four but only one can be implemented? How is that possible?

Bruno echoes the dissatisfaction, expressed by Edson earlier, that the elected demands created hopes, in the regions and among elected councillors, which were dashed in the negotiating phase of the PB. He also indicates, in his more extensive breakdown of the negotiations, that only a smaller number of the priorities could be realised. In one passage, Bruno mentions the government's selection of certain demands, that it can 'only attend to this and this demand'. The selection of particular investment priorities became the basis of a deeper examination of government management of the PB by other civil society representatives.

Robison was an affiliate of the Communist Party of Brazil (PCdoB) and a resident of Parque Andreense, a region in the wetlands area that was the location of the PB assembly analysed in Chapter 3. I had asked Robison about an investment work in a previous PB cycle that had been approved but not carried out.

V.A.: What was the reason given by the government for not implementing the public work?

ROBISON: No, no, we were able to [make the] demands, but I didn't understand the function of the PB structure. In my mind, I imagined that the three demands that we voted for would be approved, they had already been approved in the Parque Andreense assembly, and that the problem had already been resolved. I didn't know that there was this question of negotiation, but after a period of time I understood a little better how it all worked and resolved to make myself a candidate after I understood how important this participation was. But I also offered my candidature half sceptical that all this could actually make some difference. In some regards, I continue to be sceptical, especially when they set out what will be developed and what the mayor already set forth in the government plan. It is like the mayor had already thought, at the moment that he formulates the governmental plan, about the priorities [that will be elected in the regions]. He listens to the population only to say that they are being implemented.

V.A.: How is it that the demands enter into the plan?

ROBISON: It can't be explained in this way. Rather, it is that the government already had the intention to develop something similar in Parque Andreense; it was already a policy of theirs. When the municipal staff has a policy [idea] and then the population asks for it: there hunger meets the will to eat. They take what the population put down and put it together with what they had thought about. I could be wrong, but I still believe this to be so. It is not simply that 'the population speaks'.

Robison recalls the problem encountered by Edson in his area: that the regional assemblies created an expectation that all three priorities would be carried out. But he moves from reflecting on his particular demand to what he perceives to be the calibration of the demands elected by civil society to the plans of government. Robison's analysis of the PB is interesting because he hypothesises that the mayor, in formulating his governmental plan, anticipates what the population will request. This might be based on patterns of demand-making in previous programme cycles or on information gleaned from those close to regionally based community organisers. It suggests that the PB constitutes part of an administrative terrain which is shaped by the strategic interests and plans of political and state elites. Another resident of the wetlands, the PB councillor Murilo, summarises the problem in much balder terms: 'Can I be sincere, Victor? The government already comes with the demands that it wants'. It was, in fact, insights such as those advanced by Murilo and Robison that impelled me to question Mauricio about the privileging of government plans and priorities in the negotiating assemblies. Mauricio's admission of the practice was another case of substantive agreement between participants with different roles and responsibilities, but with divergent evaluations.

Conclusion

Civil society participants gave differentiated assessments as they reflected on the hindrances they encountered and the advantages afforded them by participatory institutions. Their specific evaluations engaged with what were at times contradictory participatory and governance ideals. Nonetheless, many participants gave closely related assessments that can be clustered together. Bruno, Edson and Robison, for example, all rebuked the superficiality of and false expectations generated in the assemblies of the PB. Edson also criticised the personal manipulation suffered by outspoken participants, while Robison gave a searching analysis of the government's tactical use of investment nominations during the PB – an interpretation that was pithily supported by Murilo. Edu more broadly denounced the power imbalance between the civil society and government councillors in the PB.

Indeed, some participants gave similar assessments of different institutions. For example, Rodrigo and Alessandra, like Edu, both noted and critiqued the power imbalance between civil society and government councillors, though in reference to the UDC rather than the PB. And at times there were points of ideological contradiction and overlap within the same narrative. Bruno, for instance, was frustrated by technical complexity in the UDC, which denied him an active role in its deliberations during the first year of his mandate. Yet he nonetheless seemed to accept this complexity as a part of state administration. In this way, Bruno's participatory ideals, and the frustration of ineffective participation, were anchored to a feature of organisational ideology: the normative basis of its technical complexity.

Assessments of the HC, however, were more positive. Bruno, in contrast to his evaluations of citizen participation in the UDC and the PB, gave the HC a very favourable review. It seems that the collegial culture of the HC accorded with Bruno's participatory ideals, though he recognised its limited capacity to deliver investments.

Government participants, perhaps surprisingly given their different roles and responsibilities, often had substantive agreement with their civil society counterparts but had divergent interpretations. That was not the case, however, for the HC. Matheus largely shared Bruno's positive assessment when he stated that it provided the conditions for 'truthful', that is, unguarded communication. This institution, lacking the resources, power and status, of the UDC and the PB, allowed the contradictions of power and participation to remain latent. These emerged as Matheus broached participation in the PB: it is only then that he employs the metaphor of internality, justifies defensiveness as a natural reaction, and hence suggests that, were it to come to a contest between groups, he would side with the government team.

Mauricio's testimony, as the PB director, is perhaps the most interesting of all, but because of its concordance with, rather than divergence from, the assessments of civil society participants. In fact, he agrees with many of the major criticisms levelled at the PB. He confirmed Robison's and Murilo's charge that the administration used the available nominations to push through government plans and policies, and in so doing, framed citizen participation as an elective exercise subordinate to the prerogatives and exigencies of governance, as defined by state officials. This was precisely the power imbalance noted by Edu; and it also reflected the assessments of Alessandra and Rodrigo, though in reference to the UDC, who suggested that the state representatives 'felt they had power' and would only make 'slight [changes to urban policy and planning] only' if they agreed with them. But while Mauricio substantively agreed with this cluster of participants, his divergent interpretation drew on organisational ideology. Indeed, the fact that participants from other institutions similarly noted the electiveness and dependency of citizen participation suggests that Mauricio's interpretation of participation was shared by others in the administration – and part of a more expansive organisational ideology that was realised in action. His boss, the director of finance in the local administration, certainly seemed to share these beliefs when he stated in the negotiating phase of the PB, related in Chapter 3, that, 'It is a privilege of yours [to participate]'

Mauricio's status and his role in the administration may have been decisive factors in his adherence to organisational ideology, and the way participation was subordinately coupled to beliefs that privileged the administrative order. The interviews from other, tenured public servants suggest that such ideological tensions are diminished at lower-levels in the command structure. Here, protected by secure employment contracts, and thus the whims and prerogatives of the mayor, employees such as Bianca and Vanessa were able to identify with their civil society counterparts as activists rather than as spokespersons of the government. Despite their diminished influence, they proved vitally important allies for civil society organisations.

The relaxation of ideological tensions and contradictions among these activist public servants is suggestive of a paradox of power (and participation) that can be related to the findings of earlier chapters. In the previous two chapters I argued that state power tended to crystallise in those participatory spaces where there was most at stake, when powerful organisations were represented and where key decisions were being made. This may be called the first paradox of power, that substantive barriers to the participation of the lay public are erected when it matters most. A second paradox of power is that, in those decisive moments, the most senior members of the administration felt that the deployment of state power was simply an exigency of governance and thus normatively justified.

6
Backstage

Public performances place a premium on observing certain codes of conduct. They often take place in front of large numbers of the public and, at times, representatives of powerful organisations. When the performers are public servants or political appointees, they give a highly visible demonstration of their technical skills and aptitude in safeguarding the reputation and interests of the government. Indeed, as events organised by the public administration, Santo André's participatory assemblies often presented an idealised version of local governance (see Scott 1990: 18) – one which, among other things, obscured the practices of personal brokerage and influence that stray some distance from the liberal ideal. But in Chapter 5 we also saw charges of manipulation and clientelism that hinted at other features of political reality that until now have been largely unexplored. In this chapter I pick up these threads and investigate, through a series of case studies, some of the complex and dynamic interconnections between what might be called the front and backstage of participation.

I borrow the term 'backstage' from Erving Goffman (1957), who differentiated, in his dramaturgical approach, between the different performative expectations and attendant cultural norms that condition human behaviour in distinct social milieux. For Goffman, the front stage is purposely subject to techniques of impression management and staging arrangements, generally by a team of actors to create coherent performances (ibid.: 116, 125). The use of theatrical metaphors evokes both the intentionality of the performance, which plays to an audience, and the suppression from public view of much that this performance implies. The self-censorship of the front stage is relaxed in life backstage – understood as a different social rather than physical milieu – an informal sphere of communication and interaction (ibid.: 114, 127). It is backstage and among one's peers that secrets can be shared (ibid.: 141). Although the terms front stage and backstage fittingly relate to the kind of performances we have seen in participatory assemblies – since, at times, there was literally and not just figuratively a front and backstage – Goffman applied them to the diverse social conditions found in mental institutions, restaurants, community life in the Shetland Islands and routine human interaction, which was developed further in his interactionist approach (Goffman 1963, 1967, 1969). That is to say, Goffman's analytical dichotomy applies not only to performances for large audiences but also to the dynamic processes of behavioural regulation operative in social intercourse in general.

However, there are difficulties in studying the backstage that are best acknowledged frankly. The same conditions that make front-stage performances somewhat pre-planned and choreographed also make them disposed to participant observation: they are plainly visible, and often allow the presence of outsiders – including interfering ethnographers – that makes whatever transpires therein verifiable by others. For example, the way that senior officials pushed favoured priorities through the structure of the participatory budget (PB), something detailed in Chapter 3, was able to be confirmed by both civil society and government participants in Chapter 5. Analysing the backstage of participation, and its indirect contribution to front-stage behaviour, also implies moving from more to less ideal conditions for substantiating arguments. There is the problem not only of verification but also of concealment: many features of the backstage are normatively proscribed in public performances because they carry negative connotations in other social contexts. While I believed fieldwork colleagues to be exceptionally forthcoming in our informal discussions and recorded interviews, the relationship between a researcher – one explicitly seeking information for the purposes of publication – and a fieldwork colleague is almost inexorably plagued by similar considerations to those applying to the front stage. I had to balance the need to maintain good rapport, and decent and honest relationships with my friends and fieldwork colleagues, with the acquisition of information. As will become clear in the following section, even the most informal gatherings were social spaces where other performative calculations were being made and where certain matters were still taboo. Studying the backstage thus involved a kind of uncovering and exploration based on testimony and episodes of social interaction that are still self-conscious performances. Indeed, careful elisions and diplomatic concealments are constitutive of the backstage and were a very real hurdle I encountered. With this in mind, I am more tentative and circumspect in the hypotheses I advance.

While the front stage of citizen participation describes a discrete social space, the backstage speaks to a much broader social and political reality. In the space of a chapter only some interconnections between front and backstage can be explored. Some of these interconnections are derived from the front stage itself, from episodes in public assemblies or attendant, informal social gatherings that intimate backstage interactions and relationships. In the first case study, I explore an episode from a participatory assembly where a civil society participant was purportedly cautioned by a high-status official. It was a caution that was interpreted – in a small, informal gathering of participants – as a warning that carried potentially lethal consequences. I relate the interpretation of this caution to a pervasive backstage narrative in Santo André: the murder of Celso Daniel, the former mayor. The following two case studies both explore cases of clientelism. The first draws on a front-stage outburst between two actors with whom we are already familiar: Edu, the civil society councillor on the Municipal Budget Council (MBC), and Mauricio, director of the PB. It illustrates how reciprocal relationships between members of the political elite and community leaders may have influenced the public performances analysed in previous chapters. The second concerns a failed attempt by a city councillor to gain control of a residents' association. This case demonstrates that social activists were not simply 'acted on' by vote-seeking politicians; rather, they had their own tactical resources for dealing with unreliable patrons and pursuing important works for their community. In the analysis of these two cases, I advance a more nuanced portrayal of patron–client relationships than is at times given in the academic literature. The final case explores a relationship that, while not 'backstage' and clientelistic in a strict sense, was criticised as if it were by diverse social activists in the city. That is, I examine the awarding of a lucrative government contract to the Movimento de Defesa dos Direitos de Moradores em Favela (MDDF), a *favela* residents movement historically renowned for its mobilising capacity. I consider how the outsourcing of state services through community organisations creates incentives for maintaining cordial relations with the government, and may be thus considered a kind of front-stage clientelism that performs a similar compromising function to its backstage counterpart, though legitimised by technocratic language and a technical focus on projects. Through this analysis we also gain insight into the moral universe of community actors in Santo André, who often harshly judge others for close attachment to the political elite.

The exploration of these issues was often instigated by breaks, ruptures or signals in front-stage behaviour, or associated social gatherings, which indicated important relationships or influences that were not immediately apparent. In this chapter I tease and flesh out these issues on the basis of interview and observational data. Here, I seek to show the kinds of political and personal influences that often bubble beneath the surface of front-stage performances and at times percolate into public view. But many of the issues treated in this chapter, such as patron–client relationships and the 'NGOisation' of a social movement, are recognised as important features of local politics, and of recent political change, in Brazil; they are not merely arbitrary issues that happened to surface during fieldwork, but are rather suggestive of pervasive features of the socio-political landscape that can also influence citizen participation.

A Caution and Its Interpretation

The following occurred during a sequence of weekly meetings held by the civil society representatives of the MBC, already addressed in Chapter 3. As part of the biennial cycle of the PB, civil society participants are asked to submit potential changes to the internal regulations of the institution. They decided to meet on Monday nights, in an amphitheatre and in the absence of government employees. Unlike the regular meetings managed by the PB director, they were highly informal. The following episode of social interaction indicates that other performative norms were being negotiated even in a more informal gathering of civil society peers where social performances were less strictly regulated.

After one of the meetings, several of us gathered in the hall outside and chatted as we ate sandwiches. It was here that one regional representative confided in the group her experience with one of the administrative elites (not serving on the MBC). She had apparently been complaining to the government, who had, as a way of silencing her, offered her a government post. She refused the offer, already being satisfied with her current job, after which she was issued with a warning: 'You had better shut your mouth, understand?' An air of seriousness came over the gathering. Another councillor warned her that she needed to be careful with this kind of information, that such accusations need to be either made formal and public, or she ought to just shut up about it – otherwise, she 'risked getting a bullet in the head' (*senão vai acabar com uma bala na cabeça*). There was a sense during the recounting of a private exchange between an individual citizen and a high-status official that the meeting had entered into shadowy territory, and several of those in the small group seemed visibly uncomfortable. Then another councillor chimed in: 'Hey, you can't talk about all that ... This guy [meaning me] is going to go back to Australia, and you know what he's going to say about us?'

It was, it is important to note, just one individual's account, and there was no proof that the administration, or some highly placed individual within it, would have, or had in the past, violently persecuted a citizen for verbal criticism. But there was a very real belief that it was a possibility. The reaction to the disclosure is also interesting on two counts. First, one of the group present suggested that such talk was dangerous even in a small group of one's peers. It either needed to be made public, making any physical retribution riskier for the administrative elite or individual concerned, or not spoken about at all. Second, it showed how local pride was perhaps a consideration for fieldwork colleagues who may not like to have Santo André's name blackened by the reporting of threats and coercion, even when they may have disapproved of the threats. The above example shows that the backstage was not simply a space of informality and trust, but rather a context where different performative calculations were being made. Indeed, there was some disagreement over what constituted an appropriate topic for conversation. While one actor perceived the gathering to be a context in which a very sensitive subject could be broached, others disagreed, for reasons of local pride or concern for personal safety.

Over the course of my fieldwork, certain fieldwork colleagues similarly identified administrative and political elites and associates who had threatened or blackmailed them in the past, though physical threats were rare. In the extract given above, there was no explicit physical threat: that was the interpretation of one of the individuals in the small gathering. But why would a warning from a high-status official be interpreted as carrying such possibly dire consequences? The murder of the former mayor, Celso Daniel, provides, I think, one of the reasons.

Several official enquiries into Daniel's murder in 2002 did not find substantive evidence to contradict the version of events proffered by the gang that kidnapped him: that he was a random victim chosen after their original target, an affluent businessman, had eluded them, and that on discovering his identity the gang had a minor shoot him to death on the Estrada das Cachoeiras in Juquitiba, in the southern zone of São Paulo.[1] Various details of the crime are suspicious. Daniel's bodyguard, Sérgio Gomes da Silva, the 'Shadow', claimed that his brakes and transmission failed when their four-wheel-drive vehicle was blocked by the assailants.

Yet the police enquiry found no evidence of mechanical failure. In addition, according to several reports, seven people connected to the crime were killed or mysteriously died, including the waiter who served Daniel that night (he was leaving the restaurant when attacked) and the person who found Daniel's body.[2]

Daniel's two brothers have subsequently argued that his murder was politically motivated. According to them, Celso was part of a clique that was illegally siphoning funds from businesses and other Workers' Party donors. Apparently, Celso had decided to go public when he discovered that several members of the clique were diverting the funds into their personal accounts. His murder was thus orchestrated to prevent the public outing of the politicians involved in the scheme. Celso's brothers, Bruno and João Francisco, identified in their claims several senior figures in the Workers' Party, and consequently both Bruno and João Francisco fled to Europe in fear of reprisals.[3]

The veracity of one claim or the other is not so important here, and it seems unlikely that a political connection to the brutal crime will be established. But, perhaps precisely because it is, in the eyes of many members of the local population, unsolved, and precisely because there are doubts and suspicions about his murder, it became a powerful narrative among local residents, and particularly the civil society participants I knew well. Almost everyone had their own interpretation of what really happened. Two hypotheses, in particular, had gained currency among those close to the Workers' Party and the local government. I was told about them in cars, cafés, restaurants and people's homes. When the subject came up at a local gymnasium, the instructor told me not to talk about it in public. And when civil society participants broached the topic with me in public, they would invariably check over each shoulder to see who was in earshot before giving me their interpretation in hushed tones. The death of Celso Daniel seemed to contribute to the sense that members of the political and administrative elite were capable of using violent means to pursue their interests; it penetrated and pervaded the public space with fear. Like the talk of violence in São Paulo in general, the murder of Daniel lives on as one of many narratives that 'impose partitions, build up walls, delineate and enclose spaces, establish distances, segregate, differentiate, impose prohibitions, [and] multiply rules of avoidance and exclusion' (Caldeira 2000: 20). Referring back to the days of Brazil's authoritarian regime (1964 to 1985), a veteran social activist in Santo André was able to joke with me before our interview, when I suggested that excerpts of it might be published, that he no longer had to worry about the Department of Political and Social Order, and that the poisonous suspicion that one experienced talking on the street was thankfully gone.[4] Yet similar fears have not disappeared entirely.

The potential for backstage reprisals from members of the political elite is perhaps a consideration for civil society participants. It would certainly be strange if the caution given to the participant who recounted the story above did not at least figure as a consideration that guided future conduct, that is, if it did not curb contentious behaviour altogether. But the effect of such cautions and warnings, and their manifold interpretations, would have been more or less diffuse, and more or less effective, as they were told and retold, interwoven with and fed by narratives like the murder of Celso Daniel. Illegitimate violence may be an extreme manifestation of what John Gledhill might call 'shadow state powers' (Gledhill 1999); however, there were numerous other threats and sanctions made by political and administrative elites that were, according to fieldwork colleagues, experienced directly, and the events became circulating narratives that may have influenced their front-stage performances. It is an example that demonstrates the subtle effects of violence on democratic institutions, revealed here in performative calculations which may otherwise remain tacit, and which serves to fortify the social position of those perceived – erroneously or not – to have access to violent means (Arias et al. 2010: 4–5).

While threats may be a prime example of backstage interaction, inasmuch as they are normally secretive interpersonal exchanges, others are more widely recognised as prosaic features of local politics in Brazil. In the following case studies, I turn to clientelism, and examine some of the ways that patron–client relationships surfaced, and failed to surface, in public assemblies.

Clientelism and Co-optation

Patron–client relationships are almost ineradicably associated with Brazilian politics (see Graham 1990: 209–32; Leal 1975). Clientelism refers to a relationship between a political actor, normally in the legislature, and a client, in which the former 'exchanges votes for jobs and public services that are achieved due to her capacity to influence the executive branch' (Carvalho 1999: 135). In much liberal scholarship it is held to be prevalent in contemporary Brazil, perhaps more so in the recent democratic era than under authoritarianism (Hagopian 1996), a corrupting influence on its political institutions and deleterious to strategically unimportant social groups. But not only is clientelism criticised by liberal scholarship, it also contravenes the liberal norms of participatory assemblies.

In the following example, taken from a meeting in the negotiating phase of the PB, we see how a government actor publicly undermined a civil society participant by accusing him of acting on behalf of a political benefactor. It helps illustrate the interconnections between public performances in participatory assemblies and patrons and their clients. A second example from fieldwork shows the variegated kinds of patron–client relationships in Santo André, and the tactical resources that community organisers – often portrayed as powerless clients – can employ when dealing with vote-seeking politicians.

In earlier meetings of the negotiating phase of the PB, government councillors had presented their counter-proposal and had appeared unwilling to negotiate or compromise. This helped create a tense atmosphere, as some citizen councillors were steeling themselves for a fight in order to have the demands they favoured entered on the government's approved list of demands. Two tables were put end to end on the stage in the amphitheatre, with two civil society participants on the left-hand side, from the perspective of the audience, and two government participants on the right. At the centre of the two adjoining tables were already familiar faces: Edu, a civil society participant, sat next to Mauricio, the PB director. Mauricio had just been defending himself and the government against some of the civil society participants incensed by the prospective passage of the counter-proposal, when Edu took the microphone. To be honest, I did not clearly hear what Mauricio said to Edu, but it became apparent soon enough. The meeting, while tense and contested, had remained civil. But on hearing a barely audible comment by Mauricio, Edu immediately rose to his feet. 'There was life before Berrezza [a city councillor], and there will be life after Berrezza'.[5] Edu argued that it was absurd that he was criticised in this way. If you recall my description of his election contest in Chapter 2, Edu is a big man. He towered over and was pointing his finger within inches of Mauricio's face. The latter had clearly breached the codes of front-stage behaviour, by suggesting that Edu was acting as a proxy for Berrezza in the negotiations. He had suggested that Edu was unrelenting in his support for a crèche in Vila Luzita because of his relationship with Berrezza. But Edu's outburst did not end. It became a tirade, and for minutes he remained standing. He was furious that he could be so publicly humiliated, and several in the audience, me included, thought he might end up punching Mauricio.

A couple of the public servants in the audience interjected to try to restore order. One was a health official who stated that the meeting could not continue unless everyone remained civilised. Mauricio, by now well aware that he was at least partly responsible for the furore, sought to qualify his accusation: 'We are all linked to one candidate [of the political elite] or another, as we're all commissioned [i.e. political appointees]'. Mauricio tried to qualify one breach of professionalism with another; none of the senior staff liked where this was going. The health official, who was still standing, made the sawing hand-across-the-throat gesture at Mauricio for him to stop immediately. Edu continued, protesting that although he might have a relationship with Berrezza, his intentions for delivering investments to his area were genuine:

> I defend the construction of a crèche. Everyone in the neighbourhood has lost faith in the PB but I still decided to run [for election]. It has been a big disappointment. I will not concede [to the government counter proposal] and I will go to the end.

This was perhaps another example of Mauricio's propensity to commit gaffes. But it also vividly demonstrated the strength of performative norms, that when contravened publicly they called Edu's motives into question, and triggered an indignant outburst. Despite his explosive reaction, Edu's relationship with Berrezza would have been fairly well known. As Edu indicated to me in his interview, he had worked in the office of the legislator prior to his nomination for the PB, a post he purportedly relinquished in order to run for the PB, since those directly employed by a politician or the government are ineligible for candidature as a civil society representative. But while Edu did speak to me about his relationship with Berrezza in our interview, he did not elaborate on any ongoing arrangement.

Edu originally encountered Berrezza when he sought out an ally in the Legislative Chamber after a law under consideration would have categorised his region as 'uninhabited' had it not been amended. Berrezza gave him support for that amendment, which was passed, and a longer-term relationship between the two was established. The influence Berrezza maintained on Edu after leaving his employment is, however, questionable. He frankly admitted that his community association 'needed other avenues' to pursue their goals – a statement that I understood to mean that some form of allegiance with a political actor was necessary. But although Edu was disposed to talk about his past attachment to Berrezza, he was reticent on the matter of his ongoing relationship. Perhaps I could have pressed him on the issue, but, like Gianpaolo Baiocchi (2005: 163), in the past I had had little success when asking direct questions about ties to elected officials, and I was also committed to maintaining good rapport with Edu.

Edu's reluctance to talk specifically about his current relationship with Berrezza is perhaps better understood in the context of popular interpretations of patron–client relationships. In Santo André, so-called clients were often the objects of scorn and derision. Sometimes fairly euphemistic terms would be used. For example, a civil society councillor on the HC who was a representative of a housing association run by Edu's erstwhile and perhaps ongoing political patron was called 'Berrezza's boy' (*o rapaz de Berrezza*). More scathingly pejorative expressions were also in circulation – such as 'turned his back on the community', and, even more dramatically, 'Judas' – that were used to critically describe a community leader seen to be attached to a member of the political elite. These descriptions, however, were rarely used in direct communications with the client in question; they were normally part of private conversations about others that as a corollary underscored the moral standing of the accuser (Lazar 2008: 76). Indeed, Edu's outburst seemed not so much a challenge to the substance of the allegation (to my knowledge he did not contest Berrezza's sponsorship of the crèche), but rather a response to a breach of social convention that cast his relationship in a disparaging light and served to undermine his credibility and therefore the substance of his demands. Backstage information about his political connections was presented front stage in order to tarnish his public standing. One of the key features of Edu's angry response was therefore the attempt to redeem his injured character and salvage his community's demand by claiming that he was ultimately his own person (that is, 'there will be life after Berrezza').

In the literature on participatory institutions, patron–client relationships and their role in influencing citizen and government conduct in assemblies and attendant decision-making processes have not received in-depth study (but see Ottmann 2006). In the short space that is available here, I critique a still common portrayal of patron–client relationships. Rather than a dyadic relationship of elite domination, I maintain that clientelism describes a raft of more-or-less permanent and more-or-less tenuous and temporally restricted allegiances between members of the political elite and community organisers based on extant or prospective reciprocal exchanges (see Gay 1994, 1998, 1999; see also Koster 2012).

Edu's outburst was an example of a backstage relationship that erupted onto the front stage. In the following case study, I examine an interview with a public servant who was also involved in community organising and had a fractious relationship with a city councillor. In this case, in contrast to that of Edu, the city councillor failed to gain control of the community association and consequently failed to use its influence over the local population in participatory assemblies. It is an example which demonstrates the kinds of calculated manoeuvres that take place backstage, and in this case stay backstage. The community organiser is shown to be possessed of her own tactical nous and resources for dealing with an untrustworthy politician.

Clientelism and the Politics of the Backstage

Mauricio's attack on Edu's agency invoked a popular, derogatory conception of clients as powerless puppets of their political patrons. It is, perhaps surprisingly, a conception at times shared in academic studies which can tend to gloss over the agency of so-called clients. Here I examine and explore the case of Laura, a tenured public servant, community organiser and member of a small social movement, the MDDF, and her fractious relationship with a city councillor, with whom she had previously engaged as a supportive client. As she adroitly negotiates his advances, fights to maintain control of her community association and succeeds in electing a trusted confidant to the MBC, it becomes clear that she is far from a powerless client. Unlike the accusation levelled at Edu, Laura's defence of her community association ensured that the tenuous relationship with a city councillor failed to influence front-stage participation. Her case is suggestive of the diversity and precariousness of backstage relationships.

Before the interview, held towards the end of my fieldwork, I had seen Laura on numerous occasions. She was a member of the MDDF, and I had seen her at a meeting in a community centre near my apartment. I had also seen her at meetings of the PB and also at the town hall, where she was a tenured public servant. Our interview was held in the Department of Housing, which is down two flights of stairs from the main entrance of the town hall. Laura invited me into an office that was divided with modular partitions, their joints clipped together. These formed only thin walls, so I had little doubt that what we said was audible to those in adjacent areas. There were, in fact, a couple of senior staff members whose desks butted up against the hollow walls of the area in which Laura and I talked. In a voice just above a whisper, Laura thus began recounting her experiences as an activist.

Like Edu and many others, Laura became involved in community organising due to landownership issues. A man who presented himself as a landowner of her *favela* had demanded what she believed to be an extortionate sum for the purchase of the plot on which her house was built, and Laura doubted that he could provide legal title. After the incumbent community leader left the post vacant, Laura assumed responsibility for dealing with the landowner, collated all of the documentation relating to the sale of land, and after negotiating with the administration, the proprietor accepted a price for the land far below his initial demands. Laura then continued 'searching for ways' to improve a community that, although relatively well established, having been constructed in the 1970s, still lacked important services. 'We discovered the participatory budget … and we also searched for political strength, political support … not for assistance in services, but to facilitate our struggle'. This led her to provide support for a city councillor. 'We worked and gave a lot of support. The city councillor won [election to the Legislative Chamber], and then turned his back on us. But we continued in the struggle alone'. While Laura posits that her support of the city councillor was not motivated by 'assistance in services', there was an expectation of reciprocity. I asked Laura in what sense did he turn his back on her community.

> I went up to him and asked for the surfacing of a road … There was this uneven road, full of rocks … there was not even space [for the kids to] play … and he said that he would help. But in the end, it was us that made the petition and went to ask [the local administration]. When it was ready, he went there to receive praise for the work of other people. And we left it [without confronting him about it]. There wasn't a moment, a time to dissociate [ourselves from him], to clarify the truth [of his influence on the project].

Laura thereafter withdrew her support. It became clear that the councillor would not effectively advocate for the community, and his willingness to take the accolades stemming from the work of community organisers suggested he could not be trusted. It was not a verbally acknowledged withdrawal, but rather the councillor noticed how the community organisers distanced themselves. Laura's experience with political elites, and an appreciation of their characteristic practices, informed her decision to refrain from directly assuming the presidency of the community association: 'I was always putting someone else in front, and omitting myself [from public exposure] to avoid certain situations'. Installing another community member as the president, as it turned out, became an important means of maintaining organisational independence since, despite some estrangement, the relationship between the community association and the city councillor continued.

In the run up to the 2008 regional elections (for the MBC), the president of Laura's community association was, in Laura's words, 'co-opted', or offered employment by the city councillor. He did so in order to increase his control over an influential member of the community, and by extension, it was hoped, residents' voting preferences and conduct in participatory assemblies. But this was based on the erroneous assumption that the association president was the principal organising figure in the region. Laura's ploy of giving the presidency to someone who had little influence over the community came into effect as a long-time colleague was given an offer too good to refuse.

> I knew her very well and we were always discussing things, since I had been in touch with her since she became involved in the community association. But I said to her, 'Politics is never in the first place for us; our community is always in first place'. But he [the city councillor] offered her a position, and she said to me, 'Look, he offered me this job here, through an NGO, working in a health clinic (*posto de saúde*), and I need [employment]'. And I said to her, 'Look, I don't have the right to tell you, since you need to work, I don't have the right to say to you, "Don't accept it". But if you are going to accept it, you accept it personally. It is not the community or the association'. So I thought [with the elections in view], what am I going to do? I need to elect a councillor [for the MBC] that I trust. I needed someone who wasn't co-opted [*laughs*].

According to Laura, she herself retained control of mobilising the population, irrespective of the formal post of association president. Her plan of pulling the strings of community organisation while remaining in the background worked, though she lost a colleague, who after accepting the job at the health clinic was considered to be on the side of 'those people'. But for the time being there were more pressing matters: she needed another person to be elected to the MBC. Laura began talking to her husband, 'who hates politics', and convinced him to run for election, since he was well known in the area.

> He went and spoke to the community leaders, to mobilise support for his candidature, because I don't have much time ... And he accepted the undertaking, a responsibility – because it is a responsibility, to represent the community. On the day [of the election] I organised a bus [to take the supporters organised by the community leaders] because it's a hike. But on the day, I was worried because the time was approaching and they didn't appear. I called the community leaders to find out how they were doing. I was almost crying because it's a struggle, you know [to organise all those people], and I was scared they wouldn't show. But when I left my house I saw a crowd of people covering the street, so I was happy. So we went to the PB [assembly] and the bus did two journeys [to take the community members there].

Laura's organising efforts succeeded, as her husband won the election and became the titular representative for the region. Laura used her colleague, who assumed the presidency, as a kind of proxy, obscuring her own agency from those on the front stage. She effectively insulated the independence of the community association from a calculating political operator, and successfully nominated a trustworthy candidate to the position of regional representative on the MBC. The city councillor's attempt to seize control of the community association and the local clout it yielded was at least temporarily thwarted.

Laura's case shows how patron–client relationships operate in a strategically charged social field in which actors make tactical ploys, calculations and miscalculations. There were, of course, power imbalances. Laura lacked the resources and political connections that enabled the city councillor to poach potential allies with lucrative offers of employment. However, the power imbalance was not absolute but particular, and required specific arrangements that protected the integrity of the community association and its ability to mobilise the population. It is not a case that accords well with the picture of clientelism as a dyadic but permanently asymmetrical relationship of control. Yet, while Laura's story is one of independent organisation and mobilisation, it might have been quite different. If the city councillor had made good on his promise to surface the road, and had delivered other public works to the region, it is possible that he would have had greater sway over the community association. Even then, as Robert Gay (1999) has cogently shown, there is no reason to suppose that Laura or the association would simply have been receptive subordinates in any such relationship; rather, other social conditions would have emerged that guided and conditioned their conduct. The unsuccessful attempt of the city councillor to 'co-opt' the association through poaching its president, and an otherwise estranged relationship with the community organisers, meant that patron–client relationships had, according to available evidence, little influence on front-stage participation. The failed attempt of a member of the political elite to increase their control over the association was also a failure to influence the front stage of participation, confining their machinations, at least in this case, to the backstage.

The allegiances that obtain between vote-seeking politicians and community organisers are negotiated at some remove from public forums like participatory assemblies. Yet they can have far-reaching ramifications for front-stage participation, and can be consequential provided that citizen groups are able to influence government policy and investment decision-making. Clientelism is often criticised as a vestige of the past that impedes and impairs the liberal reforms of the present. However, there are other relationships that do not contravene liberal ideals of governance and yet may prove similarly constraining for the vitality of citizen participation. In the following section I explore such a case: the evolving relationship between a *favela* residents' movement and Workers' Party governments.

Clientelism on the Front Stage?

In a careful elision, Laura did not mention the president of the community association by name, yet I actually knew her quite well, and had met the city councillor at her house on one occasion. Both Laura and her association president belonged to the MDDF, a social movement that had been recognised as one of the most active in the 1980s, but which during fieldwork drew intense scrutiny from other community activists for its proximity to the local government. It is worth analysing this relationship in more depth, because tracing its evolving nature provides important information about the socio-political context within which Santo André's participatory institutions function. It is also germane to analyse it here because the criticism the MDDF attracted was similar to that reserved for the clients and proxies of political actors, namely that its relationship with a higher power had compromised its independence. Here, the favoured pejorative used was 'sell-outs' (*vendidos*), perhaps no less scathing than those used to describe individual clients.

The threshold for this sense of public betrayal might have been low, since similar criticisms were often quite liberally bandied about.[6] Yet when my conversations with social activists and civil society participants turned to issues of co-optation and clientelism, the MDDF was often mentioned, if not identified as a prime example. To be sure, terms like co-optation were used in an encompassing and fairly vague manner, as they often are in the academic literature. But although tarred with much the same brush by their critics, there was a notable difference between MDDF–government relations and those between politicians and their clients: rather than chiefly personal, informal arrangements between individuals, the MDDF's relationship with local government was inter-organisational and officially sanctioned. While not the subject of performances in public forums – the definition of 'front stage' employed previously in this chapter – MDDF's partnership with local government was scarcely backstage in any meaningful sense. It was not, to my knowledge, mediated or brokered by the informal influence of a city councillor, and throughout my extensive contact with the movement and its members I never became aware of any interference by members of the political elite in its internal affairs. Significantly, the critics of the movement never made any allegation to that effect: their co-opted status was held to be self-evident.

In the following section I explore and analyse the evolution of the movement from the perspective of its president, Emerson. I pay particular attention to its changing operations as it shifted from a clandestine *favela* rights organisation to a formal, service-delivery partner of local government. The MDDF–government relationship, as it stood by the time of my fieldwork in 2007, and as some critics had suggested, was potentially compromising, inasmuch as long-term financing provided a powerful incentive for maintaining the support and good will of government officials. But in this case it was an officially sanctioned relationship, and not an informal backstage arrangement that may have figured in the conduct and behaviour of movement members. I concede to the critics of the movement that the contract it undertook with local government may indeed have had political motivations. Yet in a relatively demobilised political climate, a lack of any substantial protest and contestation in the broader civil society of which the movement was a part meant that the supposedly compromised independence of the movement was hard to measure. The return to democracy and a series of progressive Workers' Party administrations helped create a political context in which cooperation was rational, productive and mutually rewarding, even if it tended to restrict the terms of that engagement to professional cordiality (see Gohn 1997: 285).

The MDDF was founded in 1977 when residents of a *favela* in Vila Palmares, a suburb of Santo André, organised to resist moves by local government to evict and demolish their homes (MDDF 2011). Community organisers coordinated with members of the Catholic clergy, and at times the media, to defend against the removal of residents from their homes – a task that required constant vigilance and coordination, since eviction and demolition would sometimes be planned for the early hours of the morning to avoid critical attention. At that time known simply as the MDF (Movement for the Defence of Favela Inhabitants), it grew to become one of São Paulo's most active social movements in the early 1980s (Jacobi & Nunes 1983), eventually growing beyond its geographic birthplace in Santo André and becoming established in São Paulo proper. The São Paulo contingent broke away from Santo André, retaining the original name of the movement, and is still active today, particularly as an advocate of improved health services in the east zone of the city (Feltran 2007).[7] The Santo André contingent then adopted the slightly modified name of Movimento de Defesa dos Direitos de Moradores em Favela (Movement for the Defence of Favela Inhabitants' Rights).

Emerson was in his third two-year term as president of the movement during my first period of fieldwork. While the movement had started in the late 1970s, Emerson became active in 1986. At that time, he moved to Vila Gamboa, and the then mayor had tried to evict its residents:

> I started to participate in the middle of 1986, where in my community, which is the *favela* Gamboa, there was at the time an attempt by the mayor to start a 'reintegration', or rather an eviction of the community. And together with other leaders of the MDDF who made contact with us – and this was when I started to participate in the movement – we resisted and struggled against eviction. At the time they were able to remove a dozen families from the area. Then there were even city councillors who lent their support to others [i.e. residents of Vila

Gamboa] to avoid eviction. We were able to avoid it and the public administration back-pedalled [on its plans].

Emerson became involved at a pivotal moment in the trajectory of the movement, as he explains.

> The MDF became the MDDF in 1988, when we also elected the movement's first directorate. Before then there was no elected directorate, just some people that ran the movement, informally and clandestinely, and who were supported by the diocesan curia and the bishop of the time, Dom Claudio, who gave a lot of support to us and helped us organise the communities. Other communities started to participate more, new leaders came to participate in the movement, becoming active in the struggle, and in the organisation of it. It was only after 1988 that we had our first *favela* urbanisation projects in Santo André.

Just as the organisation of the movement became more regulated, initiating periodic elections for its administrative positions, significant changes were also taking place in the local government, in which it had a keen interest.

> At the end of 1988 and [the start of] 1989 we were able to organise a conference, a meeting, where we were able to design an urbanisation project, assisted by other sectors, other organisations and technical assistants (*assessors*), including what was called at the time the Centre of Social and Political Studies of the ABC, an organisation that helped a lot in the development of the project. And then in 1989 the now-deceased Celso Daniel assumed executive office, through the Workers' Party, and we met with the other community leaders and delivered the *favela* urbanisation proposal to him. He accepted the proposal from MDDF and we began discussions. The Department of Housing didn't exist [at that time]. All of that institutional [structure] that you see today there in the local government in the area of housing didn't exist [in the pre-Daniel era]. The Department of Housing was created [as one of the first institutional changes].

The period Emerson describes is one of the MDDF's institutionalisation and pro-active engagement with the administration, which itself had initiated organisational and personnel changes in order to advance a progressive political agenda. Past governments had been responsible for the forced evictions of informal settlements, a string of unrealised promises (Almeida 1992: 38–39, 43) and a general neglect of the poor areas of the city. With Daniel at the helm of local government, larger issues relating to the legitimacy of social movement claims dissolved immediately. Popular movements ceased to be acrimonious opponents of government, and their relationship became more involved and complex. In fact, a friend of the movement aided in the information gathering that was the first order of business for an administration with little knowledge of the periphery. Emerson continues:

> After the mayor, Celso Daniel, had assumed ... office, he took the project [that MDDF had developed] and subsequently sent a letter, around two to three months later, asking the director of housing [in the local administration] to reformulate the re-urbanisation project, and then started to discuss which neighbourhoods should be urbanised first, and how the process of urbanisation should progress. First they did a survey of all of the *favelas* [to determine] how many *favelas* there were in Santo André, the condition they were in (*qual era a situação delas*), and this was the survey which a friend of ours from the movement helped to carry out.

A new era had begun for the MDDF, whose activities became less concerned with the protection of their communities from eviction, and which in turn became less defensive and more involved in cooperative endeavours with local government. This assumed its most concrete form when the MDDF was approached by members of the administration to manage a welfare project:

> After the urbanisation project restarted [under the new Daniel administration in 1997] we also thought about other kinds of work that could be done in the communities. So between 1997 and 1998, the administration, through the Department of Welfare, offered us the job of working with children and adolescents. At the time it was called the Brazil Child Citizen Project (Projeto Brasil Criança Cidadã).

This project completed the transformation of the MDDF from an informal and backstage *favela* rights movement into an official service partner of the government that resembles much more closely an NGO (see Foweraker

2001: 846). In Emerson's wording, the project was offered to them, seemingly unsolicited, by the administration. This may have been one of the reasons for the criticism the newfound relationship attracted from fellow activists: it was an approach from the government with an offer of long-term funding. Suspicions would have been further compounded by Emerson's admission that they were quite unprepared for such a project:

> At the time, when I assumed the project, we were without any experience at all in the area of children and adolescents, so we contracted a technical team, a group that was well known to us, with experience in working with children, that started to design the Child Citizen Project.

While a seemingly odd choice for the provision of services, given the lack of experience Emerson refers to, the MDDF did have valuable relationships with community leaders and residents that would be instrumental in attracting participants to the project. But regardless of the political or policy motivations for awarding the contract, it introduced a similar set of considerations to the movement organisers as those faced by the clients of politicians. Project financing had allowed the MDDF to establish a second permanent office in Sacadura Cabral, in a larger building than the movement headquarters in Vila Gamboa, from which its operations would be managed. Since the project began in 1999 and was due to expire in 2009, the non-renewal of the contract would have been a significant loss for the MDDF. Unlike the backstage arrangements between clients and politicians, however, it was a formal and official agreement that gave the movement's organisers and those employed by the project a powerful incentive for maintaining the goodwill and support of political appointees in the administration.

Yet the suggestion implicit in criticisms from other social activists, that movement members altered their conduct so as to acquiesce to the expectations of government officials, was difficult to substantiate or deny, since the lack of other, more contentious displays by social actors in the city during my fieldwork meant that there was little room for comparison. When I asked several activists about the last large scale social mobilisation in Santo André, their minds had to turn back to the impeachment of the Brazilian president, Fernando Collor de Melo, in 1992 – a mobilisation in which the local Workers' Party had an instrumental, organising role. Perhaps the most substantial indication of the relative tranquillity of sociopolitical relations in the democratic period came during the conservative administration of Newton da Costa Brandão, which held office from 1993 to 1996, between Celso Daniel's first two terms as mayor. A mainstay in local politics since his first term as mayor in 1969, Brandão dismantled the fledgling participatory reforms initiated by Daniel without significant protest from civil society or from Workers' Party representatives in the Legislative Chamber (Pontual 2000: 152). Cordial relations with the local administration in the post-transition era were more the rule than the exception in Santo André, particularly when the Workers' Party was in power. This became clear when we spoke about the quality of the relationship between social movements and the government.

> V.A.: I would like to ask about the relationship between the government and these social movements, how has it changed during the Workers' Party administration(s)?
>
> EMERSON: The relationship changed for the better, for certain. We have difficulties and there are problems between us, divergences, but compared to other governments, other mayors for example, it has much improved. In the local administration, the Department [of Urban Development] receives us very well, we discuss [issues together], but we have the right to agree or disagree with what the *prefeitura* does. So the relationship is good.

There remained differences of opinion, Emerson maintains, but there is no suggestion that the means for expressing disagreement would transgress the professional parameters of dialogue and deliberation that had been established. A new, technocratic language entered into circulation among MDDF members; and other aspects of community life, such as sport and entertainment, came under a remit newly expanded by extensive funding. The movement became more project and service-oriented:

> There are people who say that we are in partnership with government, and in a sense they are right in terms of projects. We partner them in respect of projects. We have [the] Child Citizen [Project]; the government provides the resources and we develop the project. Another project that we are developing now … is from the Department of Social Inclusion, [it] is a reference centre for social inclusion in Cidade São Jorge. It is a government attendance centre for the low income population, because they cannot go into the centre of town, so we can attend to them there.

Just like the clients of politicians, the MDDF had much to lose from antagonising high-status officials. However, the influence of the government on the conduct of its members was perhaps more implicit than explicit. Normative considerations, concerning the actual and future conduct of the movement vis-à-vis the government, were embedded in personal and inter-organisational relationships, a new sociability that accompanied the 'new institutionality' (Draibe 1998) that, over a period of many years, had established a framework for resolving differences of opinion, divergences and disagreements.

Although the contractual relationship established organisational incentives for cordial professionalism, individual members of organisations were clearly not bound hand and foot. The cases of Laura and her association president serve as timely reminders of the diverse individual predilections and trajectories of movement affiliates. Laura's husband became a quite vociferous proponent of the civil society demands while on the MBC, many of which were omitted from the government counter-proposals in the negotiating phase of the PB, while the association president seemed to participate less, from what I could tell, in the movement and in the public forums I attended. Awarding a lucrative financial contract to the MDDF did not eliminate its agency, as its critics suggest, but it did help alter its role in the city by creating disincentives for opposition to the government, and by establishing professionalised norms of conduct through which differences could be worked out.

Conclusion

This chapter has explored and analysed some relationships between what I have called the front and backstage of participation. Often the precise influence of the one on the other was somewhat vague and hard to make out. Yet at times it was precisely the uncertainty and latency that lent consequence to backstage exchanges and relationships. For instance, in the first case study, we saw how a caution from a senior government official was extrapolated with dramatic effect. What may have been an offhand remark from an aggravated official was considered potentially life threatening by a civil society participant. It was an interpretation nourished, I suggested, by narratives surrounding such events as the unsolved murder of the former mayor, Celso Daniel.

The second and third case studies addressed clientelism. The second vividly illustrated the performative norms of the front stage, which were contravened by Mauricio, the gaffe-prone PB director. His attempt to undermine the credibility of Edu, by indicating his ties to a city councillor, backfired, for although Mauricio succeeded in drawing attention to Edu's political ties, he badly miscalculated the potential reaction and had to back-pedal awkwardly. The third case study examined the tenuous and tactically charged encounters between a city councillor and a community organiser, Laura. Unlike the accusation levelled at Edu, Laura's was a story of failed co-optation, as she retained control of her community association through installing a proxy in the position of association president. Laura's case shows that community leaders were far from powerless clients, and were possessed of their own tactics for dealing with unreliable and predatory patrons.

The final case study explored and analysed the relationship that developed between the MDDF and local government. In contrast to the other cases, however, the MDDF had an officially sanctioned relationship in the form of a contract, which provided long term funding for the management and operation of a project. It was, if you will, a more front-stage arrangement. Yet it posed the problem of compromised independence that also applied to the clients of politicians examined earlier. The MDDF of 2007 and 2008 was a different creature to that which operated in its initial phase. It had changed with the times, even if the popular criteria by which it was often judged had not. As an organisation, the MDDF had developed closer ties with local government, perhaps encumbering what may be called the performative imperatives of the front stage on its senior personnel. But this did not prevent individual movement affiliates from pursuing individual and community interests in inventive, and at times quite outspoken, ways. Nor did it prevent the MDDF from providing services to the residents of *favelas*.

Each of these cases is distinct. Yet in all the cases in which a concrete relationship was established – that is, every case with the exception of Laura's – there was an incentive to fulfil the expectations of the powerful. Whether for reasons of personal safety, fealty or individual or collective interest, the arrangements negotiated backstage percolate into the front-stage arena of public life in ways often difficult to detect through interviews and other documentation methods of empirical social science. I have also suggested that officially sanctioned relationships between government and social movement organisations may potentially have a similar influence on the front stage of participation. In fact, as acknowledged and legitimised features of local governance, with the support of much of the global development community, their influence may grow. Relationships between institutionalised social movement organisations and different government units are becoming more common in Brazil's democratic era (see Foweraker 2001: 846). Although these socio-political partnerships may flourish, those social movement organisations (and popular NGOs) which are seen to be all too ready to ally themselves with the government will probably continue to draw the ire of social activists for their perceived disloyalty to the community. This interpretative tendency suggests that the values that accompanied the development of NGOs – which had grown with their 'backs to the state, glued to the bases of society' (Landim 1993: 29) – have endured, even in a time of significant socio-political change. But even if civil society organisations and the state develop increasingly formal ties, there will be actors like Laura who can stake out a social domain, and effectively protect it against members of the political elite, whether they reside in the local administration or the Legislative Chamber. There may, of course, also be fissures that develop between civil and political society that give rise to aggressive episodes of mobilisation that could overshadow the micro-sociological features of local politics analysed here.

Conclusion: Reimagining Participatory Democracy

Santo André's participatory institutions were intimately caught up with the local state administration, with its organisational structures and the interests and plans of its officials. In this book I have provided a particular approach to this entanglement, one that follows the experiences of the participants as they vie for membership in an institution and then take part in a series of interconnected meetings that are the core activities of the participatory institutions. This approach allows a line of causal theorising that is attentive to time, and to the ritualisation of interaction in a sequence of events. Participation, according to this analysis, is not something that comes to us as an established historical fact; rather, it is constantly being shaped and reshaped, legitimised and challenged, stirred and soothed by the rhythms and flows of social action. It is also, of course, and as others have noted, informed by other, not immediately apparent influences and interests. To this end, the analysis plotted outward, into the patterned beliefs and ideologies of state and civil society participants, and into the broader political economy of power relations in the city. This outward plotting has a dual purpose: it informs an understanding of participation by adding other factors into the causal mix, such as the influence of patronage politics and the fear of the political elite, and it also allows a picture to emerge of how Santo André's participatory institutions figure on a larger political canvas.

In political and sociological studies, much of the activity of participatory institutions that has been analysed here is assumed in the analysis and accepted as a taken-for-granted feature of organisational life. This is, in part, a consequence of the necessity of abstraction in more general studies. But it is also because the repetitive nature of participation and the prevalence of similar forms of social action can tend to 'homogenise perspectives' (Hannerz 1992: 67), to draw our attention away from everyday behavioural regularities and to focus it on the content of participation or on periodic ruptures of routine. This is problematic for institutions of participatory democracy in at least two senses. First, it is problematic because everyday interactions between state officials and members of the lay public are often shaped by power relations that inhibit more robust forms of citizen participation. Second, these patterns of interaction and situational involvement may be similarly taken for granted by participants, and hence a likely explanation for why it was so difficult to get my fieldwork colleagues in Santo André to critically reflect on them, in effect taking vital normative questions off the table. The normalisation of asymmetrical power relations in participatory institutions ought to be a key and ongoing analytical concern, even in those cases celebrated as exemplars of participatory reform.

An important source of the shared, tacit knowledge that undergirds such everyday involvements is the pervasiveness of similar social practices. The participatory institutions examined here are only a small percentage of the total number of these institutions in the city of Santo André. There were 24 management policy councils, in addition to the participatory budget, the Future Cities project and other ad hoc conferences and assemblies. In addition to the Housing Council (HC), the Urban Development Council (UDC) and the participatory budget (PB), I attended the meetings of two other management policy councils, though with less regularity, and scores of other formal and informal gatherings in the city. Despite important differences between them, there were striking similarities among the configurations of practices in the various participatory and presentational forums. The normalisation of social conduct in participatory institutions is thus bound up with a much larger knitting together of state bureaucracy with sections of the public that depend on similar situations of co-presence. These are important, proximate sources of the normalisation of conduct in participatory institutions. But the analytical net should be cast wider still, for citizen participation is indelibly shaped by the patterns of practices in wider society, in schools, public events and state rituals, and in the work meetings of organisations like the state administration (see Handelman 2004). We need to better understand the way that institutions of participatory democracy are imbricated with these other social phenomena (see Cornwall 2004: 85), and with the normalisation of power in domains of social life that may be only tenuously linked to state-organised participatory arenas. That is, we need to locate the repertoires of situational involvement in participatory institutions within larger ecologies of social practices.

The prevalence of similar practices among different participatory institutions and other public forums calls into question the discursive framing of the institutions. In other words, how is it that we come to call a forum or institution 'participatory'? Many of the so-called participatory assemblies examined in this book were comparable in their patterns of interaction and in the opportunities for engaging with state officials with other public forums that were organised by local government that did not carry the participatory label. The use of the term 'participatory', that is to say, is a successful act of signification effected by the organisers of the institution. Thus, what might be better simply termed government assemblies come to be keyed in the language offered by power-bearing officials. Even where these institutions are found to be merely 'consultative' or to 'offer little real participation', we continue to refer to them as participatory institutions. This provides a kind of legitimacy that gives life to political claims of collaborative governance, and ensures that evaluations take place within the discursive space marked out by the institutions' political sponsors. The depiction of an institution as 'participatory' perhaps should be considered a contingent and tenuous achievement rather than an accepted label. The study of participatory democracy and governance would thus perhaps do better if it discarded the language of participation altogether, not because of definitional imprecision (Cornwall & Brock 2005), which seems almost inescapable in the social sciences, but rather because it involves adopting the labels and language offered by the powerful. In place of examining differing forms of participation, it is perhaps better to begin with a minimalist definition upon which further analysis can then build. Participatory institutions, that is, generate situations of co-presence; citizen participation, voice, transparency and the other democratic aims of the initiatives are only possibilities.

This would mean foregoing the kind of academic language that may preemptively exaggerate the independence that participatory institutions have from other spheres of political and administrative life. Take, for instance, the following portrayal of participatory institutions as constituting:

> a *distinct arena* at the interface of state and society: what we term here the 'participatory sphere'. The institutions of this sphere have *a semi-autonomous existence, outside and apart from the institutions of formal politics, bureaucracy and everyday associational life*, although they are often threaded through with preoccupations and positions formed in them. As arenas in which the boundaries of the technical and the political come to be negotiated, they *serve as an entirely different kind*

of interface with policy processes than other avenues through which citizens can articulate their demands – such as protest, petitioning, lobbying and direct action – or indeed organise to satisfy their own needs. (Cornwall & Coelho 2004: 1–2, emphasis added)

The problem here is not that participatory forums *may* constitute a distinct arena of action, set apart from other fields of political activity; it is, rather, that they should not be presumed to be so before this distinction is empirically established. The relative independence of participatory forums from other spheres of political and community life is a possibility to be explored rather than assumed. Nor should it be simply accepted that participatory institutions are *entirely* different from other forms of demand-making and state–society interaction, particularly when, as was shown in Chapter 3, participatory politics can involve elements of petitioning and protest; and as shown in the MDDF–government relationship analysed in Chapter 6, social movements at times must also negotiate the boundaries of the technical and the political. To be sure, state-based actors will also have variable effects on the organisation and effectiveness of institutions of participatory democracy. However, the central role of administrative officials and political appointees in sponsoring and organising participatory initiatives should make it a central concern of scholarly analysis.

Furthermore, while the analysis must be alive to the agency of community actors, it should not be presumed, *pace* Foucault, that power relations are '*always* sites of resistance' (Cornwall 2004: 81, emphasis added), particularly when the ethnographic evidence indicates otherwise. Dissent and contestation between participants and organisers, when it takes place, does not necessarily signal a critique of the role of state actors or an attempt to alter the normative parameters of participation, since contestation often implies a 'restatement of the value of the order that permits its expression' (Handelman 1976: 438). Institutions like the PB can prefigure contestation, but they also mobilise a normative architecture that shapes the kinds of contestation that are possible. This may be only partially set out in formal institutional designs and attendant regulations. It is thus important to examine the contours of resistance, the degree to which it operates within the normative confines of institutions, and to analyse the processes that normalise and reproduce power relations in participatory institutions.

Santo André's participatory institutions are, like other formal organisations, 'rooted in highly institutionalised contexts' (Garsten & Nyqvist 2013: 11) that help to cast the manifestations of state power as mundane routine. But this qualifies rather than discounts the potential for change and creative agency on the part of participants. In this book I have examined the active and ethnographically accessible practices through which power relations are expressed and reproduced in participatory institutions. Implicit in any such theorisation is the promise that modifications to these practices – to the rituals, the symbolic expressions of power and the spatial organisation of participation – will have some attitudinal, cognitive or behavioural consequence. In the first half of this concluding chapter I pursue this normative interest more explicitly and explore the possibilities for reform based on the findings of the book. I propose changes to some of the ritualised social phenomena that have been examined, and speculate as to how these might change expectations and, potentially, patterns of behaviour. I engage in dialogue with the findings of earlier chapters, not for the purposes of summary and closure, but rather to offer up and reflect on what the substantive analysis of the book might provide for participatory reformers. These are exploratory contributions to the ongoing debate over the potential for participatory reform in representative democracies – motivated more by the enduring enthusiasm of Santo André's activists for participatory democracy than by my own personal convictions – with a particular focus on how some of these insights might apply to other participatory reform efforts in Latin America and elsewhere. Some of the practices, structures and behavioural patterns that have been examined are plainly more disposed to this kind of normative reflection than others. Indeed, portions of the analysis might indicate challenges facing participatory reformers without offering solutions. But those too are important to note.

It may be fruitful to make proposals based on empirical analysis, however modest in their potential scope. Yet they can mean little if there is no political will to implement them. In the second half of the chapter, I examine local support for the participatory project in Santo André against the backdrop of a widely noted de-radicalisation of the political goals and rhetoric of the Workers' Party. Reflecting on the Lula administration's reforms at the national level and the Carlos Grana administration in Santo André, I finally consider the reasons for the unending appetite for participatory reform in Brazil.

Rituals and Institutional Structures

In Chapter 2, I cast the initial events for participants-to-be as rituals that are part of a larger process of ritualisation. The elections and induction ceremonies served various purposes, for example, as a space for choreographed social dramas and celebrating the life of a loved public servant. But they also introduced the new members to the participatory institution in ritual processes that located participants in a socially and spatially hierarchical relationship with state officials that drew from the structure of graded authority within the administration. Elections and induction ceremonies were thus what Don Handelman called 'events of presentation', which are the 'dominant forms of occasion that publicly enunciate and index lineaments of statehood, nationhood, and civil collectivity' (Handelman 1990: 42). In other words, the preliminary ritual events of a biennial term on a participatory institution are part of a coherent ensemble of social occasions that articulate and help reproduce in participatory assemblies the formal power structures of local government, through nesting membership in the institution within a broader symbolic framework of statehood, collective identity and belonging.

The effect and influence of these rituals derives from their preparatory role in a series of similar gatherings, rather than as standalone events. In the UDC, for example, the symbolic hierarchy of local government extends over the participatory institution: there, the highest ranking government officer from the relevant department, the secretary of urban development, also held the foremost position on the Executive Committee as president of the UDC. In a similar but slightly different case, the highest-ranking individual from the Department of Participatory Budgeting and Planning, Mauricio, assumed the de facto position of president of the Municipal Budget Council (MBC), even though it was unspecified in the formal hierarchy of the institution. That is to say, during the elections and induction ceremonies, the individuals who occupied the *espaço nobre* ('noble space') in the front region and who formally admitted the inductees into the participatory institution were also, in the cases of the UDC and the PB, those who would assume similarly pre-eminent positions in the meetings of the institutions. While there was a second dimension to these rituals, which opened up opportunities for resistance and contestation, something we saw most vividly in the PB, the risk of inuring lay participants to the power and authority of state officials warrants that such occasions be brought within the scope of normative theorising.

As I see it, the changes that could be made to these rituals can be one of two kinds: either by modifications to personnel that maintain the ritual form, or by modifications to the form itself. In the first instance, the ritual process can remain exactly the same, the process of composing the table can remain, and high-status officials can be the principal actors who formally admit participants-to-be into the institution. But rather than high-status state officials, they could be the outgoing representatives of civil society who were ending their tenure in the institution. This retains the livery and hence some of the symbolic status of the institution and its executive positions, but eliminates any ritual acts that signal hierarchical relations between administrative officials and the new participants. Regarding the second, modifications of form would entail a more radical renewal of the induction process and are open to any number of possible changes. For example, the induction could be organised entirely by civil society groups with a minimal presence of government staff. Or, state officials might still play a significant role in the ceremony, but without reference to their status within the administration. If, as Richard Fox suggests, 'domination has to be constantly re-created' (cited in Kertzer 1988: 175), then altering the symbolically charged processes through which power relations are reproduced may help refigure those relationships, even if only modestly.

Spatial Organisation

As instances of a larger process of ritualisation, we should consider how power relations are spatially mapped out, not only in the initial rituals but also in the routine meetings of the institutions. Even though participatory meetings and assemblies might be spatially organised in any number of ways, I will confine my reflections to the two principal types examined in Chapters 3 and 4: the cinema-style, 'sociofugal' format, seen in the meetings of the UDC and the PB, and the circular, 'sociopetal' type that obtained in the meetings of the HC. Both the circular and the cinema-style types anticipate and help produce different patterns of behaviour. The cinema-style format differentiates and divides the participants by locating a smaller number in the front region – a region that was often sacralised in the process of 'composing the table'. It was from this area that a minority, commonly senior members of the administration, coordinated and regulated the larger assemblies of Santo André's participatory institutions.

Yet not all front regions are the same. We saw in the negotiating phase of the PB that making space in the front region for participants provided opportunities – that is, normatively accepted opportunities – for participants to voice their opinions. We also saw, however, that experience and oratorical nous play a role in determining whether those opportunities can be exploited by civil society representatives. Those charged with organising participatory assemblies might thus consider alternating the position of chairperson and those occupying the front region, so as to avoid the reification of control by a minority of state officers and/or civil society representatives of long standing. There might also be greater experimentation with the make-up and composition of the front region, in a way that grants lay participants time to prepare and perfect their performative skills so as to allay the apprehension that was on show in the negotiating assemblies of the PB.

The circular, sociopetal format, in contrast, was conducive to cooperative forms of behaviour since it does not spatially segregate participants into distinct groups. This we saw borne out in the meetings of the HC, the most collegial of the participatory institutions examined here. While there were clearly other factors that contributed to the egalitarian culture of the HC, such as its size and the composition of its membership, the material arrangements of its meetings enabled face-to-face contact and communication between all its members. Its spatial organisation thus contributed, however moderately, to the open-ended deliberations of the institution. Smaller, sociopetal meetings might provide a means for encouraging less hierarchical participatory meetings for reformers who seek to improve the conditions of public deliberation, even if that does come at the cost of representativeness. However, it should not be presumed that fostering cooperation is necessarily desirable. A distinguishing feature of the PB, for instance, was its ability to generate tension and to articulate the interests of community actors, a necessary component of which was the separation of civil society as a group distinct from the state, which allowed its constituent members to develop plans and strategies that they would execute during negotiations. Orchestrating adversarial interactions between spatially separated civil society and state representatives might be appropriate when state officials and other administrative actors have contradictory plans of their own, or are unwilling unless required to listen to the demands from civil society.

In broad terms these suggestions draw attention to the content and the form of participation (see Abers et al. 2014). Participatory reformers need to pay greater attention to the way that behavioural habits may override cognitive messaging. The point is perhaps best made with a fieldwork example, which is taken from the introductory phase of the PB, when all civil society representatives on the MBC take part in quite extensive educational sessions. The first education session was held by a Workers' Party intellectual who warned of the depredations of international finance capital and outlined the importance of active citizenship, against a backdrop of an image of Karl Marx which was projected onto the wall behind him. To all appearances, the session was designed to steel the participants for a fight in the coming weeks, as it was held prior to the negotiating phase. But it also demonstrated the way that a radicalisation of rhetoric is often, in participatory and socialist gatherings, coterminous with conservative social forms. That is to say, the sessions in which the intellectual underscored the importance of their participation and its radical potential were still organised by the administrative staff, and civil society members were largely receptive attendees at the session. The practices through which state representatives would coordinate the key assemblies in the upcoming weeks were reiterated, just as the participants were being braced for the negotiations. It is thus unsurprising that civil society representatives, when permitted a place on the front stage in the negotiating phase, seemed so ill at ease. Civil society educators need to be aware that the normativity of the social form of assemblies may help to undermine unspecific exhortations to be 'active citizens'. For participatory assemblies to live up to the name, civil society members must become organisers and coordinators of the assemblies, or else their gatherings may merely be, to borrow the words of Marco Nogueira, 'spaces [that are] regulated by the state and filled with civil society' (Nogueira 1998: 222).

Refiguring Administrative Structures and Norms

A number of insights might be drawn from other aspects of the analysis, for those who seek to deepen citizen participation in governance affairs. One of the foremost examples, and one foreshadowed in the section above, concerns the coordination and moderation of assemblies. It is perhaps strange that there has not been greater popular and academic scrutiny of who occupies the executive positions in participatory institutions. In fact, important normative questions concerning the allocation of power in Brazil's participatory institutions are often avoided in the literature. A common argument runs that the relationship between participatory institutions and the state cannot be prescribed in the abstract and that each case will require its own design, based on local conditions, on the policies and issues to be deliberated, and on the demands and desires of the social and political actors constituting the institution. This is a reasoned position given the diversity of participatory institutions in Brazil and the disparate and ever-changing socio-political conditions of which they form a part. In recent Brazilian history, the question of how popular organisations should interface with the state, if indeed at all, has been a vexatious one (see Gohn 2000: 282; Mainwaring 1987: 151; Teixeira 1996). Yet, if we accept that there are to be participatory institutions, even short of accepting their desirability in all areas of government, then these ought to generate a kind of creative tension with local administrations and their internal patterns of power.

The analysis of Santo André's participatory institutions suggests a couple of simple ways to generate such tension. One way is to mandate that the foremost executive position of every participatory institution is to be held by a civil society representative. Of course this would not dispose of, or necessarily diminish, the influence of senior state officials over the determinations of the institution. We could imagine, quite easily, situations where the president of the institution would become a position that is 'merely symbolic'. However, since the position of president has socially accepted responsibilities and prerogatives, it may also furnish a cultural resource that could be used by civil society actors. You may recall, for example, how in Chapter 4 Vanessa used her position as president to foster open-ended deliberations in the meetings of the HC and advance the interests of civic associations. There were, of course, other factors that affected Vanessa's ability to influence the deliberations of the HC and its informal culture; but the presidency did provide socially accepted dispositions of consequence. She adopted critical positions towards the administration, was more receptive to the concerns of *favela* associations and solicited the views of other participants in a way that the presidents of the UDC and the PB did not. Reserving executive positions for civil society participants may help to disrupt the tendency for government hierarchies to be reproduced in participatory forums, as it did in the HC, and to increase the probability that the institution is receptive to civil society groups and their concerns. It may also help to ensure that administrative projects that are brought before the institution are presented in non-specialist terminology, something that would be particularly welcome in institutions like the UDC or Mexico's Consultative Councils for Sustainable Development. There is no reason why civil society presidents would be necessarily more inclined to follow Vanessa's example (see Schönleitner

2006). But it would increase the likelihood that the holders of the foremost positions in participatory institutions would be less beholden to the administrative and political elite.

There are other, plainly important normative questions concerning the makeup and functioning of Santo André's participatory institutions. Perhaps the most obvious pertains to the composition of their membership (Fung 2003: 342). If groups such as members of state agencies and departments tend to produce coherent public displays – due, among other things, to the imperatives of public performances (Goffman 1957: 107; Scott 1990: 55) – then it is little surprise that state representatives normally vote together and seldom publicly dispute and argue among themselves. The HC was successful as a participatory space in part because its civil society participants were largely representatives of disadvantaged social groups. While governments may like to include a broad range of social and commercial actors in participatory institutions, if for nothing else than to please special interest groups, this can provide an opportunity for already advantaged groups to further advance their interests (Fung 2003: 347–8). In many cases, this prevents thoroughgoing deliberation and enables decision-making within the institution to become routinely controlled by senior state officials, who effectively choreograph their team's performances.

One partial remedy would be to allocate civil society members the majority of seats, but to give the mayor the power to override the decisions of the institution (in the case of management policy councils). This would ensure that government staff would have a greater incentive to explain the prospective policy changes to civil society members in terms they are able to understand, though they would, crucially, still control how those issues were framed. In addition, mayors who are continually vetoing and overriding civil society decisions would establish a track record of resistance to the decisions of civil society representatives that could be interrogated. Another quite simple modification would be to channel all voting through an anonymous ballot system. If there is group pressure to ensure that the voting practices of all government staff are uniform, then an anonymous ballot would protect the identities of the public servants whose contrarian beliefs might displease their superiors.

If the imperatives of group membership pose one kind of performative problem for participatory democracy, then the manner in which those performances are shaped by audience type is another. This was revealed in the analysis of the PB in Chapter 3, where I noted how differently state representatives acted in the negotiating phase than they did in the regional assemblies. In the latter, government staff underscored the importance of citizen participation, were generally welcoming and outlined the many achievements that had been achieved by the PB in years past. In the former, however, state representatives were curter, more determined and at times even threatening, as counter-proposals were pushed through with little real debate and deliberation. Such a performative differentiation recalls Goffman's notion of 'audience segregation' (Goffman 1957: 57), and underscored how performances are tailored and adapted to certain audiences. However, this segregation could be countered to improve transparency without altering the structure of the PB.

A video recording of negotiations would be one relatively simple way that greater transparency could be fostered. It would be relatively inexpensive, could be posted online or distributed via DVD or other data recording device, and would enable a much more broad-based scrutiny of the government's willingness to engage in public-spirited debate. While sitting through hours of negotiating assemblies might test the patience and resolve of all except the most committed activists, it could nonetheless increase disclosure of government responses to the demands that were chosen during regional assemblies. Furthermore, it might discourage representatives from civil society who might be representing demands motivated by narrow self-interest or those of a political patron.

The Rationalisations of State Power

A number of important questions are raised by these suggestions. For example, to what extent can altering the rituals and spatial configurations of assemblies shape the attitudes and expectations of state and civil society representatives towards citizen participation? How might excluding state officials from participatory meetings improve the prospects of generating dialogue and exchange among participants? How might allowing non-state actors to design the agendas and content of assemblies counter the prevalence of technically specialist discourse and help foster more fulsome episodes of citizen participation? Finally, to what extent can a non-state actor – that is, an unremunerated activist – (co-)organise assemblies in such a way that is relevant to the internal decision-making processes of local government? A major challenge to the promise of participation is that state actors have powerful 'rational' claims that justify their prominence in participatory institutions. This was made clear by Celso Daniel when he defended the role of high-status government officials in Santo André's participatory institutions on practical grounds:

> If the presence of representatives of the government is not a qualified presence, if the representatives do not speak in the name of the government, the role that the [Management] Councils can assume as a space of formulating and defining public policies is reduced. If the presence of representatives of the government is a qualified presence, if they speak in the name of the government and know and are able to defend positions without having to stop the meeting in order to consult with the Secretariat or any other person, the situation is completely different. (Daniel 2000: 128)

The presence of senior officials was justified on the basis of their authority to implement decisions, and thus to be able to avoid time-consuming consultations. Efficiency is improved, according to this logic, but so too is the capacity of the participatory institution to formulate and design public policy. The power of senior officials constitutes the source of a number of meritorious effects, not least of which is the empowerment of the participatory arena. An extrapolation of this logic would hold that interference with the internal circuits of decision-making authority, either through creating participatory institutions lacking senior officials or by minimising the influence of state officials on deliberations, would create inefficiencies and ineffective government policies. In one sense this accords with Mauricio's depiction in Chapter 5 of citizen participation as burdensome, an intrusion of the uninformed public. It may indeed be 'easier to make the budget in the local administration ... without the participation of the population', as Mauricio claimed, given the well-trodden path of decision-making processes within the administration. But such declarations of efficiency or any other accompanying assumptions about technical superiority should also be treated cautiously, for they are not only references to an empirical reality; they are rationalisations of state power that help to define reality according to the interpretations of the powerful (see Flyvberg 1998: 117).

The evaluations of civil society participants, and particularly those who live on the periphery of the city, would paint a quite different picture of state action. Behind the bureaucratic rationality of state power, the competent discourse of its actors and exhortations of the logic and specialisation of its technocrats lies a history of urban development that has often been haphazard and focused on beautifying the upper-class areas of the city, though this history has taken a somewhat different turn under Workers' Party administrations (Almeida 1992). Santo André's urban landscape has more than its share of 'white elephants', works that were promised by one politician or another on election day and then abandoned when the funds dried up. While these are treated with a combination of dismay and wry humour by many of Santo André's residents, they are emblematic of the different ways that power carves out a discursive space in which it operates. The ability of political patrons to sponsor particular works, which often contravene urban planning principals and are at times left to become half-finished relics, receives none of the close, public and technical scrutiny experienced by the proposals of the lay participants of the city's participatory institutions, which are groomed and moderated in myriad ways. It is a kind of distrust, I would argue, that derives less from the technical deficiencies of their plans than it does from their relative lack of political authority.

More profound attempts at instituting participatory democracy involve accepting some measure of risk, the risk that citizens will demand a service that is not prioritised by the administrative elite or another kind of service or public work altogether. The motivation to advance participatory reform in Brazil has come under scrutiny in recent years, as the Workers' Party that was formed in the ABC region and that sought to remake Brazilian politics according to a new, participatory ethos has experienced a period of de-radicalisation.

Participatory Democracy and the Workers' Party

It might be well and good to proffer suggestions for participatory reform and to debate and discuss how the participatory project might advance. Yet these remain merely academic if the motivation to modify, experiment and extend the reach of citizens in participatory institutions is not shared by other social and political actors. In what remains of this concluding chapter I explore the contours of political support for participatory democracy by relating the case study of Santo André to the changes and continuities within the Workers' Party as a whole.

Participatory democracy has been an enduring ideal of the Workers' Party since its emergence in the early 1980s. It has gone by various appellations and has been conceived in the context of quite disparate political strategies, but there has nonetheless been an ongoing valorisation of the citizen's active role in the affairs of government that likely derives from the founders' experience of the military regime, the party's socialist origins and the influence of liberation theology (Abers 2000: 59). But despite the currency of participatory ideals in Workers' Party rhetoric, the commitment to participatory reform by sitting governments has been far from uniform. This is unsurprising given the ideological diversity of the party, the individual beliefs of politicians and their cliques, regional differences, the shifting terrain of electoral competition and the correlation of forces in different socio-political milieux. The political-administrative conditions of each state and municipality also alter the prospects for developing and maintaining effective participatory institutions. Even if the mayor or governor is behind the reform effort, resistance might be met in the Legislative Chamber or in the bureaucracy itself (see Denaldi & Dias 2003: 319).

The Workers' Party has experienced significant change since its birth in Sion College in 1980. Socialism is no longer the prominent ideal it once was. Though it still has purchase among much of the party faithful, it was famously discarded by Lula in his ultimately successful presidential campaign in 2002 (Samuels 2004: 1004). Indeed, Workers' Party discourse, more broadly, was moderated as it entered the fight for the votes of the political centre (see Amaral 2003; Singer 2012). The picture painted by Wendy Hunter on this point could not be clearer: 'The main story of the [Workers' Party]'s evolution between 1989 and 2002 is that of a radical programmatic party that became transformed into a catchall party' (Hunter 2005: 472). Yet despite such unequivocal evaluations, André Singer has drawn attention to divergent tendencies within the party, and he notes seemingly contradictory facts by way of illustration. For instance, while the presidential campaigns have been unmistakably pragmatic and conservative, numerous party congresses have reaffirmed the party's socialist convictions (Singer 2010: 90). These divergent aspects of the party are what Singer calls the 'two souls' of the Workers' Party.

Participatory democracy, or rather 'radical democratisation', is, Singer suggests, part of the soul of the Workers' Party that was forged in Sion College and that has endured despite the pragmatism of recent years (ibid.: 109). Singer speaks specifically of the Lula government's participatory reforms, which have included dozens of national conferences that brought together thousands of citizens as evidence of this other soul. It is interesting that Singer notes the participatory reforms implemented by Lula at the federal level, for they provide an illustrative example for the participatory reform effort in Santo André. That is, on the one hand Lula's participatory reforms have been undoubtedly productive and, depending on one's interpretation of the term, participatory. Seventy-two national conferences were organised during Lula's two terms in government, which in total involved 5.6 million participants and passed 14,000 resolutions (Baiocchi et al. 2012: 224). Lula's successor, Dilma Rousseff, organised 23 national conferences in her first three years, indicating that while the pace may be slowing, there remains broad-based support for national, participatory conferences. In terms of sheer numbers – that is, the numbers of people, conferences and issues discussed – the Lula and Rousseff administrations have been ground-breaking in their championing of participation.

Closer inspection, on the other hand, reveals the practical limitations of this participation. Baiocchi, Braathen and Teixeira conclude that the national-level participatory efforts were 'much less radical than those experienced at the local level' (ibid.: 235), and add, 'The Lula government did not have a clear strategy for participatory democracy, and perhaps more important, it has not enhanced any discussion of passive v. active conceptions of society participation in government' (ibid.: 235). Yet despite the fact that the massive mobilisation of the population had apparently negligible practical influence on federal government policy, Baiocchi, Braathen and Teixeira observe that:

> Lula's government was much more open to social movements than previous governments. Although few concrete policies were introduced, the 'ritual' of going to Brasilia to attend meetings, councils and conferences has had a positive effect in comparison with the various forms of disqualification, if not repression, that they were subject to under previous presidents. (ibid.: 236)

Yet what the authors did not observe is that the recognition of participants – understood here as part of a broader 'politics of recognition' in which the Workers' Party was engaged (Krischke 2004) – is an almost inevitable consequence of any formal participatory venture. Participatory reforms might be radical or conservative, empowering or co-optative, but the participants will almost always receive some kind of formal recognition from the state as legitimate actors in the business of government.

This is a political dividend enjoyed by progressive and participatory administrations whose terms of reference are perhaps not the high ideals of participatory democracy, but rather a historical backdrop of authoritarian and populist government. Any concession from on high – whether it be policies or investments, or recognition and validation – can be, and often is, interpreted as a social gain. The influence of civil society over government policy and decision-making might be episodic or negligible, and yet government officials can point to histories of exclusion, and to former mayors, as Avamileno was wont to say, 'who would rarely come out to this part of the city'.[1] Indeed, the evaluative quandary of citizen participation is that participation always provides something, whether that is a new proximity to power-holders, recognition of the poor, information and education or some measure of control over policies and investments. It is why the selectivity involved in formulating the research approach in the study and evaluation of participatory democracy is so important. Additionally, it is also why the believers in participatory democracy can always find some justification for their commitment. That is not to denigrate or belittle the social gains that they indicate. Recognition is important; and even having face-to-face contact can help attune power holders to the existence and needs of the popular classes. These are real, legitimate gains. But they do pose an evaluative problem, and not only for academics, for whom the selective framing of the research problem can indelibly affect the evaluation of the participatory institution.

I now turn to examine the local branch of the Workers' Party in Santo André, which has not been spared many of the changes experienced by the party at the national level.

The Workers' Party and Participatory Democracy in Santo André

In my interview with the then president of the Workers' Party in Santo André, Tiago Nogueira, I asked about the de-radicalisation of the party:

> V.A.: In the academic literature abroad there is a tendency to observe that the Workers' Party has moderated. Do you think that the party has changed?
>
> T.N.: Yes. The Workers' Party was [at the beginning] just attached to social movements, and had almost no institutional presence. When after 1988 the party started to win dozens of mayoral, state and now federal government elections, we started to have a much more institutional character (*cara*) and have less to do with the social movement. It is not that we do not have [a presence in the social movement], but you have, I will say it but it might sound strong, a certain 'co-optation'. The director

of an NGO, or of a popular movement, she comes to the administration. So rather than being there struggling [with organising the popular movement], she ends up giving an explanation: 'It can't be implemented as you'd like [the demand the popular movement wants], so there has to be a bit of patience'. So there is a certain moderation of the militancy of the Workers' Party – this is real, I cannot deny it. It would be correct if we had a socialist strategy, I believe in this. We have to have one foot in the institutional and one in the social movement, 'a foot in each canoe', and have a larger objective, which is the transformation of things. That is the radicalisation of democracy, to be able to emancipate people. So I would say that today we suffer from a process of moderation.

If Tiago's ideological beliefs derive from 'the soul' of the Workers' Party, to borrow Singer's phrase, that was born in Sion College, he also acknowledges another, emergent and increasingly pragmatic soul of the party at the local level. A brief comparison of Workers' Party propaganda confirms that party rhetoric has also clearly moderated. One small but highly visible example of de-radicalisation is the administration's motto. During Celso Daniel's first term in office, the local administration borrowed the expression of French Marxist Henri Lefebvre that had been adopted by the Urban Reform Movement: 'Right to the City'. The slogan of the second Avamileno term, in contrast, was the more instrumentalist and pragmatic: 'A New Time to do More'. The rhetoric and high ideology that had disappeared from Lula's presidential campaigns had, by Daniel's third term and the administration of his immediate successor, João Avamileno, similarly faded from the official discourse of the Workers' Party government of Santo André.

Workers' Party rule in Santo André was interrupted when Dr Aidan Ravin, of the centre-right Partido Trabalhista Brasileiro (Brazilian Labour Party) won power in 2008. Ravin dissolved the PB and several other participatory forums that were enacted by the Daniel and Avamileno administrations. However, the management policy councils were legal entities that could not be so easily disbanded. A Workers' Party candidate was restored to mayoral office when Carlos Grana won power in 2012 as the head of a leftist coalition under a motto – 'The best for Santo André' – that, like the official media statements of the Avamileno administrations, lacked the Marxist hue of Daniel's early years. However, despite the de-radicalisation of rhetoric, there was a renewed attempt to refigure and broaden the scope of some of the city's participatory institutions. For instance, the PB, reintroduced with 20 regions rather than 19, was expanded in three ways. First, participation was permitted as part of the government's multi-year plan that guides and shapes government policy for the entire three-year term in office. Second, a digital presence for the PB was launched, which allows residents to propose and vote on works for their region via the internet. Third, participatory budgeting for children was launched in 2013, a programme which involved 35,000 children, who expressed through music and drawing what they would like for the city. Two representatives per school were elected who would report to their classmates on the progress of works that they presented at the regular meetings of the PB.[2] The expansion and development of the PB is suggestive of the place of participation in the imaginary of Workers' Party activists and officials, for whom it serves as the distinguishing characteristic of the party. Yet the return to participatory governance has gone hand in hand with a much more frank representation of the contingent role of participation in the Grana administration. For instance, in the first edition of *Nossa Santo André* (Our Santo André), a government newsletter published in the first months of Grana's administration, the editorial observes that participation remains:

> [the] mark and method of the democratic governments [of the Workers' Party], but that does not mean that the government abandons its role, but rather [it] *takes into consideration* the view of the population, which *can contribute suggestions* that serve to improve the quality of life [in the city].[3]

If the recent expansion of citizen participation in Santo André has coincided with a more circumspect attitude towards devolving or sharing power with the population, then it coincides with a trend begun in the Daniel years. That is, most of the existing participatory institutions in Santo André, including the PB, the HC and the UDC, were developed during or after Celso Daniel's second administration, just as the Worker's Party's socialist discourse and the aim of radical cultural change was fading from view. In this way the administration in Santo André shares an important characteristic of participatory reform at the national level (see Baiocchi et al. 2012), namely that the impulse to create participatory forums en masse was paired with a negligible commitment to sharing or devolving state power to participatory institutions.

This proliferation of participatory institutions enables the two souls of the Workers' Party to live side by side. It permits Workers' Party governments to occupy a valued discursive space, to cast its political leaders as nurturing and benevolent, and to position the party as advancing participatory reform over new policy-making and administrative terrain. Meanwhile, institutions are created out of a formally consistent symbolic order that have highly variable practical effects and influence over state action (see Herzfeld 1992: 28). In such a context it becomes particularly important to avoid confusing terminology, and to disentangle the rhetoric of participation and the practical possibilities of citizens' influence. In this book I have shown how participatory institutions not only mask 'the political under the cloak of neutrality' (Shore & Wright 2003: 7), for they also disguise state power under the cloak of a participatory rhetoric that is substantiated through bringing together state and community actors in ritualised social practices. As Michael Herzfeld notes, the 'maintenance of power relies on the reification of meaning through its conflation with form' (Herzfeld 1992: 120). Perhaps the greatest risk is thus that participation becomes identified, in the public imaginary, with conservative social forms that offer little real opportunity for citizen control over state decision-making. Critical scholarship has an important role in contrasting the rhetoric of participation with the play of power in instances of participatory democracy, and ensuring that unequal power relations do not become part of the uninterrogated domain of assumed, everyday knowledge.

Coda

Social activists in Santo André find themselves in a position that is perhaps quite similar to that of many of their counterparts in Brazil and Latin America. While they may be critical of the city's participatory institutions, they stop short of condemning them completely. Even those who describe them as 'farcical', 'cosmetic' or 'controlling' still find the proximity and access to state actors and decision-making processes preferable to the alternative. The city's participatory institutions, though far from ideal, are grudgingly accepted, for they provide recognition, information and a tenuous and qualified kind of influence over local government policy and decision-making.

Even though state representatives pushed through their favoured demands in the PB, civil society was still able to select many of the priorities from which those demands were chosen. The population still had an influence on state investment, albeit more indirect than was often touted by the official rhetoric. In the UDC, although there was little real influence, citizens still had access to official decision-making processes and information about legislative change. Finally, while the HC had little by way of resources or administrative influence, it still provided a vital forum for civic associations to discuss their issues, to procure advice from administrative staff and to build relationships and share information. The imperfections and contradictions of Santo André's participatory institutions were plain to see, and yet they still provided important means for addressing social issues with wider public involvement than was the historical norm.

Much of this book has focused on the formal spaces of participation. But there is also a more pervasive sociality of activism that endures, and indeed thrives, in the everyday interactions and discussions between community actors, public servants and elected officials, and that percolates into the arenas of formal politics in ways that are hard to detect. In these dense webs of socio-political relationships the lines between the state, civil society, community organisations and the Workers' Party at times become impossibly blurred. Indeed, it is a paradox of participation that it is precisely in those spaces where deliberation is held to take place that ideal forms of government are paraded and thereby preserved, and where, at the same time, imperatives of public performances impel administrative representatives to appear cohesive and hierarchically organised. Participatory forums, that is, become a space where an imagined socio-political reality is projected, and in which state and society are cast as two elements of a dyadic relationship, with one subordinate to the other. It may be hard for participatory democracy to thrive in a hierarchical society, but that is precisely the challenge that faces those who yet believe in the promise of participation. For the dream to be renewed and to take shape, it will have to fashion a set of organisational and cultural materials that are not so indebted to the existing political order.

Notes

Introduction

1. The football team is so-called after the Portuguese explorer João Ramalho who founded a small settlement, Santo André da Borda do Campo, from which the modern city derives its name.
2. All translations in this book are my own.
3. I recognise that Handelman's theorisation of public events was an attempt to develop conceptual alternatives to ritual (Handelman 2006). However, I find his description of the form of public events useful for the framework used in this book, and Catherine Bell's theory of ritualisation (Bell 1992, 2009) helpful for developing a diachronic approach to citizen participation. Here is not the place to evaluate the relative merits of Handelman's conceptual moves.

Chapter 1

1. Health Councils are the foremost exception to this rule and have a tripartite representative system. Half of their participants must be made up of services users. The other half is divided equally between government agents and private health providers.
2. The actual wording in the Constitution is not 'right to the city', but rather 'to guarantee the well-being of its inhabitants', which largely mirrored the content of the MNRU's demand.
3. 'Estatuto da Cidade' ('Statute of the City'), Federal Law No. 10.257/0, 10 July 2001.
4. Floor area ratio is used in urban planning regulations to control housing density. It refers to the ratio between the total floor area of the building, normally measured in square meters, and the space of the plot on which it is erected. A ratio of 1:1 means, for example, that a one-storey building can be built over the entire surface of the plot.
5. The territory of the city was divided, for the PB, into 18 regions between 1997 and 1999, but from 1999 to 2000 the number of regions rose to 19 (Pontual 2000: 163). Since 2013, this number has risen to 20.

Chapter 2

1. Pseudonyms are used for all participants in this study, including the public servants and political appointees who work in the administration. The gender of research participants may also have been changed to further protect their identity. Real names are only used for elected officials, such as the mayor and deputy mayor, political party officials who chose to have their name disclosed,

and other public officials who did not directly take part in the study but whose name is included due to their historical role in the administration.
2. A word of clarification may be necessary concerning the MBC and the PB. As mentioned in Chapter 1, the MBC is the chief decision-making organisation of the PB that consists of both civil society and government representatives. At times in the text it is necessary to specifically refer to the MBC, since it had a separate stream of meetings and particular rites of membership, while at other times it is necessary to refer to the PB as a whole. In this sense it is different from the other two participatory institutions examined here, since the analysis of the HC and the UDC focuses on their monthly assemblies and does not frequently refer to the meetings of their constituent organisations.
3. Throughout the text I use an unusual term for the research subjects of this book. I use the expression 'fieldwork colleagues', preferring it to the more common terms 'research informants' or 'key informants'. That is because the term 'informants' implies a discrete and unilateral relationship. By using the expression 'fieldwork colleagues' I hope to convey what was a more reciprocal, collegial and variegated set of relationships than is suggested by the popular alternatives.
4. Another regional representative on the MBC, José, for example, far from being an ambitious community leader, was nominated to the MBC seemingly by accident. During the election process in his region, a friend of his told him to go to the front of the hall where he was nominated, then seconded. Not only was José's election to the MBC entirely unplanned, he was also spontaneously elected as a representative to the Pastoral de Saúde. Although José's experience of sequentially unplanned appointments was unique, the difference between the two cases does show how diverse the election processes were for different councillors of the MBC.
5. The minutes of the HC and the UDC attest to this similarity.
6. UDC, 'Internal Regulations of the Municipal Council for Urban Policy', meeting minutes of the first extraordinary meeting of the UDC, 23 February 2005, chap. 4, art. 16.
7. It is possible that the vice-president willingly renounced the opportunity to act as the chairperson in the absence of the council president. Yet this is still an aspect of the informal power of senior government officials, insofar as the management of the participatory assemblies was perhaps easier, less challenging and more convenient than as was the case for civil society participants.
8. MBC, 'Internal Regulations of the Council of the Participatory Budget', meeting minutes of the first extraordinary meeting of the UDC, 12 June 2007, chap. 3, art. 3.

Chapter 4

1. UDC, 'Internal Regulations of the Municipal Council for Urban Policy', meeting minutes of the first extraordinary meeting of the UDC, 23 February 2005, chap. 3.

2. See UDC, 'Internal Regulations of the Municipal Council for Urban Policy', meeting minutes of the first extraordinary meeting of the UDC, 23 February 2005, chap. 3, art. 11.
3. Municipality of Santo André, 'Santo André City Master Plan', Law No. 8.696 2004, preamble and art. 1.
4. Municipality of Santo André, 'Municipal Decree No. 15.561', 30 May 2007, art. 1.
5. Included in these items were: a clarification over the regulatory processes necessary for funds to be disbursed to civic associations, a summary of the funds destined for works carried out by civic associations in past years, and a clarification over the ways in which municipally funded investments can be carried out by associations.
6. For example, an investment of R$100,000.00 was approved for works sponsored by SERVCOOP (the council president's organisation). During fieldwork, the exchange rate between the Brazilian real and the US dollar was R$1 to US$0.56.
7. I was unable to ascertain the exact amount of the municipal housing fund. However, the income for the fund controlled by the HC over the period 2005 to 2008 was forecast at R$123,525.25 (US$69,174.14) per year (PMSA 2006: 223).

Chapter 5

1. Indeed, perhaps it is the burden of public participation that leads to such different evaluations from government and civil society councillors. For example, in Silvana Tótora and Vera Chaia's comparative study of management policy councils, government councillors from São Paulo and Santo André's education and health councils believed the government had much greater commitment to the councils and that the councils had more influence over government affairs than their civil society counterparts (Tótora and Chaia 2002: 91–92).
2. Bianca is here criticising the administration for accessing money that had been earmarked for housing and under the control of the HC in order to fund works that were nominated at the PB. That is, she is criticising the administration for not exclusively using money from general revenue.
3. The senior officers in the administration are appointed by the mayor and are often connected to the mayor's political party. However, they are tenuously employed because they serve at the pleasure of the mayor, do not have the secure employment rights of public servants, and are often dismissed when a mayor from a competing political party is elected.

Chapter 6

1. Minors are often used by gangs to perform murders, as they are not subject to the harsh penalties and long prison sentences that apply to adults.

2. A large amount has been written on Celso Daniel's death in the press. See e.g. H. Freitas and Marina Novaes, 'Promotor diz que Celso Daniel foi morto porque "sabia demais"', *Terra*, 10 May 2012 (available at: http://noticias.terra.com.br/brasil/policia/promotor-diz-que-celso-daniel-foi-morto-porque-sabia-demais, 42cb0a43aa1da310VgnCLD200000bbcceb0aRCRD.html, accessed 2 February 2010), and the editorial 'Caso Celso Daniel: 10 anos, oito mortes e uma dúvida', *Repórter Diário*, 19 January 2012 (available at: http://www.reporterdiario.com.br/noticia/328360/caso-celso-daniel-10-anos-oito-mortes-e-uma-duvida/, accessed 13 January 2013).
3. See 'O Mandante e o Coveiro', *Jornal Opção*, 21 April 2012 (available at: http://www.jornalopcao.com.br/posts/reportagens/o-mandante-e-o-coveiro, accessed 13 January 2013).
4. The Department of Political and Social Order was closed down in 1983. During the period of the authoritarian regime its São Paulo branch was responsible for the torture and murder of dissidents (see Huggins et al. 2002).
5. A pseudonym has been used for this elected official.
6. A common expression of one of my fieldwork colleague's was 'everything's manipulated!'
7. See also the website of the MDF (www.mdf.org.br).

Conclusion

1. This quote is taken from the regional meeting of the PB in Region G, 26 May 2008. But it was also a point made by him and several of his staff on other occasions.
2. *Nossa Santo André*, Edição 1, Ano 1, Informativo 1, 2013, p.1.
3. *Nossa Santo André*, Edição 1, Ano 1, Informativo 1, 2013, p.7, emphasis added.

References

Abers, Rebecca N. (2000) *Inventing Local Democracy: Grassroots Politics in Brazil*. Boulder, CO: Lynne Rienner.

Abers, Rebecca N., Lizandra Serafim & Luciana Tatagiba (2014) 'Repertórios de interação estado-sociedade em um estado heterogêneo: a experiência na era Lula'. *Dados* 57(2): 325–57.

Abravanel, Harry (1983) 'Mediatory Myths in the Service of Organizational Ideology'. In Luis R. Pondy, Peter J. Frost, Gareth Morgan & Thomas C. Dandridge (eds), *Organizational Symbolism*, Vol. 1: *Monographs In Organizational Behavior and Industrial Relations*. Greenwich, CT: JAI Press.

Acioly Jr., Claudio, Andre Herzog, Eduardo Sandino & Victor H. Andrade (2003) *Participatory Budgeting in Santo André: The Challenge of Linking Short-Term Problem Solving with Long-Term Strategic Planning in a Brazilian Municipality*. Rotterdam: IHS.

Adams, Brian (2004) 'Public Meetings and the Democratic Process'. *Public Administration Review* 64(1): 43–54.

Almeida, Antônio de (1992) *Movimentos sociais e história popular: Santo André nos anos 70 e 80*. São Paulo: Editora Marco Zero.

Alvarez, Sonia E. (1993) '"Deepening" Democracy: Popular Movement Networks, Constitutional Reform, and Radical Urban Regimes in Contemporary Brazil'. In Robert Fisher & Joseph Kling (eds), *Mobilizing the Community: Local Politics in the Era of the Global City*. Newbury Park, NJ: Sage.

Amaral, Oswaldo E. (2003) *A estrela não é mais vermelha*. São Paulo: Garçoni.

Angell, Alan (1998) 'The Left in Latin America Since c. 1920'. In Leslie Bethell (ed.), *Latin America: Politics and Society Since 1930*. Cambridge: Cambridge University Press.

Apthorpe, Raymond (1997) 'Writing Development Policy and Policy Analysis Plain or Clear: On Language, Genre and Power'. In Chris Shore and Susan Wright (eds), *Anthropology of Policy: Critical Perspectives on Governance and Power*. London: Routledge.

Arias, Enrique D., Daniel M. Goldstein & Neil L. Whitehead (2010) 'Violent Pluralism: Understanding the New Democracies of Latin America'. In Enrique D. Arias, Daniel M. Goldstein & Neil L. Whitehead (eds), *Violent Democracies in Latin America*. Durham, NC: Duke University Press.

Arretche, Marta T.S. (1999) 'Políticas sociais no Brasil: descentralização em um estado federativo'. *Revista Brasileira de Ciencias Sociais* 14(40): 111–41.

—— (2010) 'Federalismo e igualdade territorial: uma contradição em termos?' *Dados* 53(3): 587–620.

Assies, Willem (1994) 'Urban Social Movements in Brazil: A Debate and its Dynamics'. *Latin American Perspectives* 21(81): 81–105.

Avritzer, Leonardo (1997) 'Um desenho institucional para o novo associativismo'. *Lua Nova* 39: 149–74.

—— (2002a) *Democracy and the Public Space in Latin America*. Princeton: Princeton University Press.

—— (2002b) 'Modelos de deliberação democrática: uma análise do orçamento participativo no Brasil'. In Boaventura de Sousa Santos (ed.), *Democratizar a democracia*. Rio de Janeiro: Civilização Brasileira.

—— (2003) 'Reflexões teóricas sobre o orçamento participativo'. In Leonardo Avritzer & Zander Navarro (eds), *A inovação democrática no Brasil*. São Paulo: Cortez Editora.

—— (2006) 'Reforma política e participação no Brasil'. In Leonardo Avritzer & Fátima Anastasia (eds), *Reforma política no Brasil*. Belo Horizonte: Editora UFMG.

—— (2009) *Participatory Institutions in Democratic Brazil*. Baltimore: Johns Hopkins University Press.

Avritzer, Leonardo, & Brian Wampler (2004) 'Participatory Publics: Civil Society and New Institutions in Democratic Brazil'. *Comparative Politics* 36: 291–312.

Baba, Marietta (1989) 'Organizational Culture: Revisiting the Small-Society Metaphor'. *Anthropology of Work Review* 10(3): 7–10.

Bachrach, Peter, & Morton E. Baratz (1962) 'Two Faces of Power'. *American Political Science Review* (56)4: 947–52.

Bailey, F.G. (1965) 'Decisions by Consensus in Councils and Committees'. In Max Gluckman & Fred Eggan (eds), *Political Systems and the Distribution of Power*. London: Tavistock.

Baiocchi, Gianpaolo (2003) 'Emergent Public Spheres: Talking Politics in Participatory Governance'. *American Sociological Review* 68(1): 52–74.

—— (2005) *Militants and Citizens: The Politics of Participatory Democracy in Porto Alegre*. Stanford: Stanford University Press.

—— (2006) 'Inequality and Innovation: Decentralization as an Opportunity Structure in Brazil'. In Pranab Bardhan & Dilip Mookherjee (eds), *Decentralization and Local Governance in Developing Countries: A Comparative Perspective*. Cambridge, MA: MIT Press.

Baiocchi, Gianpaolo, Einar Braathen and Ana C. Teixeira (2012) 'Transformation Institutionalized? Making Sense of Participatory Democracy in the Lula era'. In Kristian Stokke and Olle Törnquist (eds), *Democratization in the Global South: The Importance of Transformative Politics*. London: Palgrave Macmillan.

Baiocchi, Gianpaolo, Patrick Heller & Marcelo Silva (2011) *Bootstrapping Democracy: Transforming Local Governance and Civil Society in Brazil*. Stanford: Stanford University Press.

Banck, Geert (1990) 'Cultural Dilemmas Behind Strategy: Brazilian Neighbourhood Movements and Catholic Discourse'. *European Journal of Development Research* 2(1): 65–88.

Barber, Benjamin (1984) *Strong Democracy: Participatory Politics for a New Age*. Berkeley: University of California Press.

Barczak, Monica (2001) 'Representation by Consultation? The Rise of Direct Democracy in Latin America'. *Latin American Politics and Society* 43(3): 37–59.

Bell, Catherine (1992) *Ritual Theory, Ritual Practice*. New York: Oxford University Press.

—— (2009) *Ritual: Perspectives and Dimensions*. New York: Oxford University Press.

Bevilaqua, Ciméa (2003) 'Etnografia do estado: algumas questões metodológicas e éticas'. *Campos* 3: 51–64.

Bevilaqua, Ciméa, & Piero de C. Leirner (2000) 'notas sobre a análise antropológica de setores do estado brasileiro'. *Revista de Antropologia* 43(2): 105–40.

Bloch, Maurice (1989) *Ritual, History and Power: Selected Papers in Anthropology*. London: Athlone Press.

Bourdieu, Pierre (1977) *Outline of a Theory of Practice*. Cambridge: Cambridge University Press.

Brandão, Marco Antonio (2003) *O socialismo democrático do partido dos trabalhadores: a história de uma utopia (1979–1994)*. São Paulo: Annablume.

Bruce, Iain (2008) *The Real Venezuela: Making Socialism in the Twenty-First Century*. London: Pluto Press.

Caldeira, Teresa P. (2000) *City of Walls: Crime, Segregation, and Citizenship in São Paulo*. Berkeley: University of California Press.

Caldeira, Teresa P., & James Holston (2014) 'Participatory Urban Planning in Brazil'. *Urban Studies* 52(11): 1947–61.

Cameron, Maxwell A., Eric Hershberg & Kenneth E. Sharpe (2012a) 'Voice and Consequence: Direct Participation and Democracy in Latin America'. In Maxwell A. Cameron, Eric Hershberg & Kenneth E. Sharpe (eds), *New Institutions for Participatory Democracy in Latin America: Voice and Consequence*. New York: Palgrave Macmillan.

—— (2012b) 'Institutionalised Voice in Latin American Democracies'. In Maxwell A. Cameron, Eric Hershberg & Kenneth E. Sharpe (eds), *New Institutions for Participatory Democracy in Latin America: Voice and Consequence*. New York: Palgrave Macmillan.

Cardoso, Ruth L. (1983) 'Movimentos sociais urbanos: balanço crítico'. In Bernardo Sorj & Maria H.T. Almeida (eds), *Sociedade e política no Brasil pós-64*. São Paulo: Editora Brasiliense.

Carvalho, José M. (1999) *Pontos e bordados*. Belo Horizonte: Editora UFMG.

Carvalho, Sonia N. (2001) 'Estatuto da cidade: aspectos politicos do plano diretor'. *São Paulo em Perspectiva* 15(4): 130–35.

Castilho, Sérgio R., Antonio C. Lima & Carla C. Teixeira, eds. (2014) *Antropologia das práticas de poder: reflexões etnográficas entre burocratas, elites e corporações*. Rio de Janeiro: Contra Capa.

Chauí, Marilena (2000) *Cultura e democracia: o discurso competente e outras falas*. São Paulo: Editora Cortez.

Collins, Randall (2004) *Interaction Ritual Chains*. Princeton: Princeton University Press.

Cornwall, Andrea (2004) 'Spaces for Transformation? Reflections on Issues of Power and Difference in Participation in Development'. In Samuel Hickey & Giles Mohan (eds), *Participation: From Tyranny to Transformation?* London: Zed Books.

Cornwall, Andrea, & Karen Brock (2005) 'What do Buzzwords do for Development Policy? A Critical Look at "Participation", "Empowerment" and "Poverty Reduction"'. *Third World Quarterly* 26(7): 1043–60.

Cornwall, Andrea, & Vera Schatten Coelho (2004) 'Spaces for Change? The Politics of Participation in New Democratic Arenas'. In Andrea Cornwall and Vera Schatten Coelho (eds), *Spaces for Change? The Politics of Participation in New Democratic Arenas*. London: Zed Books.

Cornwall, Andrea, Jorge Romano & Alex Shankland (2008) 'Brazilian Experiences of Participation and Citizenship: A Critical Look'. IDS Discussion Paper 389. Brighton: Institute of Development Studies, University of Sussex.

Cornwall, Andrea, & Alex Shankland (2013) 'Cultures of Politics, Spaces of Power: Contextualizing Brazilian Experiences of Participation'. *Journal of Political Power* 6(2): 309–33.

Cymbalista, Renato, & Paula F. Santoro (2009) 'O plano diretor na luta pelo direito à cidade'. In Renato Cymbalista and Paula F. Santoro (eds), *Planos diretores: processos e aprendizados*. São Paulo: Publicações Pólis.

Dagnino, Evelina, Alberto J. Olvera & Aldo Panfichi (2006) 'Para uma outra leitura da disputa pela construção democrática na América Latina'. In Evelina Dagnino, Alberto J. Olvera & Aldo Panfichi (eds), *A disputa pela construção democrática na América Latina*. São Paulo: Paz e Terra.

Dahl, Robert (2000) *On Democracy*. New Haven: Yale University Press.

DaMatta, Roberto (1986) *Explorações: ensaios de sociologia interpretativa*. Rio de Janeiro: Editora Rocco.

Damo, Arlei S. (2006) 'A peça orçamentária: os sentidos da participação na política a partir do OP porto-alegrense'. In Claudia Fonseca and Jurema Brites (eds), *Etnografias da participação*. Santa Cruz do Sul: EDUNISC.

Daniel, Bruno (2003) 'O orçamento participativo no seu devido lugar: limites colocados por seu desenho institucional e pelo context brasileiro-reflexões sobre a experiência de Santo André nos períodos 1989–1992 e 1997–2000'. Ph.D. diss. São Paulo: Catholic University of São Paulo.

Daniel, Celso (1988) 'Sociedade: participação popular'. *Revista Teoria e Debate*. Available at: http://www2.fpa.org.br/portal, accessed 9 March 2008.

—— (1990) 'As administrações democráticas e populares'. *Espaço e Debates* 30: 11–27.

—— (1996) *Poder local e socialismo*. São Paulo: Editora Fundação Perseu Abramo.

—— (2000) 'Conselhos, esfera pública e co-gestão'. *Revista Pólis* 37: 121–33.

Das, Veena, & Deborah Poole, eds. (2004) *Anthropology in the Margins of the State*. Oxford: Oxford University Press.

Denaldi, Rosana, & Solange G. Dias (2003) 'Limites da regularização fundiária: a experiência do município de Santo André'. In Pedro Abramo (ed.), *A cidade da informalidade: o desafio das cidades latino-americanas*. Rio de Janeiro: FAPERJ.

Dias, Solange G. (2001) 'Democracia representativa x democracia participativa: participação popular no plano local e emergência de um novo paradigm democratico'. Masters diss. São Paulo: University of São Paulo.

Draibe, Sonia (1998) 'A nova institucionalidade do sistema brasileiro de políticas sociais: os conselhos nacionais de políticas sociais'. Cadernos de Pesquisa do NEPP 35. Campinas: Unicamp.

Dulles, John W.F. (1973) *Anarquistas e comunistas no Brasil*. Rio de Janeiro: Editora Nova Fronteira.

Durkheim, Emile (1965 [1912]) *The Elementary Forms of Religious Life*, trans. Joseph Ward Swain. New York: Free Books.

Edwards, Jeanette (2005) 'Idioms of Bureaucracy and Informality in a Local Housing Aid Office'. In Susan Wright (ed.), *The Anthropology of Organizations*. London: Routledge.

Fassin, Didier (2000) 'La supplique: stratégies rhétoriques et constructions identitaires dans les demandes d'aide d'urgence'. *Annales* 55(5): 955–81.

Feltran, Gabriel de S. (2007) 'Vinte anos depois: a construção democratic brasileira vista da periferia de São Paulo'. *Lua Nova* 72: 83–114.

Ferguson, James, & Akhil Gupta (2002) 'Spatializing States: Towards an Ethnography of Neoliberal Governmentality'. *American Ethnologist* 29(4): 981–1002.

Fernandes, Florestan (2005 [1975]) *A revolução burgesa no Brasil: ensaio de interpretação sociológica*, 5th edn. São Paulo: Editora Globo.

Flores, Fidel P., Clayton M. Cunha Filho & André Luiz Coelho (2011) 'Democratic Theory, Representation and Participatory Institutions in Bolivia, Ecuador and Venezuela'. Paper presented at the European Consortium for Political Research General Conference, University of Iceland, Reykjavik, 25–27 August.

Flyvberg, Bent (1998) *Rationality and Power: Democracy in Practice*. Chicago: University of Chicago Press.

Foweraker, Joe (2001) 'Grassroots Movements and Political Activism in Latin America: A Critical Comparison of Chile and Brazil'. *Journal of Latin American Studies* 33(4): 839–65.

French, John D. (1992) *The Brazilian Workers' ABC: Class Conflict and Alliances in Modern São Paulo*. Chapel Hill: University of North Carolina Press.

French, John D., & Alexandre Fontes (2005) 'Another World is Possible: The Rise of the Brazilian Workers' Party and the Prospects for Lula's Government'. *Labor: Studies in Working Class History of the Americas* 2(3): 13–31.

Friendly, Abigail (2013) 'The Right to the City: Theory and Practice in Brazil'. *Planning Theory and Practice* 14(2): 158–79.

Fung, Archon (2003) 'Recipes for Public Spheres: Eight Institutional Design Choices and Their Consequences'. *Journal of Political Philosophy* 11(3): 338–67.

Futrell, Robert (1999) 'Performative Governance: Impression Management, Teamwork, and Conflict Containment in City Commission Proceedings'. *Journal of Contemporary Ethnography* 27(4): 494–529.
Gaiarsa, Octavio A. (1968) *A cidade que dormiu três séculos*. Santo André: Editora Prefeitura Municipal de Santo André.
—— (1991) *Santo André ontem, hoje e amanhã*. Santo André: Editora Prefeitura Municipal de Santo André.
Garsten, Christina, & Anette Nyqvist (eds). 2013. 'Entries: Engaging Organisational Worlds'. In Christina Garsten and Anette Nyqvist (eds), *Organizational Anthropology: Doing Ethnography in and among Complex Organizations*. New York: Pluto Press.
Gay, Robert (1994) *Popular Organization and Democracy in Rio de Janeiro: A Tale of Two Favelas*. Philadelphia: Temple University Press.
—— (1998) 'Rethinking Clientelism: Demands, Discourses and Practices in Contemporary Brazil'. *European Review of Latin American and Caribbean Studies* 65: 7–24.
—— (1999) 'The Broker and the Thief: A Parable (Reflections on Popular Politics in Brazil)'. *Luso Brazilian Review* 36(1): 49–70.
Geertz, Clifford (1973) *The Interpretation of Cultures*. New York: Basic Books.
Genro, Tarso (2003) 'Crise democrática e democracia direta'. *Democracia e Política* (Series 3) 6: 9–23.
Giddens, Anthony (1979) *Central Problems in Social Theory: Action, Structure and Contradiction in Social Analysis*. London: Macmillan.
—— (1984) *The Constitution of Society: Outline of the Theory of Structuration*. Cambridge: Polity Press.
Gledhill, John (1999) 'Official Masks and Shadow Powers: Towards an Anthropology of the Dark Side of the State'. *Urban Anthropology* 28(3/4): 199–251.
Goffman, Erving (1957) *The Presentation of Self in Everyday Life*. London: Penguin Books.
—— (1963) *Behavior in Public Places: Notes on the Social Organization of Gatherings*. New York: Free Press.
—— (1967) *Interaction Ritual: Essays on Face-to-Face Behavior*. Garden City, NY: Anchor Books.
—— (1969) *Strategic Interaction*. Philadelphia: University of Pennsylvania Press.
Gohn, Maria da G. (1997) *Teorias dos movimentos sociais: paradigmas clássicos e contemporâneos*. São Paulo: Edições Loyola.
—— (2000) 'O papel dos conselhos gestores na gestão urbana'. In Ana C.T. Ribeiro (ed.), *Repensando a experiência urbana na América Latina: questões, conceitos e valores*. Buenos Aires: CLASCO.
—— (2001) *Conselhos gestores e participação sociopolítica*. São Paulo: Cortez Editora.
Goldfrank, Benjamin (2003) 'Making Participation Work in Porto Alegre'. In Gianpaolo Baiocchi (ed.), *Radicals in Power*. London: Zed Books.
—— (2007) 'The Politics of Deepening Local Democracy: Decentralization, Party Institutionalization, and Participation'. *Comparative Politics* 39(2): 147–68.

Goldstein, Daniel (2003) *The Spectacular City: Violence and Performance in Urban Bolivia*. Durham, NC: Duke University Press.
Goldstein, Donna (2003) *Laughter Out of Place: Race, Class, Violence, and Sexuality in a Rio Shantytown*. Berkeley: University of California Press.
Goode, Luke (2005) *Jürgen Habermas: Democracy and the Public Sphere*. London: Pluto Press.
Goodwin, Charles (2009) 'Professional Vision'. In Alessandro Duranti (ed.), *Linguistic Anthropology: A Reader*. Malden, MA: Blackwell.
Gordon, Colin (1991) 'Introduction'. In Graham Burchell, Colin Gordon & Peter Miller (eds), *The Foucault Effect*. Chicago: University of Chicago Press.
Graham, Richard (1990) *Patronage and Politics in Nineteenth-Century Brazil*. Stanford: Stanford University Press.
Hagopian, Frances (1996) *Traditional Politics and Regime Change in Brazil*. Cambridge: Cambridge University Press.
Hall, Edward (1963) 'A System for the Notation of Proxemic Behavior'. *American Anthropologist* 65(5): 1003–26.
—— (1966) *The Hidden Dimension*. New York: Doubleday.
Handelman, Don (1976) 'Re-thinking "Banana-Time"'. *Urban Life* 4(4): 433–48.
—— (1990) *Models and Mirrors: Towards an Anthropology of Public Events*. Cambridge: Cambridge University Press.
—— (2004) *Nationalism and the Israeli State: Bureaucratic Logic in Public Events*. Oxford: Berg.
—— (2006) 'Conceptual Alternatives to Ritual'. In Jens Kreinath, Jan Snoek & Michael Stausberg (eds), *Theorizing Ritual*. Leiden: Brill.
Handelman, Don, & Galina Lindquist, eds. (2005) *Ritual in Its Own Right*. New York: Berghahn.
Hannerz, Ulf (1992) *Cultural Complexity*. New York: Columbia University Press.
Hansen, Thomas B., & Finn Stepputat, eds. (2001) *States of Imagination: Ethnographic Explorations of the Postcolonial State*. Durham, NC: Duke University Press.
Herzfeld, Michael (1992) *The Social Production of Indifference: Exploring the Symbolic Roots of Western Bureaucracy*. New York: Berg.
Hilbert, Richard A. (1987) 'Bureaucracy as Belief, Rationalization as Repair: Max Weber in a Post-Functionalist age'. *Sociological Theory* 5: 70–86.
Holston, James (2008) *Insurgent Citizenship: Disjunctions of Democracy and Modernity in Brazil*. Princeton: Princeton University Press.
Huggins, Martha K., Mika Haritos-Fatouros & Philip G. Zimbardo (2002) *Violence Workers: Police Torturers and Murderers Reconstruct Brazilian Atrocities*. Berkeley: University of California Press.
Hunter, Wendy (2005) 'The Normalization of an Anomaly: The Workers' Party in Brazil'. *World Politics* 59: 440–75.
IBGE (Instituto Brasileiro de Geografia e Estatística) (2003) 'Perfil dos municípios brasileiros – gestão pública, 2001'. Rio de Janeiro: IBGE. Available at: http://www.ibge.gov.br, accessed 20 November 2008.

—— (2010) 'Perfil dos municípios brasileiros – gestão pública, 2009'. Rio de Janeiro: IBGE. Available at: http://www.ibge.gov.br, accessed 2 August 2011.

Irazábal, Clara (2005) *City Making and Urban Governance in the Americas: Curitiba and Portland*. Aldershot: Ashgate Publishing.

Jacobi, Pedro, & Edson Nunes (1983) 'Movimentos populares urbanos, participação e democracia'. *Ciências Sociais Hoje* 2: 25–62.

Jara, Felipe J. Hevia de la, & Ernesto I. Vera (2012) 'Constrained Participation: The Impacts of Consultative Councils on National-Level Policy in Mexico'. In Maxwell A. Cameron, Eric Hershberg & Kenneth E. Sharpe (eds), *New Institutions for Participatory Democracy in Latin America: Voice and Consequence*. New York: Palgrave Macmillan.

Jessop, Bob (2008) *State Power: A Strategic-Relational Approach*. Cambridge: Polity Press.

Junior, Caio P. (1965 [1942]) *Formação do Brasil contemporâneo*, 8th edn. São Paulo: Editora Brasiliense.

Keck, Margaret (1992) *The Workers' Party and Democratization in Brazil*. New Haven: Yale University Press.

Kertzer, David I. (1988) *Ritual, Politics and Power*. New Haven: Yale University Press.

Klink, Jeoren, & Rosana Denaldi (2011) 'O plano diretor participativo e a produção social do espaço: o caso de Santo André (São Paulo)'. *Scripta Nova*. Available at: http://www.ub.es/geocrit/sn/sn-382.htm, accessed 28 November 2012.

Koster, Martijn (2012) 'Mediating and Getting "Burnt" in the Gap: Politics and Brokerage in a Recife Slum, Brazil'. *Critique of Anthropology* 32(4): 479–97.

Koziol, Geoffrey (1992) *Begging Pardon and Favor: Ritual and Political Order in Early Medieval France*. Ithaca, NY: Cornell University Press.

Krischke, Paulo (2004) 'Políticas de reconhecimento uma novidade das políticas sociais do PT?' *Civitas* 4(2): 337–52.

Landim, Leilah (1993) 'A invenção das ONGs: do service invisível à profissão impossível'. Ph.D. diss. Rio de Janeiro: Federal University of Rio de Janeiro.

Lavalle, Adrian Gurza (2011) 'Após a participação: nota introdutória'. *Lua Nova* 84: 13–24.

Lazar, Sian (2008) *El Alto, Rebel City: Self and Citizenship in Andean Bolivia*. Durham, NC: Duke University Press.

Leal, Victor Nunes (1975 [1948]) *Coronelismo, enxada e voto*. São Paulo: Alfa-Omega.

Lefebvre, Henri (1968) *Le droit a la ville*. Paris: Anthropos.

Lincoln, Bruce (1994) *Authority: Corruption and Corrosion*. Chicago: University of Chicago Press.

Lipsky, Michael (1980) *Street-Level Bureaucrats: Dilemmas of the Individual in Public Services*. New York: Russell Sage Foundation.

Lüchmann, Lígia H.H. (2002) 'Possibilidades e limites da democracia deliberativa: a experiência do orçamento participativo de Porto Alegre'. Ph.D. diss. Campinas: State University of Campinas.

Lucio Cardoso, Adauto (2003) 'A cidade e seu estatuto: uma avaliação urbanística do estatuto da cidade'. In Luiz C. de Q. Ribeiro and Adauto Lucio Cardoso (eds), *Reforma urbana e gestão democrática: promessas e desafios do estatuto da cidade.* Rio de Janeiro: Editora Revan.

Lukes, Steven (2005) *Power: A Radical View*, 2nd edn. New York: Palgrave Macmillan.

Lupien, Pascal (2015) 'Mechanisms for Popular Participation and Discursive Constructions of Citizenship'. *Citizenship Studies* 19(3/4): 1–17.

McCarthy, Michael M. (2012) 'The Possibilities and Limits of Politicised Participation: Community Councils, Coproduction, and Poder Popular in Chávez's Venezuela'. In Maxwell A. Cameron, Eric Hershberg & Kenneth E. Sharpe (eds), *New Institutions for Participatory Democracy in Latin America: Voice and Consequence.* New York: Palgrave Macmillan.

McComas, Katherine, John C. Besley & Laura W. Black (2010) 'The Rituals of Public Meetings'. *Public Administration Review* 70(1): 122–30.

Mainwaring, Scott (1987) 'Urban Popular Movements, Identity, and Democratization in Brazil'. *Comparative Political Studies* 20(2): 135–9.

—— (2006) 'The Crisis of Representation in the Andes'. *Journal of Democracy* 17(3): 13–27.

Marcus, George E. (2000) 'Introduction'. In George E. Marcus (ed.), *Para-Sites: A Casebook against Cynical Reason.* Chicago: University of Chicago Press.

Maricato, Erminia (2010) 'The Statute of the Peripheral City'. In Celso S. Carvalho and Anaclaudia Rossbach (eds), *The City Statute: A Commentary.* São Paulo: Cities Alliance and Ministry of Cities.

—— (2011) 'A cidade sustentavel'. Paper presented at the 9th National Union Congress for Engineers (CONSEGE), Porto Velho, Rondônia, 7–10 September.

Maya, Margarita L. (2010) 'Caracas: The State and Peoples' Power in the Barrio'. In Jenny Pearce (ed.), *Participation and Democracy in the Twenty-First Century City.* New York: Palgrave Macmillan.

Maya, Margarita L., & Luis E. Lander (2011) 'Participatory Democracy in Venezuela'. In David Smilde and Daniel Hellinger (eds), *Venezuela's Bolivarian Democracy: Participation, Politics, and Culture under Chávez.* Durham, NC: Duke University Press.

MDDF (Movimento de Defesa dos Direitos de Moradores em Favela) (2011) 'Movimento de defesa dos direitos de moradores em favela'. Available at: www.mddf.org.br, accessed 8 November 2011.

Melo, Marcus, & Flavio Rezende (2004) 'Decentralization and Governance in Brazil'. In Joseph Tulchin and Andrew Selee (eds), *Decentralization and Democratic Governance in Latin America.* Washington: Woodrow Wilson Center for Scholars.

Mitchell, Timothy (2006) 'Society, Economy, and the State Effect'. In Aradhana Sharma & Akhil Gupta (eds), *The Anthropology of the State: A Reader.* Malden, MA: Blackwell.

Moisés, José A. (1990) *Cidadania e participação: ensaio sobre o plebiscito, o referendo e a iniciativa popular na nova constituição*. São Paulo: Marco Zero.

Montambeault, Francoise (2011) 'Overcoming Clientelism Through Local Participatory Institutions in Mexico: What Type of Participation?' *Latin American Politics and Society* 53(1): 91–124.

Morton, Gregory Duff (2014) 'Modern Meetings: Participation, Democracy, and the Language Ideology in Brazil's MST Landless Movement'. *American Ethnologist* 41(4): 728–42.

Nicolini, Davide (2012) *Practice Theory, Work, and Organisation: An Introduction*. Oxford: Oxford University Press.

Nogueira, Marco A. (1998) *As possibilidades da política*. São Paulo: Paz e Terra.

Nuijten, Monique (2003) *Power, Community and the State: The Political Anthropology of Organisation in Mexico*. London: Pluto Press.

Nylen, William (2002) 'Testing the Empowerment Thesis: The Participatory Budget in Belo Horizonte and Betim, Brazil'. *Comparative Politics* 34(2): 127–45.

Ortner, Sherry B. (1984) 'Theory in Anthropology Since the Sixties'. *Comparative Studies in Society and History* 26(1): 126–66.

—— (2006) *Anthropology and Social Theory: Culture, Power and the Acting Subject*. Durham, NC: Duke University Press.

Ottmann, Goetz (2006) 'Cidadania mediada : processos de democratização da política municipal no Brasil'. *Novos Estudos* 74: 155–75.

Passarelli, Silvia H., & Rosana Denaldi (2006) 'Evolução urbana e história da habitação em Santo André'. In Rosana Denaldi (ed.), *Plano municipal de habitação*. Santo André: Editora Prefeitura Municipal de Santo André.

Peirano, Mariza (2002) 'A análise antropológica de rituais'. In Mariza Peiran (ed.), *O dito e o fato: ensaios de antropologia dos rituais*. Rio de Janeiro: Relume Dumará.

Pellizzoni, Luigi (2001) 'The Myth of the Best Argument: Power, Deliberation and Reason'. *British Journal of Sociology* 51: 59–86.

Perlman, Janice (2010) *Favela: Four Decades of Living on the Edge in Rio de Janeiro*. New York: Oxford University Press.

Pires, Lilian R.G. Moreira (2007) *Função social da propriedade urbana e o plano diretor*. Belo Horizonte: Editora Fórum.

Pires, Valdemir (2007) 'Controle social da administração pública: entre o político e o econômico'. In Alvaro M. Guedes and Francisco Fonseca (eds), *Controle social da administração pública*. São Paulo: Editora UNESP.

Pontual, Pedro (1998) 'Participação Popular no ABC: experiências e concepções'. Polis Papers No. 3. Available at: http://www.direitoacidade.org.br/publicacoes/participacao-popular-no-abc-experiencias-e-concepcoes/, accessed 7 September 2008.

—— (2000) 'O processo educativo no orçamento participativo: aprendizados dos atores de sociedade civil e do estado'. Ph.D. diss. São Paulo: Catholic University of São Paulo.

Postero, Nancy (2010) 'The Struggle to Create a Radical Democracy in Bolivia'. *Latin American Research Review* 45(S1): 59–78.

Postill, John (2010) 'Introduction: Theorising Media and Practice'. In Birgit Bräuchler and John Postill (eds), *Theorising Media and Practice*. Oxford: Berghahn Books.
PMSA (Prefeitura Municipal de Santo André) (1991) 'Santo André: cidade e imagens'. Santo André: Editora Prefeitura Municipal de Santo André.
—— (1992a) 'Santo André: direito à cidade'. Santo André: Editora Prefeitura Municipal de Santo André.
—— (1992b) 'Santo André: participação popular'. Santo André: Editora Prefeitura Municipal de Santo André.
—— (1999) 'I conferência municipal de cidadania e direitos humanos de Santo André'. Santo André: Editora Prefeitura Municipal de Santo André.
—— (2004) 'Plano diretor participativo de Santo André, 2002/2004: processo de discussão pública e lei comentada'. Santo André: Editora Prefeitura Municipal de Santo André.
—— (2006) 'Plano municipal de habitação'. Santo André: Editora Prefeitura Municipal de Santo André.
Reich, Gary (1998) 'The 1988 Constitution a Decade Later: Ugly Compromises Reconsidered'. *Journal of Interamerican and World Affairs* 40(4): 5–24.
—— (2007) 'Constitutional Coordination in Unstable Party Systems: The Brazilian Constitution of 1988'. *Constitutional Political Economy* 18(3): 177–97.
Remmer, Karen L. (1992) 'The Process of Democratization in Latin America'. *Studies in Comparative International Development* 27: 1–24.
Rezende, Denis A., & Clovis Ultramari (2007) 'Plano diretor e planejamento estratégico municipal: introducção teórico-conceitual'. *RAP Rio de Janeiro* 41(2): 255–71.
Ribeiro, Ana C.T., & Grazia de Grazia (2003) *Experiências de orçamento participativo no Brasil: period de 1997–2000*. São Paulo: Editora Vozes.
Rippy, J. Fred (1966) *British Investments in Latin America*. Hamden: Archon Books.
Rogers, Denns, Jo Beall & Ravi Kanbur (2011) 'Latin American Urban Development in the Twenty-First Century: Towards a Renewed Perspective on the City'. *European Journal of Development Research* 23(4): 550–68.
Rolnik, Raquel, & Nadia Somekh (2000) 'Governar as metrópoles: dilemas da recentralização'. *São Paulo em Perspectiva* 14(4): 83–90.
Roscoe, Paul B. (1993) 'Practice and Political Centralisation: A New Approach to Political Evolution'. *Current Anthropology* 34(2): 111–24.
Sader, Eder (1988) *Quando novos personagens entraram em cena: experiências, falas e lutas dos trabalhadores da Grande São Paulo (1970–80)*. São Paulo: Paz e Terra.
Samuels, David (2004) 'From Socialism to Social Democracy: Party Organization and the Transformation of the Workers' Party in Brazil'. *Comparative Political Studies* (37)9: 999–1024.
Santos, Boaventura de S. (1998) 'Participatory Budgeting in Porto Alegre: Toward a Redistributive Democracy'. *Politics and Society* 26(4): 461–510.
—— (2005) 'Two Democratics, Two Legalities: Participatory Budgeting in Brazil'. In Boaventura de S. Santos and César A. Rodrígues-Garavito (eds), Law and *Glo-*

balization From Below: Towards a Cosmopolitan Legality. Cambridge: Cambridge University Press.

Schatzki, Theodore (1996) *Practices and Actions: A Wittgensteinian Critique of Bourdieu and Giddens*. Cambridge: Cambridge University Press.

—— (1997) 'Practices and Actions: A Wittgensteinian Critique of Bourdieu and Giddens'. *Philosophy of the Social Sciences* 27(3): 283–308.

—— (2001) 'Introduction: Practice Theory'. In Theodore Schatzki, Karin Knorr Cetina & Eike von Savigny (eds), *The Practice Turn in Contemporary Theory*. London: Routledge.

Schönleitner, Günther (2006) 'Between Liberal and Participatory Democracy: Tensions and Dilemmas of Leftist Politics in Brazil'. *Journal of Latin American Studies* 38: 35–63.

Scott, James C. (1990) *Domination and the Arts of Resistance: Hidden Transcripts*. New Haven: Yale University Press.

—— (1998) *Seeing Like a State: How Certain Schemes to Improve the Human Condition Have Failed*. New Haven: Yale University Press.

Scott, John (2001) *Power*. Cambridge: Polity Press.

Sennett, Richard (1980) *Authority*. New York: Vintage Books.

Sharma, Aradhana, & Akhil Gupta, eds. (2006) *The Anthropology of the State: A Reader*. Malden, MA: Blackwell.

Shore, Chris, & Susan Wright (2003) 'Policy: A New Field of Anthropology'. In Chris Shore and Susan Wright (eds), *Anthropology of Policy: Critical Perspectives on Governance and Power*. London: Routledge.

Singer, André (2010) 'A segunda alma do partido dos trabalhadores'. *Novos Estudos* 88: 89–111.

—— (2012) *Os sentidos do Lulismo: reforma gradual e pacto conservador*. São Paulo: Companhia das Letras.

Singer, Paul (1983) 'Movimentos de bairro'. In Paul Singer and Vinicius C. Brant (eds), *São Paulo: o povo em movimento*, 4th edn. Petrópolis: Editora Vozes.

Smith, Aaron, & Bob Stewart (2011) 'Organizational Rituals: Features, Functions and Mechanisms'. *International Journal of Management Reviews* 13: 113–33.

Souza, Claudia V. Cabral de (2007) 'Santo André: instrumentos utilizados na elaboração do plano diretor participativo para viabilizar a participação e a negociação entre os atores'. In Laura Bueno and Renato Cymbalista (eds), *Planos diretores municipais: novos conceitos de planejamento territorial*. São Paulo: Annablume.

Souza, Marcelo Lopes de (1999) *O desafio metropolitano: um estudo sobre a problemática sócio-espacial nas metrópoles brasileiras*. Rio de Janeiro: Bertrand Brasil.

Starbuck, William H. (1982) 'Congealing Oil: Inventing Ideologies to Justify Acting Ideologies Out'. *Journal of Management Studies* 19(1): 1–27.

Stepan, Alfred (1988) *Rethinking Military Politics*. Princeton: Princeton University Press.

Tambiah, Stanley J. (1979) 'A Performative Approach to Ritual'. *Proceedings of the British Academy* 65: 113–69.

Tatagiba, Luciana (2002) 'Os conselhos gestores e a democratização das políticas públicas no Brasil'. In Evelina Dagnino (ed.), *Sociedade civil e espaços públicos no Brasil*. São Paulo: Paz e Terra.

Teixeira, Elenaldo (1996) 'Movimentos sociais e conselhos'. *Cadernos ABONG* 7(15): 7–21.

Toseland, Ronald, & Robert Rivas (2005) *An Introduction to Group Work Practice*. Boston: Allyn and Bacon.

Tótora, Silvana, & Vera Chaia (2002) 'Conselhos municipais: decentralização, participação e limites institucionais'. *Cadernos Metrópole* 8: 69–102.

Turner, Victor (1969) *The Ritual Process: Structure and Anti-Structure*. Chicago: University of Chicago Press.

Van Vree, Wilbert (1999) *Meetings, Manners and Civilization*. London: Leicester University Press.

Vianna, Luiz Werneck (1997) *A revolução passiva: iberismo e americanismo no Brasil*, 2nd edn. Rio de Janeiro: Editora Revan.

Vigevani, Tullo (1989) 'Movimentos sociais na transição brasileira: a dificuldade de elaboração do projeto'. *Lua Nova* 17: 93–109.

Villaça, Flávio (2005) 'As ilusões do plano diretor'. Available at: http://www.flavio-villaca.arq.br/pdf/ilusao_pd.pdf, accessed 2 March 2009.

Wampler, Brian (2007) *Participatory Budgeting in Brazil: Contestation, Cooperation, and Accountability*. University Park: Pennsylvania State University Press.

—— (2008) 'When Does Participatory Democracy Deepen the Quality of Democracy? Lessons from Brazil'. *Comparative Politics* 41(1): 61–81.

Wolf, Eric (2001) *Pathways of Power: Building an Anthropology of the Modern World*. Berkeley: University of California Press.

Wood, Geoffrey (1985) 'The Politics of Development Policy Labelling'. *Development and Change* 16(3): 347–73.

Index

Abers, Rebecca, 5, 17, 174, 181
Accountability, 6, 11
Administrative
    and organisational authority, 1, 13, 45, 112, 126, *see also* state power; ideology, 20, *see also* ideology; structures 55, 115, 172, 175
Alvarez, Sonia, 23
Apthorpe, Raymond, 97
Anthropology of the state, 14
Arretche, Marta, 24
Assemblies. *See* meetings
Authority, 2, 13–14, 16, 39, 45, 52, 56, 64, 73, 99, 112, 126, 179
    decision-making, 25, 179; federal 24, 27; status and, 75; state and governmental, 81, 82–4, 113, 180
Avritzer, Leonardo, 6, 18, 25, 27, 75, 85–6, 109

Baiocchi, Gianpaolo, 5–6, 14, 18, 27, 75, 152, 182, 185
Bell, Catherine, 19, 42–3, 65, 67, 76, 83
Bourdieu, Pierre, 15–16, 18, 83, 88
Bureaucracy, 17, 92, 97, 99, 168–9, 181

Cardoso, Ruth, 7
Citizenship rights, 24, 27, 31, 33, 36, 64, 83
City council. *See* Legislative Chamber
City Master Plan, 85–6, 93
    and participation 125–6, 133–5; and technical complexity, 96–9, 105; history of, 25, 27–8; in Santo André, 35–36, 91, 111–12
Clientelism, 1, 10, 21, 33, 57, 100, 143, 145, 149–57, 165
Collins, Randall, 19, 42–3, 51, 79

Conferences, 5, 35, 44, 46, 91, 93, 98, 100, 108, 112, 160, 181–2
Constitution, 1, 11–12
    of 1988, Brazilian 8, 22–7, 38–9, 57, 85, 97–8
Co-operation, 15, 77, 159, 174
Co-optation, 100, 126, 149, 158, 165, 183
Contestation, 38, 67, 158, 170, 172
Cornwall, Andrea, 14, 83, 168–9, 170
Councils. *See* Management Policy Councils

Dagnino, Evelina, 15
DaMatta, Roberto, 52
Daniel, Bruno, 3, 6, 30, 148
Daniel, Celso, 4–6, 30–3, 36–9, 136, 160–1, 163–4, 178–9, 184–5
    murder of, 30, 145, 147–9
Decentralisation, 24, 27, 38–9
Deliberation, 17–18, 25
    and co-ordination, 17, 105, 113; and spatial organisation, 19; and technical language, 99; in Santo André's participatory institutions, 28, 56, 61, 78, 94–5, 99, 103–4, 107, 112–31, 131, 134, 163, 117–79, 187; open-ended, 14, 105–6, 110, 174, 176; over material goods, 109
Democratisation, 9, 23, 26, 39
    radical, 121
Durkheim, Emile, 45, 59

Elections, 120, 183
    mayoral, 4–5, 9, 30, 37, 110, 121, 132, 180; presidential, 8; to participatory institutions, 41–3, 47–8, 50–2, 62–5, 75, 151, 155–6, 172

Empowerment, 6, 179
Executive. *See* Administration

Favelas, 2–4, 26, 34–5, 101–2, 129, 154, 157–61, 165, 176
French, John, 8, 29–30

Giddens, Anthony, 15–16, 18–19, 87–8, 94
Goffmann, Erving, 41, 45, 59, 78, 93, 143–4, 177–8

Hall, Edward, 19, 87, 89
Handelman, Don, 18, 42, 65, 168, 170, 172
Hierarchy, 45, 51, 54, 56, 59–61, 63, 65, 83, 99, 119, 172–4, 187
  formal 101; government, 111, 119–20, 127, 176. *See* administrative structures

Ideology, 184
  administrative and organisational, 20, 114–15, 117–18, 123–9, 140–1; anti-capitalist, 7; of participatory democracy, 128
Investment, 12, 26, 29, 81, 107–10, 117, 130, 151, 183, 186
  decision-making, 11, 37, 71, 82, 157; priorities, 5, 10, 37, 48, 68, 75–6, 80, 119–21, 124, 138, 140

Jessop, Bob, 18, 108

Latin America, 9–10, 13, 34, 171
Laws, 11–13, 25, 27–8, 35–6, 87, 91, 97–8, 125, 133, 135–6, 151
Legislative Chamber, 30, 36, 71, 84, 91–3, 109, 111–12, 163, 181
  and clientelism, 51, 134, 151, 154; and the budget, 37–8, 68
Lincoln, Bruce, 19, 87

Mainwaring, Scott, 7, 10–11, 176

Management Policy Councils, 47, 56, 60, 130, 168, 177, 184
  comparison of, 85–6, 88; history of, 22, 25, 28, 39
Maricato, Erminia, 111
Meetings, 25, 35–8, 60, 67–8, 76–9, 83, 121, 129, 168, 178
  and agenda items, 95–6, 106; and participatory democracy, 16; the form of, 17–18, 46, 59, 87, 93–4, 104–5; and the formality of, 66; and the informality of, 99–100, 103, 106, 108; and the temporal organisation of, 90–2; the management of, 63, 102
Military, 2, 6–7, 9–10, 181

NGOs, 5, 36, 44, 60–1, 92–3, 155

Ortner, Sherry, 15–16

Participatory budgeting, 5–6, 66, 79, 82
  and cultural transformation, 32; biennial cycle of, 68; emergence in Santo André, 36–8; under Carlos Grana administration, 184–5
Participatory democracy, 9–10, 13–18, 20–1, 27, 41–2, 66, 108, 113–15, 120, 177, 180–3
  ideology of, 128; reimagining, 168–71; tensions between organisational membership and, 124
Participatory governance, 10, 185. *See* participatory democracy
Patronage, 1, 10, 33, 100, 167
PDS, 9, 23
PFL, 23
Pontual, Pedro, 6, 32–3, 37, 163
Practice approach and theory, 15–16, 21, 43, 88
PSOL, 132
PT. *See* Workers' Party

Rights, *See* Citizenship rights
Rituals, 41–3, 51, 64–5, 168, 171–3, 178

São Paulo, 3–4, 8, 28–9, 47, 86, 100, 147–8, 159
Sale of Building Rights, 36, 95, 111, 126–7
Santo André, 2–4
  citizen participation in, 4–6, 16–18, 30–6, 39–40, 42, 54–5, 59–61, 86, 113, 143, 167–8; history of, 28–30
Santos, Boaventura de Sousa, 5, 108
Schatzki, Theodore, 16, 43, 88
Scott, James, 75, 103, 133, 143, 177
Shore, Chris, 65, 186
Spatial configurations, 19, 89, 104, 178
Social movements, 4–5, 8, 23, 100, 103–4, 125, 153, 182–4
  NGOisation of, 157–61, 163–6
Socialism, 22
  and Workers' Party, 30–2, 181
State power, 6, 13–14, 16, 18, 21, 67, 86, 108, 171, 186
  enactments of, 112–3, 142; expressions and symbolisations of, 4, 46, 55, 64–5, 72; rationalisations of, 178–9; ritualisations of, 83–4
Statute of the City, 25, 27, 85, 97

Unions, 4, 8, 23, 30, 101
  metalworkers' 60, 62, 111
Urbanisation, 35, 105, 130
  of favelas, 160–1
Urban Reform Movement, 22, 26–7, 30, 184

Villaça, Flávio, 85, 111
Violence, 148–9
Voice, 20, 125, 129, 169
Voting, 149–50, 181
  in conferences, 100; in participatory institutions, 47, 49, 50–1, 62, 75–6, 78–82, 95–6, 105, 107, 109, 118, 125, 130–2, 135–7, 155, 177, 185; public, 1, 59, 65, 109

Zones of Special Social Interest, 35–6, 93, 111, 125